AF866228

CLINICAL SUPERVISION IN THE REAL WORLD

This practical guide provides support for mental health practitioners as they develop their approach to clinical supervision, drawing on the authors' extensive experience of counseling and psychotherapy to bring readers into the "real world" of clinical supervision.

Chapters introduce the essential responsibilities and tasks of a clinical supervisor and place emphasis on the development of a Competence-Oriented Model of Clinical Supervision, upon which a philosophical foundation for supervision can be built. Integrating up-to-date research with case vignettes and practical resources, the text discusses philosophies of clinical supervision and explores themes that often define a supervisor's contextual world, from professional ethics and legal issues to the personal development of both the supervisor and the supervisee.

Affirming and encouraging professional development as well as identifying a range of common challenges, *Clinical Supervision in the Real World* is a key resource for aspiring clinical supervisors looking to build their own philosophy of supervision.

Francis A. Martin, PhD, is Director of The Center for Clinical Training in Nashville, Tennessee, USA, and has maintained a career-long focus on providing psychotherapy. Currently, he focuses on advancing the professionalization of clinical supervision and reforming psychotherapy.

Janet P. Turner, PhD, is a licensed professional counselor, counselor educator/supervisor, and assistant professor in the School of Professional Counseling, Lindsey Wilson College, Kentucky, USA. Dr. Turner provides leadership and training through The Center for Clinical Training.

CLINICAL SUPERVISION IN THE REAL WORLD

A Practical Guide to Ethics, Legal Issues, and Personal Development

Francis A. Martin and Janet P. Turner

Routledge
Taylor & Francis Group
NEW YORK AND LONDON

First published 2020
by Routledge
52 Vanderbilt Avenue, New York, NY 10017

and by Routledge
2 Park Square, Milton Park, Abingdon, Oxon, OX14 4RN

Routledge is an imprint of the Taylor & Francis Group, an informa business.

© 2020 Francis A. Martin and Janet P. Turner

The right of Francis A. Martin and Janet P. Turner to be identified as authors of this work has been asserted by them in accordance with sections 77 and 78 of the Copyright, Designs and Patents Act 1988.

All rights reserved. No part of this book may be reprinted or reproduced or utilised in any form or by any electronic, mechanical, or other means, now known or hereafter invented, including photocopying and recording, or in any information storage or retrieval system, without permission in writing from the publishers.

Trademark notice: Product or corporate names may be trademarks or registered trademarks, and are used only for identification and explanation without intent to infringe.

Library of Congress Cataloging-in-Publication Data
A catalog record for this book has been requested

ISBN: 978-0-367-34070-4 (hbk)
ISBN: 978-0-367-34071-1 (pbk)
ISBN: 978-0-429-32376-8 (ebk)

Typeset in Minion
by Apex CoVantage, LLC

This book is dedicated to supervisees and their clinical supervisors. We hope that your clinical service brings you immense professional fulfillment. As you demonstrate your personal and professional skill, compassion, and generosity to improve the lives of your clients, may your life be improved, too.

CONTENTS

CHARTS

INTRODUCTION

As the title indicates, the purpose of this book is to offer guidance that will help readers to develop their approach to clinical supervision. In addition, it is intended to introduce many of the basic and essential responsibilities and understandings that inhere in good clinical supervision. And it is intended to provide guidance, including structure and content, for those who wish to develop a philosophy of clinical supervision. Based on our collective, long experience in providing clinical services and clinical supervision and preparing others to provide clinical supervision, our hope is that others will gain from our experience. More than gaining from our experience, though, our much larger hope is that all of us who provide clinical services will energetically pursue ways to improve our professional services for clients. This hope emerges from solid and accrued evidence that the effectiveness of counseling and psychotherapy continues to decline. For example, a reader may refer to Goldberg et al. (2016) for partial but clear confirmation of this evidence.

A comment about our intended style of writing may be useful for readers. While we wish to respect and comply with the normative standards of writing, intellectual discourse, and professional accountability, we wish also to communicate as well as we can. Flowing from our shared commitment to the idea that clinical supervision involves a relationship between a supervisor and a supervisee, although others are sometimes involved, we assume that we may reasonably take the prerogative of writing to readers or "speaking" to them in a conversational manner. We exercise this prerogative somewhat rarely and always with appropriate caution.

The goal of the book is to help interested individuals to develop their approach to clinical supervision. As a way to orient them to achieving this goal, we offer two vignettes from real clinical supervision experience. Presented in the Introduction, they are intended to be an invitation to readers to consider questions and issues that may arise in clinical supervision. The names of the individuals in these vignettes have been replaced with pseudonyms. Also, these two vignettes may appear to be somewhat non-typical of issues that may arise in clinical supervision. Despite this appearance, each one of them represents larger, more general issues that often arise in clinical supervision. In the first vignette, the broad question involves challenges to contracting between clinical supervisors and their supervisees. The second vignette introduces sensitive challenges around questions about a supervisee's clinical judgment and her inappropriate expression of her religion. Both of these vignettes receive attention later in the book in Chapter 14, "The Experience of Clinical Supervision," with emphasis on how a clinical supervisor may respond to each of these supervisees.

Vignette – Franklin and Charles: In October, a prospective supervisee – Franklin – and a possible clinical supervisor met for the first time. Franklin had contacted the supervisor – Charles – for the purpose of beginning post-degree clinical supervision in his pursuit of a license as a professional counselor.

Franklin described his situation. He completed his master's degree in mental health counseling at a state university that offers an accredited training program. Shortly after completing his graduate degree, Franklin got married. He and his wife are now expecting their first child. Franklin began to practice psychotherapy in a small mental health center located in a small city approximately twenty-five miles from a major metropolitan area. He expressed doubts about his ability to pay for supervision, adding that his new employer does not provide clinical supervision. Otherwise, Franklin appears to be well prepared to begin his work toward getting a license to provide mental health care. His consultation with Charles indicates that he understands the regulations, laws, and professional ethics within which he will practice. In addition, Franklin appears to have made his pursuit of a license an appropriately high priority.

Charles maintains an independent clinical practice as a psychologist. Based on training as a clinical supervisor, Charles meets the requirements of his state for those who provide clinical supervision services for prospective licensees. He sometimes meets with supervisees in the agency where they are employed but usually meets with them in his clinical office.

Following the initial consultation, Franklin and Charles agreed to meet again. Most of the second meeting completed the requisite tasks that inhere in clinical supervision. These tasks included completing an informed consent agreement, exchanging copies of liability insurance certificates, discussing expectations of both the supervisee and the supervisor, agreeing about an approximate schedule for meetings, establishing plans for managing crises, and more.

The singularly sensitive feature of the discussion between Franklin and Charles involved the question of how to handle fees. Franklin indicated that paying for clinical supervision would be a serious challenge, and Charles indicated understandable sensitivity to this challenge. Charles proposed that Franklin may be able to help with ongoing research, in lieu of payment. Somewhat enthusiastically, Franklin said that he would love to help with research. At the end of this discussion, Franklin and Charles agreed that Franklin would take specific tasks related to research, with specific clarity about how Franklin would receive completed questionnaires and tabulate information from them. They created a schedule by which Charles would ensure that the questionnaires would be sent to Franklin and the tabulations would be returned to Charles.

The scheduled supervision meetings called for Franklin and Charles to meet for at least one hour each week. The planned schedule for reporting information was printed on a calendar, with each having a copy. The schedule called for Franklin to bring tabulated information to Charles approximately every sixty days. The initial box of completed questionnaires was sent to Franklin in a timely manner. The first date for reporting tabulations came. Franklin brought the information that he had tabulated, which included approximately one-tenth of the agreed amount. He stated that he has been overwhelmed by demands at work and preoccupation with his wife's pregnancy. When the second reporting date came, Franklin brought no information from the questionnaires that had been delivered to him. In a congenial manner, he reported that he had been terribly busy, especially with the demands of his employment as a psychotherapist. In response to the two meetings in which Franklin brought much less than he had agreed to bring, he and his supervisor discussed what should happen as they looked forward to scheduled reporting dates and to ongoing clinical supervision meetings. Following Franklin's recommendation, the new plans called for Franklin to receive questionnaires and to tabulate information from a slightly smaller number of them and to bring the tabulated information to a scheduled supervision meeting, approximately every sixty days. At the next reporting date, Franklin brought no information from the questionnaires that had been delivered to him.

Obviously, the situation with Franklin and Charles is not a good one. As you reflect on their situation as if it were yours, what questions would you try to answer? As a means of transitioning this discussion into developing a philosophy of clinical supervision, you might want to consider the following questions:

In preparing for clinical supervision for Franklin, what did Charles do well? Or what did he do poorly?

Based on this vignette, do you conclude that bartering for clinical supervision services is a professionally accountable thing to do?

What, if any, specifically legal issues may be involved in this vignette?

What, if any, specifically ethical issues may be involved in this vignette?

Given Franklin's apparent failure to keep his end of the bargain with Charles, what actions, if any, should Charles take? What may be the rationale for these actions?

What failures, if any, do you attribute to Charles? For example, the vignette makes no mention of a written contract between Franklin and Charles. Should Charles have known that a written contract is almost always necessary? Whose failure is larger – Franklin's or Charles's?

Should Charles regard Franklin's apparent failure to keep his end of the bargain between them as a sign of Franklin's lack of professional competence? Or should Charles conclude that Franklin lacks readiness to function in a professional role?

Should Charles suspend or terminate his professional relationship with Franklin?

When Charles bartered for his services, did he inappropriately change his role, say, from clinical supervisor to research supervisor or from clinical supervisor to researcher supervisor? If both, how compatible are these roles?

Given Franklin's apparent failure to provide information that he had agreed to provide, should Charles invalidate the supervision and clinical hours that Franklin has accrued under his supervision?

Based on this vignette, what, if any, observations about Charles's philosophy of clinical supervision may be made?

Vignette – Therapy for Kaitlyn: A common aspiration among clinical supervisors is to assist their supervisees in their attempts to develop professionally accountable clinical judgment. This aspiration is sometimes frustrated by almost all of their supervisees. However, as the following vignette illustrates, some supervisees evoke more frustration than others.

The client is Kaitlyn, a fourteen-year-old female who sat stoically, emitting no signal that she may be emotionally or cognitively present. Her sullen, avoidant manner indicates that she does not want to be in therapy. In short, she is "shut down."

Kaitlyn currently resides in a group home where she has been for almost a year. She was taken into state custody around the age of two years, when child protective service workers discovered that she was severely neglected. She was immediately adopted but was soon returned to state custody. Kaitlyn's current placement follows a turbulent history of eighteen foster care placements. In the group home, Kaitlyn has required several critical interventions. These have come from loud and belligerent behavior, fighting with other girls in the group home, initiating unwanted sexual interest toward other girls, arguing with and cursing at support staff and clinical staff, and others.

Initially, Kaitlyn was removed from her parents' home and placed with a foster family at the age of two, following substantiated allegations of neglect and abuse. Today, Kaitlyn carries physical scars from abuse from approximately birth to four years of age by her biological parents and, soon thereafter, from her adoptive parents. Her physical victimization includes beatings, cuts, sexual assault, burns with cigarettes, and more. In addition, she carries significant emotional "scars" from these experiences. During her stay in her first foster home, she became known as "the demon child," confirming the conclusion by her foster parents that Kaitlyn was aggressive, explosive, oppositional, and more. After six months in her first foster placement, the foster parents expressed their exhaustion and requested that Kaitlyn be removed from their home. In successive placements, Kaitlyn similarly exhausted her foster parents. When she was ten years of age and living in her eleventh foster home, she received abuse again, from an older foster brother and sister. They repeatedly raped Kaitlyn. These experiences seemed to "fuel the fire" of Kaitlyn's anger and oppositional behaviors.

Now, Kaitlyn receives therapy from one of your supervisees, Rachel. As Rachel began to treat Kaitlyn, she described Kaitlyn with appropriate clinical terms, allowing for conversational and somewhat colloquial descriptions during supervision meetings. After three sessions with Kaitlyn, Rachel indicated that she was no longer struggling with uncertainty about how to treat Kaitlyn. In reporting about her work with Kaitlyn, your supervisee says,

> *"I knew what to do. I got tired of hearing 'fuck you' from this kid. It's just not appropriate for a child to speak to an adult the way she speaks to me. I told her not to speak to me that way. And, I told her, 'God won't put more on you than you can handle.'" Gesturing with her hands pointing from her eyes, as if to suggest that Kaitlyn should forget her past and move into a nice future, Rachel continued, "And, I told her, 'Your eyes are for looking forward, not backward. You can't change anything in the past. You've got to look forward. You've got to have hope. This is what God wants for you.'" Rachel added, "Her attitude sucks. She will never make it this way. And, I told her, 'You're a lovely girl. God wants good things for you. And, I will never give up on you. You are precious.'"*

Obviously, the situation with Kaitlyn and Rachel raises challenges. As you reflect on their situation as if it were yours, what questions would you try to answer? As a means of transitioning this discussion into developing a philosophy of clinical supervision, you may wish to consider the following questions:

- Insofar as clinical supervisors are legally accountable for the professional behavior of their supervisees, what is your specific legal accountability in this situation?
- Which specific legal principles and/or laws may apply to this situation?
- Insofar as clinical supervisors are ethically accountable for the professional behavior of their supervisees, what is your specific ethical accountability in this situation?
- Which specific ethical standards apply to this situation?
- How do you make clinical sense of Kaitlyn?
- Rachel delivers poor professional care for Kaitlyn. How might you address this with Rachel?
- What does Rachel reveal about herself in this situation? Does she reveal incompetence? Does she reveal a strong religious faith? Does Rachel demonstrate incompetence? Does she reveal that she is a somewhat normal, beginning, and naïve clinician who is likely to develop beyond her current limitations?
- Does this situation imply that you – the supervisor – may have erred in agreeing to supervise Rachel's clinical work?

Generally, mental health care providers develop their clinical skills and competence only when they deliver mental health care services and adapt to the realities of their professional service as clinicians. Likewise, clinical supervisors develop their supervision skills and competence only when they provide clinical supervision and adapt to the realities of their professional service as clinical supervisors. The aforementioned vignettes offer illustrations of the need for supervisors to develop their supervisory skills and adapt to the realities of providing clinical supervision. As they make necessary adaptations, they make numerous decisions about how to handle a wide variety of situations with their supervisees, as the vignettes indicate. The question that this book answers is "What informs and guides their decisions?" Most of the answer is that as supervisors adapt toward becoming effective clinical supervisors, they concomitantly develop a philosophy of clinical supervision, even when they fail to clearly articulate it. Obviously, the more clearly articulated their philosophy of clinical supervision is, the more likely they are effective in providing clinical supervision. The underlying hope and expectation of the material in this book is that it will measurably assist clinical supervisors and prospective clinical supervisors in their pursuit of a philosophy of clinical supervision and effectiveness as clinical supervisors.

The structure of this book may be an important consideration for many readers. As a general statement about the structure, the operative thought was that we would attempt to bring readers inside the experience of becoming a clinical supervisor and providing clinical supervision. The first task, then, was to provide a foundation upon which understanding clinical supervision could be built. Among other things, building the foundation compelled us to answer several obvious questions, including, "What is counseling/psychotherapy?" (Chapter 1) "What is clinical supervision?" and "What is a philosophy of clinical supervision?" (Chapter 2). These are the chapters in Section I.

With the foundation laid, the next set of questions to be answered involved the necessary component parts of an approach to clinical supervision. Therefore, we sought to provide answers to these questions, including "What do I believe about conducting mental health care?" "What characterizes a good therapist?" "What do I believe about clinical supervision?" "What is the role of the supervisor?" "What is the role of the supervisee?" "How do I define a good clinical supervisor?" Answering these questions may be necessary for individuals who practice clinical supervision, but they must be answered in the context of the professional world in which clinical supervisors provide their services. Therefore, in Section III, we sought to explain the issues that define a clinical supervisor's contextual world. Specifically, we provide basic and needed information about supervision-related professional ethics, legal issues in clinical supervision, the credentials and qualifications that prospective supervisees bring to clinical supervision, how clinical supervisors develop, and how supervisees develop. We place priority on our model of clinical supervision, a competence-oriented model of clinical supervision (COMCS).

Seeking to bring readers inside the experience of clinical supervision, we discuss philosophies of clinical supervision and include Dr. Martin's philosophy of clinical supervision in Chapter 16. Then, inviting supervisors and prospective supervisors to enter the world of clinical supervision and view snapshots of this world, we provide a chapter on "The Experience of Clinical Supervision," referring to what happens during supervision sessions, defining priorities during supervision sessions, and more. However, aiming to emphasize the practical realities of conducting clinical supervision, we provide a detailed discussion of the administrative tasks in clinical supervision in Chapter 18. In the chapter,

"Helpful Practices toward Developing a Philosophy of Clinical Supervision," we recommend several actions that will enable clinical supervisors or prospective clinical supervisors to develop their approach to clinical supervision. Finally, in the last chapter, "Putting It All Together," we provide an outline of questions that, if answered by clinical supervisors, hold the promise of helping individuals to produce a useful philosophy of clinical supervision.

Our hope is that this book helps to elevate our individual and collective effectiveness in providing mental health care, particularly with reference to meeting the needs of our clients.

SECTION I

Orientation to a Philosophy of Clinical Supervision

1

WHAT IS COUNSELING/ PSYCHOTHERAPY?

Licensed counselors and psychotherapists practice in virtually every community in America. Indeed, the ubiquity of counselors and therapists who are licensed to practice independently makes them among the most numerous professionals in America. However, one of the challenges in knowing the number of licensed and practicing counselors and therapists is that "No consensus exists on which provider types make up the mental health workforce" (Heisler, 2017, p. 1). In our efforts to locate and report the number of psychologists, counselors, social workers, psychiatrists, advanced practice psychiatric nurses, marriage and family therapists, licensed pastoral therapists, and others, we reached the same conclusion as Heisler. There is no consensus about who is and who is not a mental health care provider. This conclusion alone likely causes problems that lie beyond the boundaries of our concerns in this book. For example, does the lack of consensus about who is and is not a mental health care provider raise difficult questions for consumers who wish to utilize their health insurance? Does it raise questions about the legal standing of some mental health care providers?

We can identify almost two hundred titles of licenses for mental health care providers. We can locate more than twenty thousand approaches or orientations to psychotherapy. For the purposes of this discussion, along with the titles for licensees and the number of approaches to psychotherapy, precision about the number of licensed and practicing counselors and therapists is not necessary. Still, our estimate is that the number of licensed clinicians whose license authorizes them to practice independently, including counselors, psychologists, social workers, psychiatrists, advanced practice psychiatric nurses, marriage and family therapists, licensed pastoral therapists, and others, is currently about eight hundred thousand. With a history that extends well beyond and with this number of practicing counselors and therapists, a reasonably coherent understanding of what psychotherapy is should be readily available. It is not. Therefore, the aim of this discussion is to define psychotherapy so that its useful boundaries may be understood.

Counseling and Psychotherapy

For the ease of discussion, we will try to limit the awkwardness of talking about counseling, psychotherapy, and mental health care by emphasizing that we will use these terms interchangeably, hoping that the context comfortably accommodates our decision to use one or another. So, how would you answer this question? "What is psychotherapy?" If you have a view of what psychotherapy is, what is the basis for your view? Maybe, to facilitate your thinking about answers to these questions, you may wish to consider the following statements:

Conducting psychotherapy is nicely conceived as an art.

Conducting psychotherapy is properly conceived as a science.

Psychotherapy is an expression of the providers' view of life. One provider may place a high value on achievement, while another places a high value on service. One may place a high value on religious commitment and express this through therapy, while another sternly rejects the suffusion of religion and psychotherapy.

Psychotherapy is an expression of the provider's personality.

Psychotherapy is a major health care service. As a major health care service, psychotherapy should be held to the same standards of training and practice as any other health care service.

Because psychotherapy is, above all else, properly regarded as health care, it should not place importance on the personality of the therapist, the therapist's personal values (e.g., religious beliefs or other values-oriented characteristics), or other contradictions of relevant evidence.

Psychotherapy may involve rock climbing or praying or gardening or yoga or massage – almost any activity that a therapist deems appropriate.

Psychotherapy may involve emotional upheaval. Without attention to emotional expression and awareness, therapy is not likely to be therapeutic.

Psychotherapy may provide services for terminally ill individuals, victims of sexual assault, depressed individuals, overactive four-year-old children, troubled couples, perfectionistic painters, identity-confused adolescents, or anyone else who requests therapy.

Sincerity is far more important in conducting psychotherapy than competence. In contrast, competence is far more important than sincerity in conducting psychotherapy.

No one knows what psychotherapy is. Individually and collectively, counselors and psychotherapists lack understanding of what "it" is and how it works.

Much too little is known about effective counseling/psychotherapy.

Much too little is known about effective counselors and psychotherapists.

Most practices of counseling and psychotherapy have little or no basis in reliable evidence that may support such practices.

These statements may or may not resonate positively with an individual's understanding of counseling and/or psychotherapy. Whether they resonate positively or not, an individual's thoughts about these statements and many other possible statements provide clues about the individual's conceptualization of counseling/psychotherapy. The relevance of clinical supervisors' conceptualization of counseling/psychotherapy is that it filters into or out of clinical supervision the matters that may be considered important in the process of clinical supervision.

ACTIVITY BOX

To emphasize the importance of your conceptualization of counseling/psychotherapy, you may wish to reflect on and consider each of the following statements and your response to it. Your response may provide clues about how you view yourself as a mental health care provider but also what you may expect of supervisees. As you read each statement, consider what may make this statement important or relevant to you. If you were interpreting this statement for a colleague, what might you say about it? If any, what truth about mental health care does this statement represent for you? In what ways, if any, may this statement misrepresent your views about mental health care?

1 The healing of ourselves as healers has to take place first. Bringing ourselves to wholeness, we become more sensitive to other people. In the change of consciousness that happens within us, we bring about change of consciousness in those around us and in the planet itself.

Marion Woodman (2016)

2 The therapist's job is not to be an exterminator to take things away. The job is to give the problem back to the client in a way that shows how much they need it, show its value.

Thomas Moore (2016)

3 Generous people are rarely mentally ill.

Karl Menninger (2017)

4 What the doctor fails to see in himself, he will either not see at all in his patient or see grossly exaggerated.

Carl Gustav 1985 p. 237)

5 Experience is not what happens to you – it's what you do with what happens to you.

Aldous Huxley (2017)

6 Psychotherapy theory turns it all on you: you are the one who is wrong. If a kid is having trouble or is discouraged, the problem is not just inside the kid; it's also in the system, the society.

James Hillman (2017)

7 The level of differentiation is the single most important aspect distinguishing a therapist from a technician. Differentiation is the ability

to maintain a non-anxious presence in the face of another's anxiety. It does not mean being uninvolved or indifferent. It is the ability to tolerate pain for growth.

David Schnarch (2017)

8 If we can give up attachment to our roles as helpers, then maybe our clients can give up attachment to their roles as patients and we can meet as fellow souls on this incredible journey. We can fulfill the duties of our roles without being trapped by over-identification with them.

Ram Dass (2011)

9 Like most human behavior, violence has meaning: it only seems "senseless" or "meaningless" to the extent we are unable – or unwilling – to decode it.

Stephen A. Diamond (1996)

10 If we seek to be loved – if we expect to be loved – this cannot be accomplished; we will be dependent and grasping, not genuinely loving.

M. Scott Peck (2003)

Following these considerations, how may counseling/psychotherapy best be conceptualized? No doubt, many counselors and therapists likely do not question what it is that they do, let alone worry about how psychotherapy may be conceptualized. The number of such counselors and therapists may be declining. For example, if they read Holden and Barker's article (2018), they will encounter a list of more than 450 approaches to counseling and therapy that almost all professional mental health care providers would regard as very unusual, if not inappropriate and unethical. For example, they refer to "Angelic Channeling" (p. 2), "Clairvoyant Psychotherapy" (p. 4), and "Harmonic Medicine" (p. 6). Woolfolk (2015) described the condition of psychotherapy as being "very much in flux," when he refers to the ubiquity of psychotherapy and the proliferation of the forms and approaches to psychotherapy. In 1997, when Alvin Mahrer (1999) was honored by the American Psychological Association for his distinguished contributions to psychotherapy, he suggested that perhaps there is no such thing as psychotherapy. We do not necessarily support the observations and views of these authors, but we conclude with them that psychotherapy is currently jeopardized by several major deleterious influences on it. Each of these influences requires more explanation than the scope of this chapter allows. Nevertheless, the list of deleterious influences includes the following, among others.

- The persistent decline of competence among mental health care providers (e.g., Goldberg et al., 2016; Spengler & Pilipis, 2015).
- The proliferation of training programs, with little or no evidence to support the extraordinary variety of them. A training program may prepare its

graduates to be licensed as very conservative "Christian therapists," while another one prepares its graduates to practice "contemplative psychology," while another prepares its graduates to practice "integral psychotherapy," and so on. Further, the size of graduate programs that lead to licensing as mental healthcare providers may be as small as thirty (30) graduate semester hours or as large as one hundred 10 (110) graduate semester hours, with most programs scattered somewhere in between these numbers. The inconsistency may be located within numerous colleges and universities. A review of the website of Loyola University in Chicago will confirm that within the University, graduate preparation for social workers may require as little as twenty-eight (28) semester hours (Loyola University Chicago, 2019a) or for counseling psychologists may require as many as one hundred ten (110) semester hours plus an internship (Loyola University Chicago, 2019b).

- The near total lack of regulation of practice may be the most crippling, deleterious influence on psychotherapy. While the lack of regulation may be assessed in a variety of ways. The way that we have assessed it is through gathering information from the websites of licensed and practicing counselors and psychotherapists. In short, we have identified more than 20,000 orientations or approaches to counseling and psychotherapy. Other observers have raised this issue. They include O'Donohue and Lilienfeld (2013) who decried, "we are deeply concerned about the large number of professional psychological services sold and delivered that are not evidence-based" (p. xi). Holden and Barker (2018), Singer and Lalich (1996), Thyer and Pignotti (2015), and Thompson (2010), among many others, have observed the proliferation of aberrant approaches to therapy and the lack of regulation that allows them to proliferate.
- The proliferation of codes of ethics.
- Clearly, the three largest professional associations – the American Counseling Association (ACA), American Psychological Association (APA), and National Association of Social Workers (NASW) – justifiably promote their respective codes of ethics. Many of their members, though, position themselves to require their compliance with numerous other codes of ethics. Among the many codes of ethics that may require compliance, the following may be easily located.

American Art Therapy Association (AATA, 2013)
American Association of Christian Counselors (AACC, 2014)
American Association of Marriage and Family Therapists (AAMFT, 2015)
American Association of Marriage and Family Therapists, Approved Supervisor Designation (AAMFT, 2019a)
American Association of Pastoral Counselors (AAPC, 2012)
American Association of Sexuality Educators, Counselors, and Therapists (AASECT, 2014)
American Counseling Association (ACA, 2014)

American Group Psychotherapy Association (AGPA, 2002)
American Mental Health Counselors Association (AMHCA, 2015)
American Psychiatric Association (2013)
American Psychological Association (2017)
American School Counselor Association (ASCA, 2016)
Approved Clinical Supervisor, through the Center for Credentialing Education (CCE, 2016)
Association for Addiction Professionals (NAADAC, 2016)
Board Certified Music Therapist, through the Certification Board for Music Therapists (CBMT, 2011)
Certified Career Adjustment Associates, through the Commission on Rehabilitation Counselor Certification (CRCC, 2009)
Certified Eating Disorders Specialist, through the International Association of Eating Disorders Professionals (IAEDP, n.d.)
Certified Group Psychotherapist, through the American Group Psychotherapy Association (AGPA, 2002)
Certified Rehabilitation Counselor (CRCC, 2017)
Certified Sex Therapist, through the American Association of Sexuality Educators, Counselors, and Therapists (AASECT, 2014)
Certified Vocational Evaluation Specialists (CRCC, 2009)
Certified Work Adjustment Specialists (CRCC, 2009)
International Expressive Arts Therapy Association (IEATA, n.d.)
Master Addictions Counselor (NAADAC, 2016)
National Association of Social Workers (NASW, 2017)
National Career Development Association (NCDA, 2015)
National Certified Addiction Counselor, Level I (NAADAC, 2016)
National Certified Addiction Counselor, Level II (NAADAC, 2016)
National Certified Adolescent Addiction Counselor (NAADAC, 2016)
National Certified Clinical Mental Health Counselor, through the National Board for Certified Counselors (NBCC, 2016)
National Certified Counselor (NBCC, 2016)
National Certified School Counselor (NBCC, 2016)
National Clinical Supervision Endorsement (NAADAC, 2016)
National Endorsed Student Assistance Professional (NAADAC, 2016)
National Endorsed Co-Occurring Disorders Professional (NAADAC, 2016)
National Certified Peer Recovery Support Specialist (NAADAC, n.d.a)
Nicotine Dependence Specialist (NAADAC, 2016)
Professional Certified Coach, through the International Coach Federation (ICF, 2015)
Registered Expressive Arts Therapist, through the International Expressive Arts Therapy Association (IEATA) (n.d.)
Registered Play Therapist, through the Association for Play Therapy (APT, 2016)
School-Based Registered Play Therapist (APT, 2015)
United States Association for Body Psychotherapy (USABP, 2007)

If an individual counselor is a registered play therapist, a certified clinical mental health counselor, an approved clinical supervisor, a member of the American Art Therapy Association, and a member of the American Counseling Association, with which code(s) of ethics should she or he comply? Should the individual comply with all of them, even when standards in one code may be in conflict with standards in another code? When clinical supervisors or administrative supervisors comply with a code of ethics that is different from their supervisees' codes of ethics, which code should be followed?

While there may be no "best" conceptualization here or elsewhere, we have struggled to develop our conceptualization of what people frequently refer to as "counseling," "psychotherapy," or "mental health care." Within the scope of this book, our discussion of what psychotherapy is must necessarily be briefer than we would wish to make it. Indeed, the answer to the question about what psychotherapy is appears in a much larger document that is not yet published. Our answer to the question involved two major parts. One is what psychotherapy *is*, and the other is what psychotherapy is *not*. First, we describe what psychotherapy is.

What Psychotherapy Is

Just as those who need and receive treatment are extraordinarily complex, the phenomenon of psychotherapy is likewise complex. This is an acknowledgment of the potential of making a positive contribution to a discussion about the conceptualization of psychotherapy but also an acknowledgment of the formidable limitations in attempting to make such a contribution. For now, the answer to the simple question, "What is psychotherapy?" should be regarded as a genuine and serious effort but one that comes with an invitation to others to add their ideas and help shape the discussion.

Broadly, psychotherapy is about health. The four major mental health care associations (i.e., American Counseling Association, American Psychological Association, National Association of Social Workers, and American Association of Marriage and Family Therapists) came from different kinds of histories that may be broadly characterized as social services and social sciences. Although they came from widely different histories, these four groups of mental health care providers demonstrated their interest in and concern about providing services for their respective clients. However, in responding to the problems that they conscientiously addressed, as Hightower (1988) and others have noted, "Psychologists [along with the others] have not devoted enough of their energies to the study of psychological health" (p. 527). He adds, "We have too seldom asked how the healthy person lives." To further establish his emphasis, Hightower concludes,

> *By analogy, it would be as though in deciding to discover the potentials of the human body, athletes and coaches studied the physical prowess of the average person and chronic medical patients – and never examined the factors associated*

with the success of Olympic gold medal winners. We can learn the human potential for positive mental health only by studying individuals who have achieved it. (p. 527)

Despite the deficiency to which Hightower refers – and which most mental health care providers, no doubt, readily recognize – collectively, the mental health care community has occupied itself with identifying and minimizing, if not eliminating, various mental, emotional, and relational problems and much less with identifying clear criteria for their success in seeing mental health emerge from these adversities. Looking toward their future, mental health care providers will gain significant benefits for themselves and their clients if they clearly define and energetically promote mental health – that is, know very well what "health" is – and require it of themselves. One of the likely and unfortunate outcomes of the failure of the mental health community to define and aspire to helping its clients to achieve mental health is that it has failed also to define and necessitate mental health in its members. This means that counselors and psychotherapists can be unhealthy and maintain their roles as providers of mental health care services.

Numerous individuals, including Eric Erikson, Gordon Allport, Carl Rogers, and Abraham Maslow, have developed sophisticated conceptualizations of mentally healthy individuals. The current and future need, though, is that "something" beyond these conceptualizations should be developed. As a clinical need and as a therapist need, the question is whether professionally accountable mental health care providers know what mental health is, whether they possess sufficient ways to recognize and measure it in themselves and their clients, and whether they can effectively develop it in themselves and their clients. Nevertheless, despite these deficiencies, mental health care and those who provide it are concerned with identifying, promoting, and facilitating mental health.

With its appropriate and necessary emphasis on health, psychotherapy will be defined as a health care service. In its current condition, it may be only marginally regarded as a health care service. To make this point, we can identify more than 1,200 titles for some form of "Christian" counseling and psychotherapy. Insofar as those who provide their services define their services as a religious activity, they fail to define it as a health care activity. Further, they risk alienating every other health care provider from them and their aberrant practices, including those who practice counseling and psychotherapy from religious orientations that are not Christian and those who practice with orientations that are not specifically religious.

Psychotherapy is health care. It is mental health care. As such, it gives primary attention to helping others to establish and maintain mental health.

Defining psychotherapy as health care likely has nearly universal appeal. However, defining psychotherapy as health care carries important consequences. One is that it aligns the work of counseling and psychotherapy with the larger health care community. As such, it shares the principles, practices, and general outlook of the larger health care community. Specifically, psychotherapy holds itself to the standards of health care that make it compatible with the standards of health care of, say, pharmacists or cardiologists or oncologists or physical therapists. Suffice it to say that if a cardiologist instructed her or his patients to massage grape jelly into their knee caps, the advice would likely cause the cardiologist to lose her or his license to practice and, maybe, suffer other adverse consequences. In mental health care, though, when conspicuously bad approaches to therapy appear frequently in the advertising and practices of large numbers of counselors and therapists, nothing of consequence happens, except for the erosion of their credibility and harm to their clients (e.g., Holden & Barker, 2018; Thompson, 2010). In contrast with the standards of the larger health care community, when a therapist advertises so-called "therapies," such as aura therapy, biblical Christian sex therapy, Indigenous healing practices, magnetic field therapy, mesotherapy, new life therapy, soul healing love, therapeutic fly fishing, Toltec wisdom, or most of the twenty thousand approaches to therapy that we have gathered from the websites of practicing therapists, nothing of consequence happens. These so-called therapies fall well below the minimal standards of normative and professionally accountable health care. Worse, they compromise the integrity of all mental health care providers and pose potential harm to the clients who receive such treatments.

As a major form of health care, mental health care must continue to refine its capacity for competently delivered services, based on the best evidence that supports its services. At least, this means that, instead of individual judgment alone, collective judgment about what constitutes professionally accountable mental health care should give direction to the practices of mental health care providers in the future.

Psychotherapy is mental health care. Within the larger community of health care and allowing for ambiguous, overlapping interests, mental health care rightly claims its role, just as other kinds of health care, such as oncology or physical therapy, claim theirs. Affirming its place, mental health care may be defined in the following manner: Mental health care is a professionally accountable service that, in a very large variety of ways, provides mental health care services for individuals, couples, and families, in response to relationship problems, environmental stressors, and mental illnesses. Taking some of its component parts, this definition of mental health care may be briefly explained in the following manner.

"Mental health care" refers to a broad range of helping services. The services may include relaxation training, anger management, interventions for ADHD, substance abuse treatment, psychological assessments, marital therapy, and many others. The range of possible mental health problems is similar to the range of possible physical health problems. If a random population of, say, three hundred adults was asked about their medical problems, the possibilities would likely include unexplained weight loss, breast cancer, irregular heartbeat, stomach ulcers, sprained ankles, high blood pressure, and many others. Similarly, the needs of individuals, families, and groups who receive mental health care appear in numerous forms.

"A professionally accountable service" refers to a high level of competence and ways of helping. Surely, this includes training in accredited (i.e., profession-endorsed) programs, profession-defined and endorsed clinical supervision, demonstrable knowledge of relevant laws and professional ethics, a license to practice, demonstrated clinical competence, active participation in clinically relevant professional associations, pursuit and utilization of the best empirically validated treatments, and other markers of professionalism.

"Treats individuals, couples, and families" acknowledges that mental health needs come in multiple forms. Individuals attend most clinical sessions, but even in the absence of important persons in their lives, the influence of these persons is usually present. For example, an adolescent male attends therapy because he is depressed. He acknowledges that his depression "really began to bother me after my friend died in a car wreck." If this adolescent male self-medicated with alcohol, his treatment may be provided in a substance abuse treatment facility, a place that almost always involves others, including those who participate in group therapy and, of course, members of his family.

"Relationship problems" refers to the fact that most needs that are served by mental health care providers involve disturbances in the primary relationships of those who seek help. Parent-child therapy, marital therapy, or complicated grief illustrates the importance of relationship problems that become the focus of treatment. Also, as a practical and psychological matter, individuals who seek treatment often do so because others in their primary relationships have demanded that they get help. This is commonly the situation in which individuals suffer with substance abuse.

"Stress" refers to the very familiar "ups and downs" of life that often, but not always, leave individuals exhausted, hopeless, and sometimes disordered. Everyone knows about stress, whether they self-consciously think about it or not. For example, they know all too well the experience of working too hard for too long and getting too tired, often causing them to wonder why they do this to themselves. Whether they do this to themselves or not, they may easily be overstressed. For example, millions of Americans remember with dread the collapse of the economy in 2008. Others remember long hours of attending to a terminally ill family member. Generally, individuals accommodate stress and adapt toward overcoming the adverse effects of stress. Others who endure normative or extreme stress will require mental health care.

"Environmental stressors" refers to stress that comes from normal and abnormal responses to stressful events that are largely external to the individual and/or family. They include many kinds of events, including the crash of a small plane that killed the family next door, multiple losses from a tornado, the sudden death of a specially loved nephew, irreparable damages from a flood, a high school band bus accident that killed a child's best friends, a house fire, a sexual assault at a summer camp, and so on. And while most individuals refuse to be intimidated by terrorists, they are sometimes acutely aware of the fact that they may be vulnerable to an attack by a terrorist or, more likely, from another school shooter.

"Mental illness" refers to many uniquely personal disturbances that call for mental health care. These include major depression, excessive anxiety, various psychoses, and so on. The term *mental illness* continues to decline as one that refers to mental, emotional, and relational problems. Whether this term or others are used, the fact is that numerous individuals suffer with serious personal disturbances. The most frequently cited definition of such disturbances comes from the *Fifth Edition of the Diagnostic and Statistical Manual of Mental Disorders* – or the DSM-5 – a publication of the American Psychiatric Association (American Psychiatric Association, 2013):

> *A mental disorder is a syndrome characterized by clinically significant disturbance in an individual's cognition, emotion regulation, or behavior that reflects a dysfunction in the psychological, biological, or developmental processes underlying mental functioning. Mental disorders are usually associated with significant distress in social, occupational, or other important activities. An expectable or culturally approved response to a common stressor or loss, such as the death of a loved one, is not a mental disorder. Socially deviant behavior (e.g., political, religious, or sexual) and conflicts that are primarily between the individual and society are not mental disorders unless the deviance or conflict results from a dysfunction in the individual, as described above.*
>
> (p. 20)

To try to be useful in describing "mental illness" or whatever it may be called, the explanations of it are too large for the purposes of this discussion. Suffice it to say that, whether this definition satisfies everyone who may want to define mental illness, it involves multiple parts that need explanation.

Counselors and psychotherapists provide services in many different kinds of settings, including psychiatric hospitals, mental health centers, specialized practice groups, solo practices, residential treatment facilities, and others. No matter what their clinical setting may be, they are acutely aware of the existential immediacy of engaging their clients in the process of change. When they are face-to-face with their clients, they do not in the moment reflect on their philosophy of therapy or various journals that report validating research for their clinical work. Instead, they focus on the needs of their clients. As such, therapists recognize that this is the priority to which they should give professional attention. Tacitly, at least, they understand that the work is paradoxically enormous but confined to the moment, general but also individual and personal. As a statement about what mental health care is, the paradox evokes as much doubt as clarity and confirmation. The idea is, though, that the existential immediacy reflects the demands with which mental health care providers are confronted and to which they attempt to respond. However, even in the existential moment of interacting with a client, it reflects also the complexity of human life and the virtually limitless ways that something may go wrong with human life. Probably, too, and more generally, it also reflects the relative immaturity of mental health care and the exigent necessity of trying to be good enough to alleviate suffering from and about almost everything. For examples, within the context of attempting to be as disciplined, objective, and professionally accountable as they can be, counselors and therapists provide services for

Persons with opioid addiction who wonder why they are still alive or whether they want to be alive.
Parents who feel plagued by a tantrum-expressive six-year-old.
A long-married couple in which a member has secretly maintained an intimate relationship with someone outside the marriage but whose secret has recently been discovered.
An adolescent girl who struggles with overwhelming memories of sexual victimization.
The banker whose board of directors tells him to get professional help because of his out-of-control anger.
A perfectionistic plumber who tortures himself with beliefs about his lack of perfection.
A guilt-saturated adult female who cannot tolerate herself as a sexually alive woman.
Recent retirees who believe that their lives have ended now that they are without their work-based identity.
A young man who reports that he and God are one.
A married couple who "don't know what to do" with their severely autistic son.
Workaholic individuals who feel confusion about why they "can't do it all."

The variety of client needs is much larger than this short list may suggest. No matter what the client need may be, psychotherapists attempt to respond to the need in many different professionally accountable ways. As they respond to client needs, they produce disciplined spontaneity, knowing that there is no guiding authority in the room with them and no unambiguously clear set of steps to follow as they conduct therapy. Therapists enact their own definition of what psychotherapy is. And it is this definition that defines "mental illness."

Psychotherapy is professionally accountable. Our review of tens of thousands of websites where licensed, practicing therapists advertise their services easily locates examples of the lack of professional accountability. So far, we have located almost 21,000 approaches to therapy. Many are credible and entirely professional, but most of them are neither credible nor professional. For example, recognizing them as unusual, we include only ten of them as illustrations. They include Seichem Egyptian energy healing, divine symbolic communication, God-designed counseling, Psychopomp work, raindrop and aroma therapy techniques, soul alignment therapy, RoHun transpersonal (soul) psychology, Usui Reiki healing, wisdom of God's Word, and the Yuen method.

Along with the idea that psychotherapy is professionally accountable, the short list of ten necessitates the question, "To what or two whom should therapists be accountable?" While the evidence leads to the conclusion that many practicing therapists lack professional accountability, many practicing therapists demonstrate the opposite of this. Such accountability may be seen in several ways.

1) Professionally accountable therapists utilize approaches to therapy that their profession endorses.
2) They seek to comply with identified standards of competence.
3) They place the needs of their clients above their own needs, in the context of providing clinical services.
4) They maintain currency with their clinical skills, specialized clinical services, relevant research, evolving ethical standards, evolving legal issues, and other indicators of commitment to professionalism.
5) They seek to maintain and enhance the viability of the profession of which they are members.
6) They monitor and seek to improve their personal well-being and their clinical effectiveness.
7) They place positive value on diversity among their peers and their clients, recognizing that potentially harmful biases should be recognized and neutralized.
8) They demonstrate that they affirm positive values, such as trustworthiness, honesty, integrity, curiosity, accurate self-awareness, service, tolerance, collaboration, democracy, justice, adaptability, grace, generosity, altruism, benevolence, and so on.

Professional accountability conforms to the expectations that inhere in empirically validated clinical practices that may be seen in research literature and best practices statements about effective, outcome-supported clinical service. Allowing for the ambiguous character of clinical service, it should, nevertheless, stand on the best available evidence for it. In contrast with the chaotic and cacophonous condition of mental health care, the future of professional accountability may require regular re-testing of providers' knowledge, examination of their skills, an assessment of the outcomes of their clinical work, their attitude(s) toward their clinical work, and their competence in completing necessary tasks (e.g., maintaining current informed consent documents and appropriate documentation of clients' progress) associated with their clinical work.

The practice of psychotherapy serves the larger social good. Clearly, psychotherapy is a professional practice, analogous to any other professional practice, such as engineering, law, teaching, or medicine. And, like other kinds of professional practice, psychotherapy serves under the aegis of values and principles that transcend and guide the practice of psychotherapy. These values and principles have long been recognized and supported by all major mental health care associations, including the National Association of Social Workers (NASW), the American Counseling Association (ACA), and the American Psychological Association (APA). Each of these associations expresses fundamental values and principles in slightly different ways but in ways that demonstrate considerable agreement. Their respective codes of ethics open with discussions of their basic values and principles. As reported in the following, clinical supervisors who are members of these associations should be cognizant of and compliant with these values and principles.

The NASW *Code of Ethics* asserts,

> *The following broad ethical principles are based on social work's core values of service, social justice, dignity and worth of the person, importance of human relationships, integrity, and competence. These principles set forth ideals to which all social workers should aspire.*
>
> (2017, p. 5)

NASW identifies six basic values and an ethical principle that accompany each value.

> *1)* **Value:** *Service:* **Ethical Principle:** *Social workers' primary goal is to help people in need and to address social problems. Social workers elevate service to others above self-interest. Social workers draw on their knowledge, values, and skills to help people in need and to address social problems. Social workers are encouraged to volunteer some portion of their professional skills with no expectation of significant financial return (pro bono service). 2)* **Value:** *Social Justice:* **Ethical Principle:** *Social workers challenge social injustice. Social workers pursue social change, particularly with and on behalf of vulnerable and oppressed individuals and groups of people. Social workers' social change efforts are focused primarily on issues of poverty, unemployment, discrimination, and other forms of social injustice. These activities seek to promote sensitivity to and knowledge about oppression and cultural and ethnic diversity. Social workers strive to ensure access to needed information, services, and resources; equality of opportunity; and meaningful participation in decision making for all people. 3)* **Value:** *Dignity and Worth of the Person:* **Ethical Principle:** *Social workers respect the inherent dignity and worth of the person. Social workers treat each person in a caring and respectful fashion, mindful of individual differences and cultural and ethnic diversity. Social workers promote clients' socially responsible self-determination. Social workers seek to enhance clients' capacity and opportunity to change and to address their own needs. Social workers are cognizant of their dual responsibility to clients and to the broader society. They seek to resolve conflicts between clients' interests and the broader society's interests in a socially responsible manner consistent with the values, ethical principles, and ethical standards of the profession. 4)* **Value:** *Importance of Human Relationships:* **Ethical Principle:** *Social workers recognize the central importance of human relationships. Social workers understand that relationships between and among people are an important vehicle for change. Social workers engage people as partners in the helping process. Social workers seek to strengthen relationships among people in a purposeful effort to promote, restore, maintain, and enhance the well-being of individuals, families, social groups, organizations, and communities. 5)* **Value:** *Integrity:* **Ethical Principle:** *Social workers behave in a trustworthy manner. Social workers are continually aware of the profession's*

> *mission, values, ethical principles, and ethical standards and practice in a manner consistent with them. Social workers act honestly and responsibly and promote ethical practices on the part of the organizations with which they are affiliated. 6)* **Value:** *Competence:* **Ethical Principle***: Social workers practice within their areas of competence and develop and enhance their professional expertise. Social workers continually strive to increase their professional knowledge and skills and to apply them in practice. Social workers should aspire to contribute to the knowledge base of the profession.*
>
> (pp. 5–6)

The ACA *Code of Ethics* says, "Professional values are an important way of living out an ethical commitment" (ACA, 2014, p. 3). This assertion precedes a list of professional values, including

> *enhancing human development throughout the life span; honoring diversity and embracing a multicultural approach in support of the worth, dignity, potential, and uniqueness of people within their social and cultural contexts; promoting social justice; safeguarding the integrity of the counselor–client relationship; and practicing in a competent and ethical manner.*

Based on these core values, the ACA *Code of Ethics* describes basic ethical principles in the following manner. "These principles are the foundation for ethical behavior and decision making. The fundamental principles of professional ethical behavior are

- *autonomy*, or fostering the right to control the direction of one's life;
- *nonmaleficence*, or avoiding actions that cause harm;
- *beneficence*, or working for the good of the individual and society by promoting mental health and well-being;
- *justice*, or treating individuals equitably and fostering fairness and equality;
- *fidelity*, or honoring commitments and keeping promises, including fulfilling one's responsibilities of trust in professional relationships; and
- *veracity*, or dealing truthfully with individuals with whom counselors come into professional contact.

(p. 3)

The American Psychological Association (APA) says that its general principles "are aspirational in nature. Their intent is to guide and inspire psychologists toward the very highest ethical ideals of the profession" (American Psychological Association, p. 3). Similar to NASW and ACA, APA identifies the following principles: Principle A: Beneficence and Nonmaleficence; Principle B: Fidelity and Responsibility; Principle C: Integrity; Principle D: Justice; and, Principle E: Respect for People's Rights and Dignity (American Psychological Association, 2017).

Along with the American Association of Marriage and Family Therapists and other professional associations, all of these professional associations affirm the importance of diversity in their respective codes of ethics. Included in their code of ethics, "Social workers are sensitive to cultural and ethnic diversity and strive to end discrimination, oppression, poverty, and other forms of social injustice" (National Association of Social Workers, 2017, p. 2). Similarly, the profession of counseling upholds the importance of "honoring diversity and embracing a multicultural approach in support of the worth, dignity, potential, and uniqueness of people within their social and cultural contexts" (American Counseling Association, 2014, p. 3). In agreement with the other associations, the code of ethics for psychologists states,

> *Psychologists are aware of and respect cultural, individual, and role differences, including those based on age, gender, gender identity, race, ethnicity, culture, national origin, religion, sexual orientation, disability, language, and socioeconomic status, and consider these factors when working with members of such groups. (American Psychological Association, 2017, p. 4)*

The importance of these values and principles is that they place a necessary, significant, professional, and clinically relevant obligation – albeit a desirable obligation – on clinical supervisors. In short, it is that clinical supervisors should relate with their supervisees and others in such ways that fulfill the expectations of these values and principles. Clinical supervisors honor diversity, autonomy, justice, competence, integrity, service, and other values and principles. Further, they aspire to assist their supervisees toward developing fidelity to these values and principles.

Clearly, the collective judgment of most mental health care providers is that these values and principles are needed ones. And, no doubt, in many situations, these values prescribe clinical judgments and actions by mental health care providers or, at least, provide constraints against appealing but inappropriate judgments. Thus, more than merely accepting these values and principles, mental health care providers should ask how they may advocate for their effective implementation. For the social good, psychotherapists should do no less than advocate for the effective implementation of these values and principles.

Psychotherapy is a profession. The question of professional accountability raises another and, possibly, a more fundamentally relevant question. It is "What is a profession?" If a profession cannot be defined by what it is or what its members have in common or an identifiable purpose and mission or more, is it a profession? In this discussion, the assumption is that psychotherapy – or other synonyms used to refer to it – is a profession. To continue toward observing what psychotherapy is, the discussion turns toward briefly defining what a profession is. A profession may be characterized by the following features:

Professions have an identifiable body of knowledge. Currently, psychotherapy lacks an identifiable body of knowledge that is broadly shared by those who practice it. Confirming this observation, are the Chinese five elements and emotion-focused therapy reasonably regarded as appropriate components of an identifiable body of knowledge? Or do embodied code-switching and cognitive behavioral therapy share an identifiable body of knowledge? How about body wisdom dialogue and dreamwork and rational emotive behavioral therapy? How about the Sufi healing circle and applied behavioral analysis? How about Bible-centered Christian counseling and dialectical behavioral therapy? Clearly, a minimally appropriate, useful, and professional understanding of psychotherapy excludes some of these approaches from belonging to the profession, although they frequently appear with many others that are also alien to the profession.

A profession has an identifiable body of knowledge and, therefore, necessarily excludes knowledge that is transparently incompatible with it. The profession of dentistry is not likely to include flood control engineering in its body of knowledge, despite the obvious importance of flood control engineering. However, just like the body of knowledge in other professions, the body of knowledge of counseling and psychotherapy has steadily expanded from the time modern psychotherapy began. It is not confined to established knowledge or to the protection of established knowledge. For example, should a professional body of knowledge include earthbody ecotherapy or Tamalpa life/art process? The boundaries around established knowledge should accommodate emerging evidence, evolving clients' needs, changing economic conditions, and revisions of laws, regulations, and professional ethics.

A profession demonstrates a specific kind of expertise. When individuals practice highly individualized, made-up nonsense or solidly evidence-supported treatments, the options may shock the practitioners on both sides. They may select either Sufism or career counseling, either past life soul retrieval or trauma-focused cognitive behavioral therapy, either astrology or child trends lifecourse model, either Christian counseling or systematic desensitization, either Native American rituals or dialectical behavior therapy, either massage or motivational interviewing, either ancient African healing or the community reinforcement approach (CRA), either light touch healing or assertive community treatment, either ancient Chinese martial arts or illness management and recovery, or tens of thousands of other options. If mental health care operates within an identifiable and truly professional body of expertise, the individual clinician cannot and should not choose both of the paired options in the preceding sentences. Instead of the current chaos and cacophony in the world of psychotherapy, members of the psychotherapy community must seek to establish expertise, including relevant standards for selecting and utilizing various treatments. Lacking agreed-upon and broadly recognized expertise, readers are encouraged to pursue relevant and useful discussions of this issue. Among many resources, the following may be helpful: Tracey et al. (2014), "Expertise in Psychotherapy: An Elusive Goal?"; Hill et al. (2015), "Therapist Expertise in Psychotherapy Revisited"; or Tracey et al. (2018), "Improving Expertise in Psychotherapy."

A profession has a function that is recognized by the members of the profession and by the recipients of its services. Accounting for the options that are named in the preceding paragraphs, a reasonable conclusion is that psychotherapy lacks identifiable functions that psychotherapists recognize or that their clients recognize. Emphasizing this conclusion, does psychotherapy have a generally recognizable function, if some of its practitioners offer Torah therapy, Muslim therapy, existential Buddhism, Sufi mysticism, and Christ-centered therapy, not to mention thousands of other similarly disparately religious views as orientations to psychotherapy? Surely, allowing for useful and necessary diversity in treatment philosophies, the needs of the clientele, training opportunities, and the specific skills of a therapist, collectively, psychotherapists should seek consensus around what constitutes the necessary functions of psychotherapy.

A profession has a set of rules that guide its members. Psychotherapy is largely unregulated. It lacks agreed-upon rules that guide its members. The evidence that easily confirms this observation may be sufficiently illustrated already. Adding to this sufficiency, individuals may receive a license to practice psychotherapy after completing a graduate program with approximately one hundred semester hours or approximately thirty semester hours or a number of semester hours between these numbers. Also, based on our review of tens of thousands of websites of licensed, practicing therapists, we have located more than twenty thousand approaches to counseling and psychotherapy. This number refers to the lack of regulation but also the desperate need for it.

A profession has a broadly recognized capacity for "self"-management. The lack of a capacity to manage itself can be easily established. For one thing, as this chapter makes clear, on a massive scale, psychotherapists "just make up stuff" and call it "therapy." For another thing, preparation for the practice of psychotherapy carries the burden of an extreme array of sizes and contents. On one extreme, a "psychotherapist" may practice "chrystal bowl sound therapy," while, on another extreme, a psychotherapist may practice mindfulness-based cognitive therapy. For another thing, licenses for psychotherapists come in an extraordinary variety. We can identify more than one hundred titles of licenses for mental health care providers. For another thing, licensed mental health care providers may hold an extreme variety of certifications. For example, a widely accepted certification may be earned in rational emotive behavioral therapy through the Albert Ellis Institute (2018). In contrast, a relatively less known certification in soul entrainment may be issued by Create Heaven Soul Entrainment Training (Soul Entrainment, 2019) and advertised by licensed mental health care providers (e.g., Kim Conway, 2018). A certification may be earned in traditional Tibetan medicine from The Tibetan Medicine Education Center (Tibetan Medicine Education Center, 2019). These facts hardly support the capacity of psychotherapy to manage itself as a profession.

For another thing, the major mental health care associations cannot represent psychotherapists who utilize their respective titles (i.e., counselor, psychologist, social worker, or marriage and family therapist), simply because only a minority of those who utilize these titles are members of associations. For example, a common assumption that the American Counseling Association (ACA) represents professional counselors, including those who provide psychotherapy for clients, is incorrect. In its recent report about membership statistics (American

Counseling Association, 2018), the ACA does not include a category or division for those who provide psychotherapy. Among its nearly 53,000 members, very few are psychotherapists. According to the National Association of Social Workers, its membership numbers around 120,000 (National Association of Social Workers, 2019). In contrast with this number, the Bureau of Labor reports, "In 2016, there were more than 680,000 social workers employed in the United States" (Bureau of Labor Statistics, 2019). These facts hardly support the idea that psychotherapy has a capacity to manage itself as a profession.

Finally, a profession has commonly recognized standards and steps through which individuals enter the profession. This includes procedures for admitting individuals to preparation programs and for licensing, among other things. Allowing for the extraordinarily diverse and often contradictory standards and methods for preparing and licensing psychotherapists, numerous other individuals enter or claim to enter the profession. The others often meet few, if any, of the standards of professional preparation that may be seen and scrutinized for professional counselors, psychologists, social workers, and marriage and family therapists. For example, a "licensed clinical Christian counselor" receives a license from the National Christian Counselors Association. Unfortunately, this license appears to require little or no professional training for providing psychotherapy. The so-called "license" may be issued to individuals who have not completed high school. Then, add these individuals to those who hold no license to practice counseling and psychotherapy but practice anyway and advertise their services online. Then, add all of these to those who provide counseling and psychotherapy through social service agencies, in which individuals provide services as counselors and psychotherapists, although many of them have little or no preparation for the delivery of such services. Many individuals – maybe enough psychotherapy pretenders to constitute around half of all psychotherapy services – practice psychotherapy who are transparently unqualified for such a practice. This raises serious doubts about whether psychotherapy as a profession has commonly understood and utilized standards and steps through which individuals change from being non-members of the profession to being members of the profession. Also, to receive a commonly recognized license as one of the major types of licenses (i.e., counselor, psychologist, social worker, marriage and family therapist), the requirements come in a huge variety of sizes and quality. With regard to size, an individual may pursue licensing as a social worker and complete only thirty graduate semester hours of preparation, while a counseling psychologist may complete more than one hundred graduate semester hours.

What Psychotherapy Is Not

Obviously, the list of ideas about what psychotherapy is not could be a lengthy one. For example, psychotherapy is not welding or plumbing. Instead of simplistically listing numerous things that psychotherapy is not, this discussion intends to describe and rebut several ideas about what psychotherapy is, according to therapists who prefer to think about psychotherapy in these ways, and what it should not be.

Psychotherapy is not ideology-driven. To an unknown degree, psychotherapy has always been driven by ideology. Mostly, the ideologies that energized psychotherapy have been more or less confined by a counterbalancing interest in freeing psychotherapy from extraneous and unrelated ideologies. For example, the first major theoretical orientation to psychotherapy, psychoanalysis, was ideological more than it was scientific, despite Freud's protests to the contrary. Among other things, Freud sought to free psychotherapy from the constraints of religious ideology, even while he was creating another ideology. Currently, though, psychotherapy is driven by ideology that is unrelated to the appropriate practice of psychotherapy more than it has ever been. Based on our review of approximately 60,000 websites of practicing psychotherapists, our observation is an easily reached and compelling one. It is that religion and other ideologies have become dominating influences in psychotherapy. To illustrate this, we can locate more than 1,200 titles for various expressions of Christian counseling and psychotherapy. The multiple titles of Christian approaches, such as Christian counseling, Mormon therapy, Christ-centered therapy, Immanuel prayer process therapy, Bible-based therapy, Christian Buddhism, Catholic coaching, and spiritual root system, accompany multitudes of other ideological approaches. In addition, we can locate another 600 titles of religious orientations to counseling and psychotherapy that represent religions other than Christianity. With the recognition that they are easily located and that the possibilities for listing here is much larger than this, the short list of ideology- and religion-driven approaches of practicing therapists strongly suggests that those who offer these approaches have contaminated counseling and psychotherapy. The short, illustrative list includes

Chassidic spirituality
Eastern mystical traditions
Formational prayer counseling
God-designed counseling
Inner healing prayer
Pneumatherapy/Christian-originated
Life between life spiritual regression
Muslim healing
Past-life soul retrieval
Shambhala Buddhist approach
Soul expansion shamanic mentoring
Spiritual cognitive therapy (SCT)
Taoist/Tantric practices
Torah-based counseling and therapy
Earth-based religions
Entheogenic shamanism
Frum therapy
Huna healing/Ho'omana
Muslim psychotherapy
John of God crystal healing bed
Magical SOULutions
Nondual Kabbalistic healing
Scriptural values counseling
Soul restoration
Soul travel
Sufi psychology
Vedic astrology
Wild feminine soul psychotherapy

Apart from their deleterious impact on the practice of counseling and psychotherapy, many of these ideologies are quite respectable. Clearly, they are valuable and quite personal to those who hold the beliefs that inhere in them. No matter how strongly their religious and other personal views are held, though, they are not appropriate expressions of counseling and psychotherapy. To make this point another way, there are numerous other ideologies that should not be expressed as counseling and psychotherapy. For example, in response to a question about the role of men and women in our economy, a sincere belief may be that men should be advanced over women. After all, such a belief holds that men are more assertive and demonstrably more capable in most areas of business than women. This example may be accompanied by other unacceptable beliefs that professionally accountable therapists reject, including the belief that homosexuals are by definition mentally ill. Sincerely held ideologies are almost always inadequate bases for conducting counseling and psychotherapy. Moreover, the ideology-driven therapies likely contribute to the decline in clinical performance among practicing psychotherapists (Spengler & Pilipis, 2015; Goldberg et al., 2016). Somewhat more broadly than ideology-driven therapies, Harrist and Richardson (2012) assert that counselors' and psychotherapists' commitment to social justice "is guided more by a disguised ideology of liberal individualism than an objective theory or value-neutral principles" (p. 38). When done well, with the interests and needs of clients taking the highest priority, psychotherapy is not an ideology, let alone a highly individualized ideology.

Psychotherapy is not a uniquely personal expression. Following a review of thousands of websites where counselors and psychotherapists advertise their approaches to therapy, an easy and correct observation is that a surprising proportion of their practice of psychotherapy is a highly individualized pursuit. More than expressing the profession of which they are parts, therapists express themselves. More than integrating solidly good evidence into their practice of therapy, they express themselves. More than responding to the specific clinical needs of their clients, they express themselves. And more than doing clinical good, they express themselves and, no doubt, sometimes help their clients, but they may also sometimes harm their clients, because of non-clinical expressions of themselves. On a massive scale, they just make up stuff and call it therapy. Surely, this includes numerous specifically religious approaches to psychotherapy, such as Bible-based sex therapy or Hassidic spirituality, but it also includes approaches such as horse-informed archetypical therapy, smileology, tabletop game therapy, and un-oriented therapy.

As judgmental as the preceding paragraph may appear to be, an important note should be added to it. The therapists who demonstrate conspicuous self-interest in their practice of therapy are a minority. To be sure, more than providing appropriate clinical services for their clients, they place a higher priority on their own needs. The size of this minority is not precisely known. Obviously, a review of the advertising on their websites does not allow this number to be precise. However, at this time, the review of thousands of websites where therapists advertise their approaches to psychotherapy leads to an estimate of the size of this minority. It is approximately twenty percent of licensed counselors and psychotherapists (Martin, in press).

Unlicensed "therapists" who advertise online should be added to this number. As individuals who express themselves while alleging to offer therapy to unsuspecting, prospective clients, these self-identified "therapists" are easily located. An unlicensed "therapist," among thousands of similar advertisers, says that she practices ancient Hebraic dream interpretation. Another "therapist" offers after-death communication. And another offers astrological consulting. Sadly, these approaches to therapy are advertised by licensed mental health care providers, too. As a group of self-expressive therapists, the unlicensed ones constitute approximately seven to twelve percent of those who advertise through websites (Martin, in press).

Psychotherapy is not "everything." Collectively, therapists try to treat every conceivable human problem. They not only treat every conceivable human problem, but they invent every conceivable way of thinking about how to conduct therapy and every conceivable method for doing therapy. So far, we have located therapists who advertise numerous activities, including hiking therapy, fly fishing therapy, circus arts therapy, piano therapy, martial arts therapy, gardening therapy, and hundreds of other activities. Some will do almost anything that comes to mind, regardless of the consequences for their clients. For added examples, other licensed therapists practice other specific activities, such as cinema therapy, biking therapy, boxing therapy, chess therapy, climbing therapy, sewing therapy, swimming therapy, vibrator therapy, video production therapy, and vocal arts therapy. They allege to provide numerous other kinds of therapies. From a compilation of more than twenty thousand "therapies" that we have gathered, the list includes nine Rites of Munay-Ki, African and Native American rituals, Arno temperament profiling, Chinese herbal medicine, HALO light therapy, intuitive healing, Karuna Reiki practice, Marconics no-touch healing, Secret Garden healing, spiritual ecstatic dance, and traditional Bhakti music. The inevitable conclusion is that counselors and therapists have determined that almost any whim, desire, impulse, or belief is sufficient as a therapeutic activity. In response to this situation, professionally accountable counselors and psychotherapists should constrain themselves to practice within the boundaries of their respective competencies and their profession-endorsed approaches to therapy. In addition, professionally accountable counselors and therapists must find ways to constrain their peers from practicing unethical approaches to therapy.

The discussion of what psychotherapy is not has emphasized that psychotherapy is not ideology-driven, psychotherapy is not a uniquely personal expression, and it is not "everything." Adding to these emphases, *psychotherapy also is not "just made up stuff."* Insofar as large numbers of counselors and psychotherapists offer approaches to therapy that have no basis in clinical reality, they pose the likelihood of harm to their clients and to the profession of which they are members. They demonstrate their failure to be professionally accountable therapists. However, their failure also requires professionally accountable counselors and psychotherapists to define what they do, comply with normative professional standards, and advance their profession so that it continues to improve the lives of their clients.

Psychotherapy is not academic. If the preparation of counselors and psychotherapists had been done well, would the mental health care community be suffering its multiple, current embarrassments? Surely, Mahrer's (1999) prescient description of major embarrassments in the condition of psychotherapy makes this clear. Among his observations, he stated, "Psychotherapists try to fix problems that are mainly unreal fictions, concocted mainly by psychotherapists" (p. 1150). When asked to explain many of their frequently used terms, psychotherapists usually stumble and stutter. For example, "What is psychotherapy?" or "What is attachment?" or "What is self-esteem?" or "What is mental health?" Taking the idea of useful fictions further, Maher says, "Psychotherapy is a pseudoscience of non-existing unrealities, measured with rigorous precision." Somewhat wryly, he continues, "Set our scientific measure-makers to the task, and they can prove the existence of schizophrenia, devil possession, elves and goblins, witches and warlocks. No problem. We have scientific measures." So, how has mental health care arrived at a time when it is both a credible profession and not a credible profession? How has it sustained the illusion of a profession? How has it maintained both the mirage of accountability and the near total lack of accountability? It has done this through its affiliation with and achievement through academic institutions. It has falsely concluded that academic achievement almost inevitably produces clinical proficiency and effectiveness. Generally, preparation programs have failed to produce competent and accountable counselors and psychotherapists. Among other products of careful analysis, the comprehensive meta-reanalysis of the robustness of the experience-accuracy effect by Spengler and Pilipis (2015) attests to this, along with Goldberg et al. (2016), Hill et al. (2015), and others.

Obviously, an argument can be made for the importance of academic training for prospective counselors and psychotherapists. As long-serving academic professionals, we endorse the argument for academic preparation of individuals who wish to become counselors and psychotherapists. However, we assert that, without intensive, major, carefully assessed clinical training, academic training lacks sufficiency in preparing minimally competent and accountable clinicians. More than the academic professionals who train them, clinicians constitute the huge majority of the members of the mental health care profession of which we are members. Academic preparation need not be diminished. Clinical preparation must become substantially much more clinical than it currently is.

Instead of merely articulating a point of view about what psychotherapy is and is not, we hope that the question of what it is and our point of view will help to shape a larger discussion. More than discussion alone, though, we hope that major reforms in counseling and psychotherapy will come from such a discussion. Toward accomplishing this, specific and major reforms are presented in Martin (*Therapy Thieves: How to Save Mental Health Care from Its Providers*, in press).

Conclusion

To be clear and succinct, counseling and psychotherapy may be defined as having the following necessary features:

Counseling and psychotherapy are about restoring, sustaining, and enhancing health.
They are about health care, sharing this pursuit with all other health care professions and providers.
They are about mental health care. To reiterate, mental health care is a professionally accountable service that, in a very large variety of ways, treats individuals, couples, and families, in response to relationship problems, environmental stressors, and mental illnesses.
They are about serving the social good.
They are about professional accountability.
They are a profession that stands apart from other professions.

Note: A very different but overlapping version of the information in this chapter appears in Martin, F. A., *Therapy Thieves: How to Save Mental Health Care from Its Providers*. Oxford University Press, in press.

2

WHAT IS CLINICAL SUPERVISION?

This chapter aims to answer two questions: What is clinical supervision, and what is a philosophy of clinical supervision? Answers to these foundational questions are ones upon which much of the remainder of this book is built. Inherent in these answers is the common belief that, usually, the practice of clinical supervision stands on the presumption that it is needed to ensure competent, professionally accountable client care, particularly by newer clinicians who are emerging into the profession. This may be understood to be its universally accepted purpose.

Additionally, a compatriotic purpose is to assist with the professional development/effectiveness of supervisees. Ensuring competence for new clinicians and facilitating their professional development rest on another presumption – namely, the belief that clinical supervisors have a point of view about clinical supervision that guides their supervision, a philosophy of clinical supervision. Instead of allowing this presumption to drift into the fog of not knowing or the haze of misunderstanding, this chapter aims to define and discuss the need for a philosophy of clinical supervision and some of its necessary dimensions.

The necessity of ensuring competence and developing professionalism may be easily stated. Clients need help, and therapists provide help. To ensure that new counselors and therapists can provide competent help, they receive profession-necessitated clinical supervision. In addition, several secondary purposes of clinical supervision may be listed. These purposes indicate that clinical supervision is intended to develop clinical skills and to express a methodology in which a supervisee needs training; to teach a specific approach to a client issue or population; to express an agreed-upon ideology; to effectuate the purpose of an organization or treatment program; to assess the program of an organization; to equip individuals to receive a license or another credential, such as a certification; and to develop clinical effectiveness.

According to Martin and Cannon (2010), "Clinical supervision is the process of training another clinician to function effectively" (p. 1). This somewhat succinct definition of clinical supervision may be helpfully augmented by adding others' definitions of clinical supervision. Here are some commonly cited ones:

Supervision is an intervention provided by a senior member of a profession to a more junior member or members. . . . This relationship is evaluative, extends over

> *time, and has the simultaneous purposes of enhancing the professional functioning of the more junior person(s); monitoring the quality of professional services offered to the clients that she, he, or they see; and serving as a gatekeeper of those who are to enter the particular profession.*
>
> (Bernard & Goodyear, 2004, p. 8)

> *Supervision is "a social influence process that occurs over time, in which the supervisor participates with supervisees to ensure quality of clinical care. Effective supervisors observe, mentor, coach, evaluate, inspire, and create an atmosphere that promotes self-motivation, learning, and professional development. They build teams, create cohesion, resolve conflict, and shape agency culture, while attending to ethical and diversity issues in all aspects of the process. Such supervision is key to both quality improvement and the successful implementation of consensus and evidence-based practices."*
>
> (Center for Substance Abuse Treatment, 2007, p. 3)

> *Supervision is a disciplined, tutorial process wherein principles are transformed into practical skills, with four overlapping foci: administrative, evaluative, clinical, and supportive.*
>
> (Powell & Brodsky, 2004, p. 11)

Taken together, these definitions provide a brief overview of clinical supervision, insofar as they emphasize several essential features of clinical supervision. These features include the following:

Supervision is the process of training another clinician to function effectively.
Supervision is an intervention provided by a senior member of a profession to a more junior member or members.
Supervision is a relationship that is evaluative and extends over time.
Supervisors monitor the quality of professional services offered to clients.
Supervisors serve as gatekeepers for those who are to enter the particular profession.
Supervision is a social influence process.
Supervisors participate with supervisees to ensure quality of clinical care.
Supervisors observe, mentor, coach, evaluate, inspire, and create an atmosphere that promotes self-motivation, learning, and professional development.
Supervisors build teams, create cohesion, resolve conflict, and shape agency culture.
Supervisors attend to ethical and diversity issues.
Supervision is key to both quality improvement and the successful implementation of consensus and evidence-based practices.
Supervision is a disciplined, tutorial process.
Supervision maintains four overlapping foci: administrative, evaluative, clinical, and supportive.

So, what is clinical supervision? It is, most importantly, a process through which good clinical care from supervisees and for clients is assured. Beyond this, clinical supervision is a relationship that involves training, intervening, monitoring, gatekeeping, observing, mentoring, coaching, motivating, evaluating, inspiring, team building, resolving conflict, serving within the constraints of professional ethics and applicable laws, supporting, and teaching. In short, while it gives attention to the highest priority of ensuring good clinical care, clinical supervision provides a process through which the professional development of supervisees may be assured.

The importance of the development of supervisees cannot be overestimated. It constitutes a secondary priority but one without which clinical supervision cannot justifiably exist. Clinical supervision assists supervisees in their professional development toward becoming effective clinicians. The development of supervisees is discussed in this book, including the material on defining an effective clinician and information about the developmental stages of supervisees.

What Is a Philosophy of Clinical Supervision?

Several researchers and writers (e.g., Bernard & Goodyear, 2009; Campbell, 2000, 2006; Martin & Cannon, 2010; Center for Substance Abuse Treatment, 2009) have given definitions of a philosophy of clinical supervision. Almost all of these definitions reside within the context of the respective, specific model or theory of clinical supervision of these researchers and writers. Several of these models or theories are discussed later. For now, an integrated and possibly a broadly acceptable definition of a philosophy of clinical supervision may be stated in the following way: A philosophy of clinical supervision encapsulates the beliefs about counseling and psychotherapy and clinical supervision that a supervisor holds and through which the practice of clinical supervision is delivered. The emphasis here should be clear. It is placed on beliefs about what is being supervised and how the practice of supervision stems from these beliefs. However, as fundamentally important as they are, a supervisor's practice of supervision should express much more than a supervisor's beliefs alone. In addition, they should express the accrued wisdom of the profession of clinical supervision as it emerges from professionally accountable service to clients and supervisees, the best evidence from peer-reviewed research, and the best evidence from the practice of clinical supervision.

From these beliefs, a supervisor answers several basic and necessary questions, with clear advantages arising from a self-conscious, deliberative effort to answer them. The alternative is to act on beliefs about supervision as if these questions are answered but without the guidance of clarity that refined answers provide. Basic questions about a philosophy of clinical supervision include the following:

What is counseling/psychotherapy?
What do I believe about conducting mental health care?

What do I believe about clinical supervision?
What is the role of the supervisor?
What is the role of the supervisee?
How do supervisees develop toward increased effectiveness?
How do I define the good clinical supervisor?
How do I conceptualize the good or excellent counselor/therapist?
What is my rationale for initiating any specific clinical supervision intervention?

The answers to these questions, along with others that may be added to the list, form the core of a philosophy of clinical supervision. Individual clinical supervisors must seek to answer these questions for themselves so that they have a coherent and professionally accountable approach to clinical supervision. The answers to these questions have been represented in numerous ways throughout the relatively short history of contemporary counseling and psychotherapy. However, at this time, there are no collective, agreed-upon answers to these questions. The meaning of these terms – *supervision, counseling, psychotherapy*, and *clinical supervision* – may be called into question by advocates of the many approaches to the practice of mental health care and clinical supervision. For example, a predictably low level of agreement about almost all features of these terms would come from advocates of solution-focused mental health care and the advocates of psychoanalysis. Likewise, low agreement is likely between advocates of emotion-focused therapy and advocates of behavior therapy. Other treatment philosophies easily offer contrasts and disagreements. With these and many other likely disagreements in view, recommended ways to answers to these basic questions are offered here, with the understanding that the answers may do more to evoke questions than to answer them. Nevertheless, the questions and answers appear throughout this book. The operative assumption is that useful and sustainable answers about clinical supervision come from each supervisor's initiative in raising basic questions about clinical supervision and seeking to establish both durable and adaptable answers.

Why Is a Philosophy of Clinical Supervision Necessary?

The short answer to this question is that a philosophy of clinical supervision is needed as an expression of professional accountability. A more complete statement is that, without it, clinical supervisors display lack of professional accountability, insofar as they cannot articulate why they do what they do, which desired outcomes they wish to achieve, how they may assist their supervisees in thinking about their development as clinicians, and much more. As noted earlier, as clinical supervisors make necessary adaptations in their role, they make numerous decisions about how to handle a wide variety of situations with their supervisees. The question is "What informs and guides their decisions?" Most of the answer is that, as they adapt toward becoming effective clinical supervisors, they concomitantly develop a philosophy of clinical supervision, even when they fail to clearly articulate it. Obviously, the more clearly articulated their philosophy of clinical supervision is, the more likely they are effective in providing clinical supervision. The underlying hope and expectation of the material in this book is that it will measurably assist clinical supervisors and prospective clinical supervisors in their pursuit of a philosophy of clinical supervision and the professional accountability that comes from their philosophy.

To be somewhat colloquial about this, the adage, "If you don't know where you're going, any road will take you there" is true. If clinical supervisors lack a clearly articulated philosophy of clinical supervision, they do not likely know where they are going. And, as a result of this, they may not know of the good they do or the harm they cause.

If mental health care providers hold little or no information and understanding of what clinical work is, they are more likely than others to fail to provide effective services to their clients. Almost universally, providers are expected to be able to articulate clinically plausible conceptualizations of their clients' problems. Supervisors look for their supervisees' ability to develop such conceptualizations. Moreover, they should look for a similar ability in themselves as clinical supervisors, with regard to how they conceptualize their work with supervisees. Likewise, a large source of failure in clinical supervision stems from the lack of clarity about the supervisor's philosophy of clinical supervision. From this observation, the need for developing a philosophy of and a rationale for clinical supervision becomes clear, regardless of the setting in which supervision is delivered.

Misguided Beliefs About a Philosophy of Clinical Supervision

Many supervisors seem to conclude that they are good clinical supervisors because they are good counselors/therapists. Unfortunately, this is probably not correct. For one thing, it is incorrect because experienced clinicians commonly hold views of their clinical effectiveness that evidence strongly suggests that they lack (Goldberg et al., 2016; Walfish et al., 2012; Spengler & Pilipis, 2015). For another thing, despite many limitations of believing that being a good counselor/therapist is a sufficient basis for being a good supervisor, many supervisors believe this. While clinical service is a necessary prerequisite for supervision, it is not sufficient. Unfortunately, the belief that effective counseling is a sufficient basis for understanding and actualizing clinical supervision is supported by many states where training for post-degree clinical supervision is not required. In most states, no evidence of training in clinical supervision or even a letter that confirms interest in clinical supervision is required. To illustrate the inherent dilemma of believing that being a good clinician is a sufficient basis for conducting clinical supervision, what may a prospective clinical supervisor need to know about vicarious liability in clinical supervision? Or what do legal precedents, such as *Simmons v. U.S. 1986* (Justia US Law, 2019) say about the accountability of clinical supervisors for the actions of their supervisees? Or what may be some of the important differences between a developmental model of clinical supervision and a reflective model of clinical supervision? Unlike clinical work with clients, clinical supervision involves knowledge and experience with vicarious liability, legal precedents about clinical supervision, and various models of clinical supervision, along with other important areas of relevance to the practice of clinical supervision. Many of these areas receive attention in this book.

If they are most effective in their implementation, the beliefs that guide clinical supervision ought not to be a mere re-statement of beliefs about counseling and psychotherapy. This is to say that many clinical supervisors make the mistake of saying something like, "I am a person-centered therapist. This is my approach to clinical supervision." While this may appear to be sufficient from the point of view of the supervisor, it leaves too much unsaid and too many questions unanswered, particularly from the point of view of supervisees and with reference to understanding the role of a clinical supervisor. Further, it omits, or even excuses, the weakness of not attempting to clarify for oneself and supervisees how supervision works. It points to the question, "How may I provide effective clinical supervision, when my supervisee holds different but entirely professional and plausible views about what counseling and psychotherapy are?" A psychotherapy-based model of clinical supervision is generally not sufficient for providing effective clinical supervision.

In their influential text on clinical supervision, Bernard and Goodyear (2004) correctly distinguish between supervision models that are grounded in psychotherapy theory and those that are grounded in a developmental model of supervision. Their distinction is important. However, while parsing concepts is a necessary and worthy pursuit, the obligations of clinical supervisors encompass much more than choosing between a psychotherapy theory-based approach to clinical supervision and a model-based approach. A philosophy of clinical supervision may begin with understanding these concepts, but it should do more than this. Principally, clinical supervisors carry the obligation of informing their supervisees about their personal-professional approach to clinical supervision. As only one indicator of this necessity, a psychodynamic-oriented supervisor, for example, should be prepared to facilitate the professional development of a supervisee when the supervisee is a cognitively oriented counselor. In other words, a supervisor may identify closely with a theory of therapy but should develop a philosophy of supervision that accounts for a broader range of thinking than a model that is grounded in psychotherapy alone generally allows. After all, effective clinical supervision requires solid experience in and understanding of therapy but as a matter of practice is much more about effectively relating with professional colleagues than discharging the obligations of a therapist.

A smart understanding of misguided beliefs about clinical supervision appears in Jane Campbell's work, *Essentials of Clinical Supervision* (Campbell, 2006). Campbell, a frequently cited author and leader in advancing useful ideas about clinical supervision, offers ten myths about clinical supervision (Campbell, 2006, p. 269), as indicated here:

> If I am an experienced counselor or psychotherapist, I automatically will be successful and effective as a supervisor.
>
> True clinical supervision is strictly for the review of cases. If you give handouts or teach, that's training, not supervision.
>
> If supervision is not going well, it's the supervisee's fault.
>
> Supervision is only for the beginners or inexperienced. If you have to be supervised, you must be deficient/incompetent.
>
> Because supervisors are professionals, diversity issues do not have to be addressed.
>
> The best feedback is direct. Tell it like you see it. There is no need to coddle supervisees.
>
> A supervisee's thoughts and feeling are not relevant to learning.
>
> Supervisors are experts, so it is important to make that clear and never admit to mistakes or that you don't know the answer.
>
> Because supervisors are totally responsible for the actions of their supervisees, the supervisor's directions should not be questioned.
>
> In order to avoid a dual relationship and becoming your supervisee's therapist, you shouldn't use your therapy skills in supervision.

Campbell's collection of myths about supervision is instructive. At least, they confirm that some clinical supervisors face the temptation to follow their misguided beliefs about their approach to clinical supervision. In addition, they tacitly emphasize the need for clinical supervisors to develop an approach that they and their supervisees may rightly see as being a professionally accountable approach.

Conclusion

This chapter calls for clinical supervisors to clarify their individual approaches and views of clinical supervision. At least, this involves clarity about their respective views of what clinical supervision is and their individual understanding of their approach or philosophy of clinical supervision. Such clarity ensures that clinical supervisors will significantly increase the likelihood that they will provide competent supervision through which the clients of their supervisees will receive competent counseling and psychotherapy. And because of their elevated and clear intentionality in providing clinical supervision, their supervisees will more likely develop their professional competence.

SECTION II

Components of a Philosophy of Clinical Supervision

3

WHAT DO I BELIEVE ABOUT CONDUCTING MENTAL HEALTH CARE?

"What do I believe about conducting mental health care?" The answers to this question have pre-occupied mental health professionals for more than a century. No matter which marker is used to date the beginning of the mental health movement, the movement is characterized at least by numerous theories of psychotherapy. Each one of these theories has largely expressed the person of its inventor. Almost all mental health professionals know that Sigmund Freud was a strong analytic thinker and that, as an expression of this, he invented psychoanalysis. Similarly, most know that Carl Rogers was a strongly intuitive and relational person and that, as an expression of this, he invented person-centered therapy. While this is much too simplistic, it makes the point that as much as mental health professionals can and should rely on the best evidence for their work that they can get, they continue to be dependent on individualistic mixtures of good evidence and uniquely personal values and points of view about life in general and about their work in therapy.

Therefore, despite the obvious potential for over-simplifying them, this discussion gives attention to four major issues. One is the conceptualization of mental illness. The second is the conceptualization of those who are treated in mental health care. The third is conceptualizing evidence for mental health care. And the fourth is conceptualizing mental health, with the emphasis on "health."

However, experienced clinical supervisors know that the components of a philosophy of clinical supervision include much more than what they may believe about conducting mental health care. Therefore, this discussion of the components of a philosophy of clinical supervision includes the following chapters.

What Characterizes a Good Therapist?
What Do I Believe about Clinical Supervision?
What Are the Roles of the Clinical Supervisor and Supervisee?
How Do I Define a Good Clinical Supervisor?

Conceptualizing "Mental Illness"

If clinicians have a clear conceptualization about what mental health care is, they likely presume to hold a conceptualization of what it is that they are treating. This may be variously identified as "mental illness," "mental disorder," "emotional disturbance," "heightened or intense stress," or other commonly and professionally used terms. While there are numerous terms that may be used, all of them stand on a number of assumptions or beliefs about what these things are – or how clinicians conceive of the problems with which they are trying to help. In turn, how they conceive of these problems determines how they deliver mental health care.

Many mental health care providers prefer not to use the term "mental illness" or similar terms. The specific terms that providers use may not be important, but their understanding of the problems they treat is important. Such an understanding calls for another definition. What is – for want of another term – a "mental disorder"? While it may evoke more objections than endorsements, the DSM may be helpful in contributing to such a definition, mainly because it is likely the most frequently cited definition of mental and emotional problems. The definition of "mental disorder" in the fifth edition of the *Diagnostic and Statistical Manual of Mental Disorders* (DSM-5, American Psychiatric Association, 2013) is as follows:

> *A mental disorder is a syndrome characterized by clinically significant disturbance in an individual's cognition, emotion regulation, or behavior that reflects a dysfunction in the psychological, biological, or developmental processes underlying mental functioning. Mental disorders are usually associated with significant distress in social, occupational, or other important activities. An expectable or culturally approved response to a common stressor or loss, such as the death of a loved one, is not a mental disorder. Socially deviant behavior (e.g., political, religious, or sexual) and conflicts that are primarily between the individual and society are not mental disorders unless the deviance or conflict results from a dysfunction in the individual, as described above.*
>
> (p. 20)

To try to be useful in describing "mental disorder" or whatever it may be called, let's take parts of the preceding definition and offer explanations of some of the terms. The important terms are these:

Action or *behavior*
Syndrome or a *cluster of actions*
Clinically significant disturbance
Kinds of clinically significant disturbances

Understanding a mental disorder starts where most individuals or families begin. In short, something happens that grabs the attention of an individual or a family. The action or behavior may be many different things. It may be a child who has chronic and frightening nightmares. It may be a teenager who hints at suicide. It may be the married person who indicates to a partner that divorce is better than being married. It may be an individual who has consumed huge quantities of alcoholic beverages over a long period of time and whose life is out of control. The point is that something happens, and it grabs attention, either within the person doing it or from others who observe it.

Action or Behavior

An eleven-year-old boy hits his sister in the face. As an unusual action, this grabs the attention of the boy's parents. His parents may know that this is a one-time event or may suspect that their son has a larger problem. However, the fact that the boy hits his sister is not the same thing as a mental disorder. This is to say that this boy's action may or may not be a sign of a much bigger problem.

Syndrome or a Cluster of Concerns

If his parents observe that this boy's action is just one of many troubling actions, they may be seeing a syndrome – or a collection of problems or actions that, taken together, point to something more serious than hitting his sister.

Just to be clear, a child – or an adult – may exhibit actions that many of us may not like or that may upset us, but these actions may not be signs of a mental disorder or something else that requires mental health care. For example, teenagers may over-indulge in drinking alcohol. This may be justifiably disturbing to their parents. However, as disturbing as this may be, it is not necessarily an indication that they need mental health care.

However, when the eleven-year-old boy hits his sister, sneaks out of his house during the night to visit his friend, breaks into the bathroom where his mother is taking a shower, uses obscenities in speaking with his grandmother, and more, he is giving us a picture of a "syndrome" or a cluster of concerns. This cluster of concerns becomes a pattern of actions that rise to a "clinically significant disturbance."

Clinically Significant Disturbance

When there is a clinically significant disturbance, treatment is necessary. Later, we will discuss how treatment works. For now, though, the idea is a simple one: *clinically significant disturbance* may refer to many different things. Typically, these things will fall into several categories, including the following:

Problems or disturbances that individuals say they have and that almost everyone else sees – for example, serious depression is often acknowledged by individuals who are depressed and by those love them.

Problems or disturbances that an individual does not see in herself or denies, while others clearly see that a serious problem is present – for example, the extremely defiant, angry child usually does not acknowledge that she has a problem, but everyone else knows that she is troubled.

Somewhat unusually, an individual or a family may be disturbed but fail to see that they give evidence of clinically significant disturbance. In these cases, mental health professionals may see the disturbance, and it, therefore, becomes clinically significant. For example, a child may be inappropriately blamed for a family's failures within the family, but because of the blaming, the family would not see the psychological harm that has caused the child to be clinically disturbed. A mental health care provider would see that the family is causing the child to be clinically disturbed.

The long definition provided earlier refers to disturbances "*in cognition, emotion regulation, or behavior*." What does this mean? Let's take each one of these kinds of disturbances and briefly discuss them.

Disturbance in Cognition

Typically, "disturbances in cognition" refers to a wide range of distorted thoughts. For example, a man who remodels homes may think about how his work is inadequate. He installed – or laid – tile on the kitchen floor for a customer and believes that he did a lousy job, while the customer believes that the newly installed tile is beautiful. The remodeler thinks that he failed, while the customer and the customer's family express delight with their new kitchen floor. Probably, the remodeler holds perfectionistic ideas about his work, and because of this, he believes his work is never good or good enough.

Disturbance in thought may appear in individuals whose spouse died. The surviving spouses conclude that they may as well be dead, too, adding to their suffering. Others can appreciate how difficult life may be for the grieving survivors but also see how their distorted thinking may add to their suffering.

Disturbance in Emotional Regulation

Often, this kind of disturbance may be easily identified simply because most mental health professionals recognize this kind of disturbance when they see it. For example, while they know that young children sometimes have temper tantrums, they somewhat easily recognize that a very small proportion of children have temper tantrums frequently, over a long period of time, and for no apparent reason. The child is emotionally dysregulated or "out of emotional control." Also, for example, a forty-seven-year-old person may show extraordinary sadness because of the belief that aging means "getting old and ugly." Allowing for ordinary concern about the implications of aging, the extraordinary sadness would be seriously out of proportion with age and aging. This individual likely exhibits emotional dysregulation.

Disturbance in Behavior

This kind of disturbance refers to actions or what an individual is doing. Just like the other kinds of disturbance, this kind of disturbance may be easily illustrated, while the possibilities for disturbance in behavior are practically endless.

Allowing for the fact that the possibilities are almost endless, here are some examples of disturbance in behavior:

A seventeen-year-old female wears clothing that covers her arms – even during the hottest times of the year so that she can hide the scabs and scars on her arms from cutting herself. She uses almost any sharp object that she can find – a razor blade, shards of glass, knives, nails, keys, and so on. Her behavior indicates not only a disturbance in behavior, but inner disturbance, too. Even without knowing what the inner disturbance is, her behavior is a kind of disturbance that is very likely a sign that she needs mental health care.

A sixty-one-year-old male sits quietly, staring at a nine-millimeter handgun, refusing to speak to anyone, and withdrawing from members of his family. The meaning of this man's situation may be somewhat unclear, but his behaviors – sitting quietly, staring at a handgun, and withdrawing from his family – strongly suggests that he likely needs mental health care.

Many individuals show signs of all of these kinds of disturbance. Showing only one of these three would be somewhat unusual. However, considering these kinds of disturbances, there are additional indicators of problems that need the attention of mental health care providers. These include "*significant distress in social, occupational, or other important activities*."

Whether we are mental health care professionals or not, most of us know about these additional indicators. For example, we know about "significant distress in social activities." We know about a historically peaceful and cooperative member of our church – or another social group – who uncharacteristically explodes in anger during committee meetings, informal conversations, or church social gatherings. Or, we know about the individual who has been employed in desirable positions, only to be repeatedly terminated. Or we know about the twelve-year-old girl who has performed at a high level of success in school, until the last six months. Recently, she has failed in every way in her schoolwork. Each of these situations pictures "significant distress in social, occupational, or other important activities." And each one indicates that mental health care is needed.

All of the features of the long definition of mental disturbance given earlier should be adjusted to fit some of the exceptions that the definition includes. For example, the definition says, "An expectable or culturally approved response to a common stressor or loss, such as the death of a loved one, is not a mental disorder." This is a way of reminding us of what we already mostly know and understand. Many unusual circumstances may cause most of us to appear to be disturbed. For example, most of us know that we may not look and behave normally in the hours following the destruction of our home by a tornado. Most of us would also not look or behave normally shortly after our child was critically injured in a bicycle accident. Our reactions to these very stressful events are truly normal reactions and not signs of mental disturbance. Under these circumstances, we may look and feel like we are mentally disturbed, but because we have reactions that are expected under these circumstances, the conclusion that we have "a clinically significant disturbance" is not appropriate.

The long DSM definition (American Psychiatric Association, 2013) also states, "Socially deviant behavior (e.g., political, religious, or sexual) and conflicts that are primarily between the individual and society are not mental disorders unless the deviance or conflict results from a dysfunction in the individual, as described above" (p. 20). This sometimes poses a real challenge for all of us, including mental health care providers. Sometimes, we must acknowledge that someone else may deviate from social norms but is not showing clinically significant disturbance, while others who are also deviating from social norms are showing clinically significant disturbance. For example, during politically heated campaigns, those who disagree with us may appear to deviate from social norms, such as expressing transparently obvious racist views, only because they seriously disagree with "my views." Usually, even if we are tempted to describe them as "crazy" or "insane" or "sick," we know better than this.

In contrast with someone with whom we may disagree, consider another person. She appears to be, maybe, in her mid-twenties. She snares the attention of everyone on a downtown street, disheveled and almost naked, while begging men to have sex with her because, as she loudly shouts, "God wants me to have the baby Jesus. You gotta help me. God wants me to have the baby Jesus. Can you help me? Praise God. Praise God. God wants me to have the baby Jesus. Can you help me?" Lacking almost anything we may know about this woman, almost everyone who sees and hears this woman would very likely conclude that her breech of social norms indicates that she is clinically disturbed.

The definition of mental health care includes a reference to "a professionally accountable" service. In the context of this discussion, this means that a supervisor's beliefs about conducting therapy determine much of what is done in clinical supervision. Extending this, much of what is done in therapy and in clinical supervision stems from the supervisor's beliefs about their clients' problems and about people in general. This is to say that both supervisors and supervisees hold beliefs about clients' problems and about people in general. Almost inevitably, these beliefs emerge during the process of clinical supervision. For example, how may a supervisor and supervisee answer the following questions: How do clinicians make sense of the ten-year-old boy who hits his sister in the face? If this boy has a problem that appears before a mental health care provider, how may the provider think about how this boy makes changes in his behavior? If this boy – or any other client – displays disturbing and/or harmful behavior, what may be the role of emotions in such behavior? And, expanding this question, what causes mental-emotional dysfunction? And, expanding this question even more, what basic assumptions may a supervisor or supervisee make about the nature of being human? Along with this question, another one may be "What characterizes a mentally healthy person?"

To read about a model of clinically conceptualizing client's issues, refer to the chapter, "An Example of a Philosophy of Clinical Supervision," under the heading, "The Conceptual Context of My Philosophy of Clinical Supervision."

Conceptualizing Those Who Receive Care

Among others, Auger (2004) has emphasized the significance of raising these questions – in the preceding section – about clinicians' beliefs about those who receive care from them. In his article, "What We Don't Know CAN Hurt Us: Mental Health Counselor's Implicit Assumptions about Human Nature," he reminds us of what mental health care providers know to be true. He confirms that, quite apart from commonly recognized and accepted theories of counseling, counselors and others hold views of themselves and other human beings that guide much of their behavior. He states, "Like all people, mental health counselors have basic assumptions about how humans behave and how change in human behavior occurs" (Auger, 2004, p. 13). He goes further, though, in concluding that these assumptions "have an important influence on case conceptualization and intervention" (p. 13). What most mental health care providers generally believe about Freud, Rogers, and Wolpe confirms that therapists may regard human beings in somewhat negative ways, somewhat positive ways, and somewhat neutral ways, among others, and that these ways of regarding human beings have specific and real outcomes in the conduct of therapy and, by extension, supervision.

Articulating a conception of those who need mental health care expands well beyond the scope of this book. As noted earlier, conceptualizing those who need mental health care has been a pre-occupation from the time that the mental health movement began. This is clearly seen in the fact that mental health care providers have practiced hundreds – if not thousands – of theoretical orientations to counseling/psychotherapy. Despite the limitations that inhere in covering theories of human behavior – broadly defined – some useful characteristics of this kind of theorizing may be necessary.

The material here rests on several assumptions about the necessity of a theory or conceptualization of human behavior. These assumptions include the following:

1) Each clinician and clinical supervisor should be able to articulate such a conceptualization / theory of human behavior.
2) A conceptualization/theory of human behavior should guide clinical decisions.
3) It should explain how individuals, families, and others develop significant disturbances and/or mental illnesses.
4) It integrates major influences on human behavior, including physiology, basic needs, social interactions, affective expressions, cognitive processes, and more.
5) It should stand on the best agreed-upon evidence available.
6) It should be available for scrutiny by other mental health care providers.

7) It should represent the clinician's commitment to ongoing professional development. This is to say that a conceptualization of human behavior is not likely to be completed and broadly agreed upon in the longest of foreseeable futures. Currently, neuroscience continues to make numerous and significant contributions to mental health care providers' expanding conceptions of human behavior, for example.

Toward what may be an unending process of conceptualizing and re-conceptualizing human behavior, the challenge of doing this confronts mental health care providers with the demand that they account for an ever-expanding and complex array of data. Because of the largeness of this demand, the details that may sufficiently represent a clear conceptualization of human behavior may appear to be much too daunting to begin. However, because clinicians will continue to provide clinical services for their clients and clinical supervisors will continue to oversee these services, they must try to develop their conceptualization skills, at least for the benefit of clients who receive treatment. Without this, they may do little more than express their personal interests that, at least on some occasions, coincide with the needs of their clients. On other occasions, they may unduly frustrate their clients or harm those whom they seek to help.

To be clear about this, when clinicians and/or clinical supervisors depend only or primarily on their individualistic preferences as guides for treating clients or providing supervision, they are delivering insufficient and, probably, unethical services. A conceptualization/theory serves as a guide for decision-making, but it also integrates the provider of services into the profession of which she or he is a member.

When a clinical supervisor meets with a supervisee, how may each of them view a client whom they discuss? Based on how they make sense of, construe, interpret, understand – they have their own word(s) for this – they select which clinical interventions to implement. How may they answer important questions about clients, such as the following?

Why is the client so angry and unreasonable?
Why does he come to counseling, faithfully pay for services, and refuse to change?
Why did she leave her husband?
Why are the identical twin boys so very different in attitude and behavior?
What is the rationale for selecting a diagnosis?
Why is she distressed about how she may utilize her training as a pediatrician to help her with service on the school board?
Why are his attitudes different toward each of his children?
Why have they decided not to have children?
How does he sustain his depression?
How may clinicians differentiate between a habit and a compulsion?
Does he really relate with his wife in very much the same manner as he relates to his mother?
Does she really use her sexuality to punish men in her life – and herself?

The questions about human behavior are virtually endless in number. Nevertheless, these questions and countless others that could be raised are ones that, at least in theory, should be answered by clinicians and their clinical supervisors. Moreover, because their answers determine much of what they may do when they meet with clients, pursuing answers to these questions inheres in the work they do. Based on the belief that clinical supervisors should have a well-defined approach to conceptualizing clients' issues, Chapter 13, "A Philosophy of Clinical Supervision," provides an example of an approach to conceptualizing clients' issues.

Conceptualizing Evidence for Mental Health Care

No doubt, a generally accepted and advanced belief among mental health care providers is that the clinical services that they deliver should be based on evidence. The concepts that have become associated with this belief are "evidence-based therapy," "evidence-based practice," "research-supported practice," "empirically validated practices," and many others. Despite this common belief, the evidence does not support it. Contrary to the belief that clinicians rely on evidence from research to support their work or even believe that they should rely on evidence from research, the evidence says that, among many other related observations,

> *The dissemination of research findings to practitioners has not, for the most part, brought practice into line with research (Tanenbaum, 2005). Less than one percent (.01%) of practicing therapists can cite or refer to any research that supports any of their practices.*
>
> (p. 111)

> *A broad and longstanding conclusion is that evidence from research plays almost no role in the practice of counseling and psychotherapy among practicing clinicians.*
>
> (Umstead, 2019, pp. 3–6)

> *Large numbers of licensed mental health care providers offer approaches to therapy that are demonstrably not research-based.*
>
> (e.g., Holden and Barker, 2018; Thyer and Pignotti, 2015; Martin, in press)

> *Empirical research actually shows that "evidence-based" therapies are ineffective for most patients most of the time.*
>
> (Shelder, 2018)

> *Professionals who claim to use evidence-based treatments rarely do.*
>
> (Brown, 2013)

> *Those who practice CBT [cognitive behavior therapy] mostly fail to practice CBT, according to the research-based evidence that supports it.*
>
> (Waller, Stringer, & Meyer, 2012)

The importance of these observations is simply that evidence from research appears to provide a rationalized "cover" for insecurities about the practice of mental health care and that the rationalization is not necessary. The evidence and the presumed belief in evidence-based treatments are useful in promoting a positive image for mental health care. However, with regard to the practice of mental health care, it hardly represents the real ways that providers practice. Based on these conclusions, this discussion answers the question, "How may clinicians conceptualize the evidentiary basis of their practice?" In response to this question, this discussion offers a hierarchy of evidence for mental health care and, as such, a way to conceptualize evidence for practicing mental health care. With the referential measure of reliability, the hierarchy of evidence includes the following levels:

Highest Level of Reliability

Blended evidence from other levels, except highly individualized judgment
Meta-analyses of randomized and controlled studies
Randomized and controlled studies
Non-randomized and controlled studies
Informal, non-randomized studies
Supervision and consultant-based evidence
Clinical experience and judgment
Highly individualized judgment

Lowest Level of Reliability

A thorough discussion of this hierarchy could endure forever. Instead of testing the limits of the patience of readers, though, a brief description of each of these levels is provided here, with the idea that readers can reflect on them and utilize them as they wish. At least, the point is that, except for judgments about the lowest item on the hierarchy, little evaluation of the levels is offered.

Highly individualized judgment: With no relevant, generally acceptable reliability, some kinds of "evidence" simply have no evidence, apart from the highly individualistic judgment of the clinician. Typically, this kind of non-evidence rests on the personal interests of the clinicians and lacks plausible clinical rationale to support the practices that emerge from these interests. For example, a clinician says, "I'm really into martial arts. I look for ways to bring martial arts into my therapy." The clinician's interest in martial arts may be indisputable, as an appropriate personal interest. However, the practice of martial arts lacks plausibility when it is integrated into mental health care. Often, highly individualized judgment may be seen in a large variety of religious practices, too, such as Bible-based prayer therapy or Mormon/LDS therapy or Chassidic spirituality or knitting therapy or trail biking therapy or feline-assisted therapy. These approaches to mental health care have no reliability of evidence. Generally, highly individualized judgment should be avoided. For one thing, these approaches to mental health care separate needed care from appropriate standards of care and best practices in mental health care. For another thing, they ensure that truly professional care cannot reasonably be offered, because they depend almost exclusively on erratic and even nonsense impulses.

With regard to highly individualized judgment, an important aside for us is this: At the time of writing, we have reviewed more than 60,000 websites where counselors and psychotherapists advertise their services. So far, over a period of six years, we continue to be shocked by what we find. We have found that among the 60,000 practicing clinicians, more than 20,000 clinical/theoretical orientations are advertised. Obviously, many of the orientations demonstrate highly individualized judgment. Sadly, examples of these eccentric and generally inappropriate approaches to therapy may be easily located. Thousands of examples of these approaches could be listed, recognizing that they represent a much larger number of inappropriate approaches to therapy. Therefore, we randomly selected twenty, only as illustrations of unfortunate and highly individualized approaches to therapy (Martin, in press). Readers are encouraged to reach their own conclusions about these approaches.

Power animal retrieval	Arcturian healing
Shamanic healing	Tarot
Archeangelic light	Meridian tapping
Past life regression	Soul retrieval therapy
Energy medicine	Vibrator therapy
Ad astra therapy	Splanka energy psychology
Vedic astrology	Theophostic healing prayer
After death communications	Alchemy
Body T'Shuva	Chakra balancing
Amazonian ayahuasca shamanism	Toltec wisdom

Clinical experience and judgment: As mental health care providers practice, they gain experience. This experience informs their judgment. At least, providers of health care expect that their experience will improve their effectiveness. Although the evidence indicates that, for a majority of providers, this is not correct (Spengler & Pilipis, 2015; Walfish et al., 2012; and Goldberg et al., 2016), experience is critically important to professional functioning, no matter what the research about professional functioning may say. This acknowledges only that providing services requires providers to "do something," without necessary regard for evidence that is external to their individual experience. Relying on experience, however, limits reliability. While the level of reliability may be low, the gains from clinical experience are virtually universally accepted as important sources of confidence in practicing mental health care.

Supervision and consultant-based evidence: All categories of mental health preparation and licensing emphasize the importance of clinical supervision as a necessary part of the process of training and licensing. The evidence confirms that supervision facilitates improvement in effectiveness of supervisees. Likewise, clinicians who pursue consultation with their peers and receive supportive, candid, long-term feedback about their clinical work show improvement in their effectiveness. Supervision and consultation facilitate improvement in clinical functioning and effectiveness, increasing the reliability of evidence that may be used in clinical practice. The evidence gathered here elevates reliability through presumably careful attention to reviews of clinical cases, although the methodology is circumscribed by the appropriate attention that is given to developing clinicians and ensuring that clients receive good care.

Informal, non-randomized studies: These studies are somewhat unusual. Nevertheless, they reflect the needs of individuals, group practices, and agencies to increase their efficiency and effectiveness. For example, if an agency provides clinical services for a broad array of clients but treats an unusually high number of eating disordered clients, it may engage its clinicians in gathering data that may increase the reliability of their practices. Many individuals and agencies wonder about their effectiveness and attempt to examine it. Insofar as they do this and add to activities that stand on lower levels of reliability, the level of their reliability rises.

Non-randomized and controlled studies: The level of reliability appears in analyses and reports about clinical services, based on researchers' attempts to explain clinical techniques, confounding observations about various aspects of clinical work, and other questions that they conclude that they need to answer. Because they are controlled studies, the level of reliability of the evidence rises above the evidence from the approaches described earlier. Extending the example from the preceding paragraph, the research-oriented questions about eating disorders encompass ones that are larger than an agency's need to know whether it is effective. These questions intend to explain observations that relate to eating disorders, generally. Researchers may ask, "During clinical intake interviews and apart from clients' stated concerns about eating-related problems, what questions should be raised or observations made that would identify individuals with eating-related problems?" The pursuit of answers to questions like this elevates the reliability of evidence.

Randomized and controlled studies: This kind of study is likely the most common. It seeks to reduce potential researcher biases by randomly selecting research subjects and establishing a control group of subjects, posing a hypothesis about a specific variable to be studied, clarifying procedures for gathering evidence, gathering evidence, and analyzing results. Because of the heightened objectivity of the results of this kind of study, the reliability of evidence rises to a level that is higher than the level of the preceding ones. The critical question about this kind of study is not so much related to the reliability of its evidence but to the applicability of its findings. In other words, are the findings relevant to the practical matter of delivering clinical services?

Meta-analyses of randomized and controlled studies: As may be readily surmised, the reliability of evidence from meta-analyses rises above the reliability of evidence from all of the preceding levels of reliability. The idea of a meta-analysis is that researchers – usually, one, two, or a team of individuals – identify similar studies and seek ways to statistically pool the evidence so that the pooled evidence becomes a more influential statement about the importance of the variable that has been studied. Again, however, a critical question involves the relevance of meta-analyses for the work that most clinicians do every day.

Blended evidence from most all but the first of these: None of the preceding approaches achieves the results that all mental health care providers, administrators, academic trainers, clinical supervisors, and researchers wish to reach. None is ideal. However, lacking an ideal body of evidence that guides clinical judgment, a combination of most of these kinds of evidence makes each of the others stronger. For example, as clinical supervisors integrate their clinical work with their supervision and with randomized and controlled studies, clinical supervision becomes stronger. More than specifying a particular combination of the kinds of evidence, clinicians and supervisors should pursue the best evidence available. On any given day, the best evidence may come only from the supervisor's clinical experience. On another day, though, the best evidence may come from a supervisee and a meta-analysis of randomized and controlled studies. It is the active and deliberative pursuit that matters.

The discussion of these levels of reliability rests on the assumption that clinical supervisors need to know about them. Why? Some of the answer has already been given in the preceding paragraph. In addition, at least, they need to know about the various levels of reliability of evidence because they are likely to be demonstrated at times by their supervisees but also because clinical supervisors themselves need to demonstrate their ability to integrate these levels of reliability of evidence into their practice of clinical supervision. They should not construct an approach to clinical supervision that stands only on their experience of providing clinical supervision.

Conceptualizing Mental Health

A peculiar deficit in mental health care is that mental health care providers generally do not hold a clinically useful concept of what mental health is. Therefore, the question, "What is mental health?" may appear to be a somewhat peculiar one, in a discussion of clinical supervision. It is raised here because it emphasizes the critical importance of the place of "health" in "mental health." Or, insofar as mental health care professionals seek to facilitate mental health in their clients, they should seek to understand what mental health is. At least, based on good evidence, they should have a number of characteristics of the mentally healthy person. Just as clinical supervisors should have clearly established observations about the characteristics of effective therapists because effective therapists are the expected outcome of clinical supervision, all clinicians should have clear conclusions about the qualities of mentally healthy individuals.

In the massive literature about mental health care, mentally healthy people, as a category of interest, almost never get attention. This is understandable. Most mental health care providers place understandable emphasis on pathology, disorder, poor functioning, or other problem-focused behaviors. Clearly, this is important. After all, treating individuals who epitomize mental and relational health is not likely to benefit anyone. Nevertheless, while the emphasis on pathology, or whatever comparable term is used, is understandable, it often establishes a clinical environment in which mental health may not be recognized, limiting thinking about mental health care to ridding clients of problems and not necessarily helping them to be healthy.

This discussion cannot erase the longstanding deficit among mental health care providers, with regard to their neglect of conceptualizing "health" in mental health. It can, though, report some of the conceptualizations that have influenced current thinking about mental health. For example, Cloninger has given considerable attention to gathering data that define the healthy personality. He writes,

> *Recent research on the relations of personality to wellbeing shows that the people who are most healthy, happy and fulfilled are those who are high in all three of the character traits of self-directedness, cooperativeness, and self-transcendence as measured by the Temperament and Character Inventory.*
>
> (Cloninger, 2013)

Others who have contributed to attempts to define the mentally healthy person include Carl Rogers, Jensen and Bergin in their report from mental health professionals, and Keyes with his emphasis on social well-being. Their conclusions about the mentally healthy person are briefly presented in the following.

Carl Rogers' Fully Functioning Person

Few influential psychotherapists have had the influence that Carl Rogers has had. He describes his optimal person as the fully functioning person, a person who exhibits three essential characteristics. These characteristics receive attention in his books, *On Becoming a Person* (1961) and *Freedom to Learn* (1969), the source from which the information here is adapted. First, the fully functioning person is open to experience (Rogers, 1969). In contrast with defensiveness and undue self-protection, the fully functioning person lives fully in the moment, living each experience for what it is and not shutting it out of awareness. A wide range of perceptions are immediately available to this person as they are experienced.

The second characteristic of the fully functioning person is that she or he lives in an existential fashion. This is a way to say that each moment is new for this person. Rogers wrote, "One way of expressing the fluidity which would be present in such existential living is to say that the self and personality would emerge *from* experience, rather than experience being translated or twisted to fit a preconceived self-structure" (1969). He continued, "It means that one becomes a participant in and an observer of the ongoing process of organismic experience, rather than being in control of it." Later in the same discussion, he wrote,

> *Such living in the moment, then, means an absence of rigidity, of right organization, of the imposition of structure on experience. In means instead a maximum of*

adaptability, a discovery of structure in experience, a flowing, changing organization of self and personality.

(Italicized emphases appear in the original)

The third characteristic is that the fully functioning person finds "his organism a trustworthy means of arriving at the most satisfying behavior in each existential situation" (1969). Such a person discovers a competent internal guide in her or his feelings, as each new situation is met. Full experiencing enables her or him to find and accept the "wisest and most satisfying personal meaning" in her or his behavior.

Jensen and Bergin's Report from Mental Health Professionals

In their study of 425 mental health professionals, Jensen and Bergin sought to determine the characteristics that are associated with mentally healthy individuals. They identified several themes around which the respondents expressed consensus and several others about which there was no consensus. According to Jensen and Bergin, the agreed-upon features of a mentally healthy individual included the following.

Competent perception and expression of feelings. This included elevated sensitivity to the feelings of others and an open, genuine and honest attitude toward others.

Freedom/autonomy/responsibility. This included responsibility for one's own actions, increased flexibility in decision making, increased self-management, and feeling appropriate levels of guilt.

Integration, coping, and work. Generally, these qualities demonstrate the individual's elevated ability to cope with change, satisfy personal needs, strive for achievement, and find fulfillment in work.

Self-awareness/growth. This includes the individual's awareness of her/his potential and a readiness to grow, along with the personal discipline needed for growth.

Human relatedness / interpersonal and family commitment. This quality of mental health indicates an ability to give and receive affection, increased respect for others, faithfulness to relationships, commitment to family needs and childrearing, and a capacity for sacrifice and unselfishness.

Self-maintenance / physical fitness. This refers to the practice of habits of maintaining physical health, including self-discipline with regard to alcohol, drugs and other potentially harmful substances.

Mature values. This means that mentally healthy individuals hold life-affirming values and principles and seek to fulfill them in the way they live.

Forgiveness. This refers to a capacity to release others from their obligations that come with imposing harm. Also, it refers to the individual's readiness to make restitution for one's own negative influence on others.

(Jensen & Bergin, 1988, p. 293)

In the end, Jensen and Bergin conclude that among mental health professionals, a consensus about the characteristics of mentally healthy individuals may be established (p. 296). Taking their view as potentially significant, it would appear to lead counselors and psychotherapists to maintain their awareness of these characteristics as goals toward which they will engage their clients in seeking for themselves.

Keyes' Emphasis on Social Well-Being

In his work toward defining mentally healthy individuals, Keyes has emphasized the social dimensions of mental health, stating, "I have argued that positive functioning includes social challenges and tasks" (Keyes, 2002). He proposes five dimensions of social well-being. His dimensions include social coherence, social actualization, social integration, social acceptance, and social contribution.

A complete picture of the mentally healthy person is not likely to be an agreed-upon reality. However, practicing mental health clinicians and their supervisors may need to remind themselves that their conceptualization of mental health substantially contributes to the goals that they wish to help their clients achieve. A clear conceptualization of the mentally healthy person helps clinicians to develop clearer ideas about their clinical work, utilize useful practices that help their clients to engage in therapy, and select beneficial clinical interventions. In addition, a conceptualization of the mentally healthy person helps clinical supervisors to identify strength in their supervisees and, where strength is lacking, to guide them toward healthier ways of functioning as clinicians and as persons.

Conclusion

To be sure, mental health care poses complexities that challenge the most intellectually capable and clinically sophisticated individuals. These complexities beg for recognition and understanding, at least, because many features of being human and the social worlds of which individuals are members will always be in various states of change or even chaos. Obviously, a view of recent history includes significant changes in gender roles, family structures, and the racial composition of America, among others. At a personal level, changes include aging, newfound friends, losses of friends and relatives to death, financial ups and downs, emotional turmoil and expense of floods and tornados, and much more. Thus, in the context of change, mental health care providers carry a unique accountability to be clear about what they believe about mental health care. This means that they will seek to achieve as much awareness as they can, with regard to their assumptions and beliefs about human nature, how their clients develop problems that require clinical attention, how counseling and psychotherapy work, and, of course, how their personal issues shape their perceptions of themselves and their clinical work. This is the importance of their answer to the question, "What do I believe about conducting mental health care?"

4

WHAT CHARACTERIZES A GOOD THERAPIST?

The quip, "If you don't know where you're going, any road will take you there," may be a good one with which to begin this chapter. Translated into the language of clinical supervision, it may read something like this: "If you don't know what clinical experience and evidence from research say about what characterizes a good therapist, how could you possibly know what you are trying to achieve in providing clinical supervision?" Expanding this question, another and more challenging question for clinical supervisors is "What is clinical thinking?" or "What is clinical judgment?" The answers to this question may take many different forms. The supervisor's answers, though, determine much of what happens in supervision. For example, is clinical thinking systematic and planned, or is it serendipitous and open-ended – or something else? Alternately, is the cognitive style of the supervisor compatible with the cognitive style of the supervisee?

A supervisor should have clear thoughts about how to define and, therefore, to recognize an effective therapist. If clinical supervisors know where they're going, they will have a substantive answer to the question "What are the characteristics of a good therapist?" Whether supervisors seek to integrate research findings into their answer to this question, they should consider their beliefs about the significance of professional actions and assets in conducting therapy. For example, what is the place of the supervisee's cognitive style, empathic understanding, curiosity, understanding of a therapist's power with clients, sensitivity to gender issues, tolerance for ambiguity, and flexibility? Beyond personal reflection on these issues, competent supervisors should seek to integrate research findings about effective therapists into the process of therapy.

Personal Assets of Highly Effective Therapists

Without trying to answer the question about the characteristics of a good therapist, the supervisor's work is likely to be weak. However, to give strength and credibility to the work, several useful resources are readily available. For example, one is the January 2005 issue of the *Journal of Mental Health Counseling*. This issue dedicates six articles to studies of "master therapists." Much of the information can help supervisors to create their own view of what good therapists are. In addition, there are numerous other reports about good therapists, including ones by Blatt et al. (1996); Eells (1999); Huhra, Yamokoski-Maynhart, and Prieto (2008); Lafferty, Beutler, and Crago (1989); Ablon and Jones (1998); Goldfried, Raue, and Castonguay (1998); Jennings and Skovholt (1999); and Skovholt and Jennings (2004), among others. For now, based on numerous research reports, suffice it to write that several of the qualities of effective therapists include the following:

Proclivity for intellectual complexity: The importance of this quality may be understood as necessary for effective mental health care because clients are almost always immensely complex. Or, to state the matter negatively, simple answers to complex human problems and linear thinking lack the cognitive assets that effective mental health care require.

Indefatigable curiosity: A truism about conducting mental health care is that clients usually contain more clinically relevant information than clinicians seek from them. In other words, pursuing clinically relevant questions with clients is almost always superior to giving information to clients.

High tolerance for ambiguity: Human beings are highly ambiguous. In response to this, mental health care providers should expect and welcome ambiguity, instead of attempting to pose solutions that defy ambiguity.

Emotional attunement: Mental health care providers who demonstrate emotional attunement, with special emphasis on their internal coherence and authenticity, function with more effectiveness than those who are out of sync with their emotions. They feel their feelings with an acuity that allows them to utilize these feelings on behalf of their clients and themselves. Based on such internal awareness, therapists increase the likelihood of being accurately attuned to their clients' emotions.

Strong relational skills: The degree to which experienced clinicians demonstrate strong relational skills is the degree to which they are effective mental health care providers. Further, these skills protect the welfare of the clients whom they serve.

Intentional and sustained self-care: Studies confirm that intentional and sustained self-care is correlated with effectiveness in mental health care. While caring for oneself may be expressed in many different ways, these studies indicate that superior self-care pervades several basic aspects of human functioning, including nourishment, rest, recreation, scheduling, exercise, and others.

Important relationships/social support: Effective therapists pursue ways to meet their relational needs. They find ways to care for others and to meet their need for care from others. Conversely, they are not usually loners or inclined to avoid others.

In the context of providing clinical supervision, the importance of these qualities is that, when supervisors possess them, they may more precisely assess how well or poorly their supervisees may be developing them. Specific ways to assess supervisees' clinical functioning appear in Chapter 12, "Supervisee Development." Ideally, all clinical supervisors would develop instruments through which they may determine that their supervisees can provide effective care for their clients. In addition, these research-discovered qualities of good and excellent clinicians give clinical supervisors important resources for helping them to understand and plan for desired outcomes for supervision and supervisees.

Clinical Judgment

The characteristics of effective mental health care clinicians are displayed in clinical judgment. Clinical supervisors examine and evaluate the clinical judgment of their supervisees. While examining and evaluating cannot describe the totality of the work of clinical supervisors, surely they constitute a necessary part. In this discussion of these essential supervisory activities, the term *clinical judgment* is used to include similar and frequently used terms, including "clinical reasoning" and "clinical decision making." The core concept that embeds in these terms is that mental health care supervisees engage in a perpetual, almost second-to-second, "tick-tock" decision making process when they provide clinical services for clients.

Among other essential characteristics of this process, it serves to humanize the interactions between a provider and a client, when it engages the client in a process of change toward mental health and when this is done well. This is to say that engaging a client in a manner that exudes understanding, warmth, respect, and more forms a useful and positive foundation for conducting therapy. Allowing for the possibility that almost anyone can humanize their interactions with others, the added, essential characteristics of clinical judgment cover much more relational territory than this.

Another essential characteristic of professionally accountable clinical judgment is that it emerges from gathering clinically relevant information from and about a client. This characteristic alone stands as an important feature of effective therapy. At least, gathering clinically relevant information provides the clinician with necessary information that contributes to the clinician's capacity to practice evidence-based therapy.

However, gathering information cannot stand alone. The information gathered from clients and possibly other sources must be aggregated into a clinically relevant understanding of the client, with the emphasis on understanding each moment of relating with the client. Further, the information from the client should somewhat naturally blend with the clinician's understanding of the client's clinically relevant needs. For example, if the client provides a useful body of information that the clinician correctly aggregates into a picture of a "performance driven and over anxious" client, the clinician may engage the client in useful and corrective reframing of her or his thinking about personal worth and her or his skewed valuing on external markers of personal importance.

Finally, as this discussion has already implied, clinical judgment means that the clinician decides to do something that she or he and other clinicians, including clinical supervisors, would regard as "treatment." It is this doing of something of which good therapists are almost constantly and intentionally aware. It may mean that the therapist says and does nothing. It may mean that the therapist directs the client to remain silent and to reflect on her or his experience of the moment. It may mean that the therapist offers support (e.g., "I really admire your courage in looking at the tragic events that have overtaken your life and deciding to overtake them"). The doing of something may be almost anything of which professionally accountable therapists can think.

The importance of clinical supervisors in developing professional, accountable clinical judgment in their supervisees cannot be overestimated. As Haderlie (2011) writes, "Although it seems intuitive that clinicians become more accurate in their decisions with experience, most results have not generally supported such a relationship (Dawes, 1989, 1994; Faust & Ziskin, 1988; Garb, 1998; Garb & Boyle, 2003; Wedding & Faust, 1989)" (p. 8). However, as Haderlie also notes, "Perhaps the most frequently-suggested means of improving clinical judgment is the provision of corrective feedback during training on judgment tasks" (p. 9). In contrast with such feedback, clinicians' insular confidence in their judgment appears to be unwarranted. As Miller et al. (2015) conclude, "Contrary to prevailing assumptions our analysis of over 40 years of research on the appropriateness of confidence uncovered that clinicians' confidence has a small but statistically significant relation with psychological assessment judgment accuracy" (p. 561).

A thorough discussion of clinical judgment and research related to it would expand this presentation beyond its intentions. However, the reader is referred to others' excellent discussions of clinical judgment. Among many truly valuable discussions, the following sources provide resourceful, thorough, and useful information: Boswell and Constantino (2015), Dawes (1989), Garb (1998), Haderlie (2011), Harding (2007), Kraus et al (2016), Lichtenberg (2009), Rock et al. (1987), Spengler et al. (2009), Walfish et al. (2012), and Miller, Spengler, and Spengler (2015). The body of research and expert opinion is far more extensive than this brief sampling may indicate. Suffice it to say that, at this time, the vigorous interest in studying clinical decision making continues to increase the likelihood that clients' needs for effective clinical services will be met.

Conclusion

The history of counseling and psychotherapy has exhibited numerous strengths and a few glaring weaknesses. One of the weaknesses is that it has invested relatively little effort in investigating, understanding, and promoting highly effective counselors and psychotherapists and goal-setting for individual practitioners and the graduate programs that prepare them for practice. This weakness leaves preparation programs bereft of clear objectives for those who complete such programs. More specifically related to this book, mental health care has maintained its commitment to clinical supervisors as a necessary feature of preparing new clinicians but has failed to establish clear and useful standards that define the capabilities of the individuals who enter the profession. This chapter is a small nudge toward helping the profession to overcome this weakness.

5

WHAT DO I BELIEVE ABOUT CLINICAL SUPERVISION?

This book discusses many important features of clinical supervision. Among these topics is the necessity of a philosophy of clinical supervision, the characteristics of an effective therapist, legal and ethical issues in clinical supervision, the role of clinical supervisors, practical considerations in providing clinical supervision, and several others. As important as these discussions may be, another consideration may be more important. It is the individual clinical supervisor, including the beliefs that the individual supervisor actualizes in the practice of clinical supervision, the supervisor identity that the individual claims, and the supervisor's capacity to provide competent clinical supervision. These are the topics to which this chapter gives attention. It is followed by chapters that expand the discussion beyond the individual clinical supervisor, to include a broader understanding of the role of the clinical supervisor, the role of the supervisee, and ways to define "a good clinical supervisor."

Much of what novice clinical supervisors think about clinical supervision likely comes from their experience as supervisees. Insofar as this generalization is correct, it suggests that they may not have reflected on many of the important challenges that inhere in the role of clinical supervisor. In other words, they may not have given sufficient attention to what they believe about clinical supervision, let alone being able to claim a professional identity as a clinical supervisor. On an individual level, this is quite understandable. However, in the larger professional world of clinical supervision, individual supervisors, including long-practicing supervisors, face numerous unsettled issues that may be encompassed in their identity as clinical supervisors. Based on leading numerous clinical supervision training events for beginning clinical supervisors, usually along with some experienced supervisors, we have observed that their expressed needs may be placed into a few commonly stated concerns. Their specific concerns receive detailed attention elsewhere in this book. For now, suffice it to list their most commonly identified concerns. They are as follows:

What are the legal vulnerabilities that come with providing clinical supervision?

How do we know that we are doing a good job in providing clinical supervision?

What happens or should happen during supervision meetings?

As I help to train clinical supervisees, how should I relate with them and evaluate their clinical performance?

Another concern may be a compilation of many different specific concerns that involves clinical supervisors' performance and accountability. Namely, how should I handle a failing or incompetent supervisee, informed consent for supervisees, contracting for services, keeping records, and many others?

Understandably, these concerns come from supervisors' need for answers about their specific duties and self-assigned definition as supervisors. In addition, they indicate that beginning and experienced clinical supervisors need to clarify their definition of themselves as supervisors and seek to establish for themselves what they believe about their work as clinical supervisors. Having answers about what they believe is also an obligation to their supervisees and the larger mental health care profession. After all, their beliefs about clinical supervision provide guidance for their work as clinical supervisors.

The concerns of novice clinical supervisors only roughly parallel the concerns of those who study and write about clinical supervision. Commonly, from the view of those who study clinical supervision, the list of epistemological concerns that inhere in clinical supervision appear in somewhat more systematic forms than those of novice clinical supervisors. Thus, framed as an individual's questions, the following concerns are ones that frequently appear in discussions of clinical supervision.

What is my definition of clinical supervision?

What do I want to achieve through clinical supervision?

What are my personal and professional assets that contribute to effective clinical supervision?

What is my model of clinical supervision?

What kind of relationship do I want to develop with supervisees?

What are the ethically sensitive issues that I am likely to encounter in conducting clinical supervision?

Does my approach to clinical supervision ensure the best of client care?

What constitutes effective clinical performance?

How do I assess supervisee performance in a professionally accountable manner?

How may I relate with my supervisees in ways that facilitate their development?

What is competent and effective clinical supervision?

Toward making these concerns relevant and useful, the last chapter, "Putting It All Together," includes a comprehensive outline of questions for clinical supervisors who want to develop a philosophy of clinical supervision. When the questions are answered by clinical supervisors, they will likely produce a useful philosophy of clinical supervision.

Many more concerns than the ones listed here need to be addressed by professionally accountable clinical supervisors. The significance of these questions is likely already easily understood by prospective and practicing clinical supervisors. After all, they should already have been practicing clinicians. And, as practicing clinicians, they understand that their view of therapy is significant in its conduct. Indeed, their view of therapy includes their professional identity as clinicians, their understanding of clients' problems, the process of change, the nature of the therapist-client relationship, and much more. In short, even in advance of beginning to provide clinical supervision, prospective supervisors know that supervisor identity – beliefs about "self" doing clinical supervision – and occupying the role of clinical supervisor come from the practice of clinical supervision. Further, as effective practice and supervisor identity develop, competence in providing clinical supervision develops, too. Therefore, the rest of this chapter discusses supervisor identity and supervisor competence, because they are essential features of a philosophy of clinical supervision.

Supervisor Identity

Presumably, mental health clinicians who make the transition into the role of clinical supervisor recognize that they hold the considerable potential of shaping the professional development and functioning of those whom they supervise. With this understandable emphasis on influencing their supervisees – an externalizing view of what they do – supervisors may not account for the changes in their way of thinking about themselves as professionals. As researchers and other professional discussants of clinical supervision have long asserted, "the transition from supervisee to supervisor marks an important change in professional identity for the clinician" (Styczynski, 1980, p. 29). Unfortunately, as Pelling writes, "There are few models that both describe and attempt to explain the development of supervisors" (Pelling, 2008, p. 236). Commensurate with these observations, this discussion affirms the importance of supervisor identity and the necessity of supervisors' attempts to clarify their supervisor identity.

A common understanding of identity is that it is highly individual. Identity is, after all, "mine." No doubt, a similar understanding of supervisor identity may be reasonably asserted. Nevertheless, several common features of a supervisor identity may be acknowledged. For example, Borders (1994) states:

> *Good supervisors seem to have many of the same qualities of good teachers and good counselors. They are empathic, genuine, open, and flexible. They respect their supervisees as persons and as developing professionals, and are sensitive to individual differences (e.g., gender, race, ethnicity) of supervisees.*
>
> (p. 1, para. 5)

Somewhat more specifically related to supervisor identity, Borders adds,

> *They also are comfortable with the authority and evaluative functions inherent in the supervisor role, giving clear and frequent indications of their evaluation of*

> *the counselor's performance. Even more, good supervisors really enjoy supervision, are committed to helping the counselor grow, and evidence commitment to the supervision enterprise by their preparation for and involvement in supervision sessions.*
> (p. 1, para. 5)

The process of acquiring many of the features of supervisor identity come with the practice of clinical supervision and skill development as a supervisor. As Pelling (2008, p. 245) says, "new supervisors gain experience and have supervision of their supervision experiences to aid in their skill development so that their identity as supervisor can be established."

Surely, beliefs about clinical supervision emerge from an individual's clinical experience as a supervisee. Receiving supervision, with all that this may include, sets numerous precedents for the novice supervisor's understanding of clinical supervision. For example, a novice supervisor who attended one of our training events emphasized his commitment to "making supervision safe for supervisees." To explain his commitment, he stated, "I had a supervisor who treated us in a rough and demanding manner. He was unduly and harshly confrontational. I decided that I would never be that way with my supervisees." Another novice supervisor reported an outlook that was very different from this. She explained,

> *I remember when I was working with a very difficult client. I was getting nowhere. I felt like a failure. And I can remember exactly what my supervisor said to me. He said, "Look, you have to recognize that your client has been practicing crazy a lot longer than you have been practicing therapy. And, your client is better at it than you are." I felt such relief. He was right about that. It was very affirming.*

Beliefs about clinical supervision emerge from supervisors' history of receiving supervision.

Just like novice clinicians, novice clinical supervisors depend on low self-efficacy and confidence and on emulation of the supervision that they received (Rodenhauser, 1994; Watkins, 2018). However, presumably, clinical supervisors develop beyond their emulation and awkwardness of being novices. As they develop, they acquire beliefs about clinical supervision with increasing clarity, gain confidence in their supervisory judgments, justly assume supervisor identity, and gain reality-based competence (Frick & Glosoff, 2018; Alonso, 1985; Stoltenberg & McNeill, 1997; Watkins, 2012a). Allowing for the many inevitable changes that come with experience, how may the emerging supervisor be characterized? The following paragraphs offer substantive but tentative answers to this question. Following these answers, the discussion then provides responses to the question, how may the competent clinical supervisor demonstrate competence?

What characterizes a clinical supervisor? The attempt to answer this question draws from the product of a recent work group within the American Psychological Association (APA). The group produced a document, *Guidelines for Clinical Supervision in Health Service Psychology* (APA, 2014), that offers several characteristics of a competent clinical supervisor. These characteristics are utilized here to refer to features of a professional identity for clinical supervisors. The group wrote,

> *The overarching goal of these Guidelines on Supervision is to promote the provision of quality supervision in health service psychology using a competency framework to enhance the development of supervisee competence ensuring the protection of clients/patients and the public.*
>
> (Executive Summary section, para. 1)

The document includes a section with a bullet-point presentation of "Assumptions of the Guidelines on Supervision" (The third subsection, of the Introduction page, no page numbers provided). Paraphrasing or citing several of these assumptions, they are utilized as answers to the question, "What characterizes a clinical supervisor?" Clinical supervisors

Demonstrate professional competency that emerges from formal education and training, including supervised supervision
Prioritize the care of the client/patient and the protection of the public.
Place a high priority on facilitating the acquisition of competence by and the professional development of the supervisee
Develop professional competence across several competency domains, including "supervisor competence; diversity; relationships; professionalism; assessment, evaluation, and feedback; problems of professional competence, and ethical, legal, and regulatory considerations" (APA, 2014)
Pursue and utilize current relevant research and other empirically validated evidence for their supervision practices
Maintain respectful, adaptive, and collaborative relationships with their supervisees and other professionals
Demonstrate responsibility for ensuring that their role is clearly understood by their supervisees and other relevant parties
Practice clinical supervision in such ways that demonstrate a positive valuing of diversity
Account for their personal values, attitudes, beliefs, interpersonal biases, and characteristic ways of interacting with others, as they conduct clinical supervision
Adhere to normative standards of professional practice, including ethical and legal standards
Affirm the importance of professional development, including the development of their supervisees, the profession of which they are members, and their personal-professional development
Engage in appropriate self-assessment
Incorporate bi-directional feedback between the supervisor and supervisee
Evaluate the acquisition of expected competencies by the supervisee, in a professionally accountable manner, including evaluations that

sometimes eventuate in the exclusion of an individual from the profession (i.e., gatekeeping)

Communicate the boundaries of clinical supervision in such ways that they distinguish supervision from other related roles, such as therapist or manager

To these, we would add three features that characterize clinical supervisor identity. They are 1) that clinical supervisors have a long and broadly based history of providing effective clinical services for clients, 2) that they promptly give attention to any problems that may impair the supervisory relationship, and 3) that they possess a demonstrated capacity for divergent and complex thinking. Collectively, all of these characteristics may be understood as ways of encouraging individual clinical supervisors to be clear about what they believe about clinical supervision and how they practice clinical supervision as expressions of their professional identity.

Taken all together, we encourage clinical supervisors to reflect on the list of supervisor characteristics. Which of these characteristics do you want to utilize as features of your supervisory functioning? Which ones would you reject? Which additional characteristics, if any, would you add to the list?

As their beliefs about clinical supervision become clear and integrated into the practice of clinical supervision, a professional identity as a clinical supervisor emerges. Within this identity, a philosophy of clinical supervision also emerges. However, more than a uniquely individual identity, professionally accountable clinical supervisors also develop an identification with the profession of which they are members. This is to say that professional identity is truly individual, but it is also an expression of their profession. Also, whether their philosophy of clinical supervision is clearly articulated or tacitly understood, clinical supervisors who claim their professional supervisor role and identity have acquired or grown a philosophy of clinical supervision, just as earlier in their respective careers, they claimed professional clinical identity. In other words, when supervisors begin to practice as supervisors, they may not know who they are as clinical supervisors. However, over time, as they provide clinical supervision, they claim the role of supervisor in a uniquely personal way and in a broadly based and professionally accountable way.

Competent Clinical Supervision

The emergence of a supervisor identity cannot predictably ensure supervisor competence. Supervisor competence, though, immutably stands as a necessary expression of a professionally accountable supervisor identity. For clinicians and their supervisors, a professionally valuable definition of competence comes from Epstein and Hundert (2002). They write, "Professional competence is the habitual and judicious use of communication, knowledge, technical skills, clinical reasoning, emotions, values, and reflections, in daily practice for the benefit of the individual and community being served" (pp. 226–227). However, as clearly conceptualized as competency may be and despite approximately two decades during which numerous research reports about competence in clinical supervision have appeared, a broadly accepted taxonomy of competencies for clinical supervisors has not yet been established. At this time, several useful definitions and taxonomies may be found, though. Generally, assumptions about competencies for clinical supervisors indicate that they should demonstrate competencies in several categories of their work, including knowledge, practice, and personal assets. The following competencies provide an example of this (Center for Substance Abuse Treatment, 2009, pp. 107–108).

Knowledge Competencies

Has knowledge of theory and intervention strategies
Has knowledge of screening, assessment, and diagnostic standards
Understands cultural and ethnic issues
Has knowledge of resources in the community
Has knowledge of current ethical guidelines and legal issues

Practice Competencies

Demonstrates mastery of intervention techniques
Is timely and thorough in documentation
Is able to develop rapport
Is able to conceptualize problems
Can respond to multicultural issues
Is able to formulate treatment goals

Personal

Demonstrates ethical behavior
Demonstrates use of good judgment and counseling skills
Is interpersonally competent
Is able to identify own strengths and weaknesses
Is able to accept and learn from feedback
Is an asset to the profession

However, the Centre's outline of competencies covers those that may be conceived as foundational. Competent clinical supervisors will likely need to demonstrate additional competencies. The additional competencies qualify a clinical supervisor as having and developing refined and superior skills in the areas of clinical assessment, diagnosis (i.e., accurate problem identification), treatment planning, and case formulation. Further, in the process of providing clinical supervision, supervisors should offer a broad array of clinical interventions that their qualified peers would judge to be superior. Elevating the significance of their clinical interventions, supervisors should demonstrate high competency in consulting, mentoring, evaluating, modeling for, and encouraging/supporting their supervisees. In addition, as a necessary adjunct to clinical supervision, competent supervisors will manage their administrative tasks effectively. (Refer to the chapter, "Administrative Tasks in Clinical Supervision.")

Conclusion

This chapter rests on the commitment to assist clinical supervisors in their needed pursuit of developing a philosophy of clinical supervision. Thus, the emphasis of this chapter is that successful clinical experience, developing and claiming a clinical supervisor identity, and persistently refining supervisory competencies are necessary and foundational components of a philosophy of clinical supervision. Further, it assumes that successful clinical experience, supervisor identity, and supervisory competence are bases on which clinical supervisors construct their role as clinical supervisors.

6

WHAT ARE THE ROLES OF THE CLINICAL SUPERVISOR AND SUPERVISEE?

Clinical supervisors enter into their role with experience as supervisees. No doubt, this experience defines for them much of what they understand about clinical supervision and expect to be in the role of clinical supervisor. Taking this into account, this chapter seeks to enlarge the frame of reference beyond an individual's experience in clinical supervision so that the respective roles of clinical supervisor and supervisee may be more broadly applied to a wide variety of professional settings and clinical clienteles.

The Role of the Clinical Supervisor

One of the most important considerations for a supervisor is how the supervisory role is conceived. Unless the supervisor has given expansive thought and study to this area, the supervisor may do little more than emulate the style of a favored clinical supervisor from the past. In actuality, a supervisor faces multiple options in defining the supervisory role (Bernard & Goodyear, 2004). Generally, the many possible roles of supervisors include being a model as a therapist, a teacher, a consultant, a supporter, and an evaluator. Supervisors need to be alert to the many options for roles and attempt to be clear about the particular role that they should take in meeting the supervisee's clinical or learning goals and professionally relevant needs. Just as supervisees develop and continually redefine their roles as counselors, supervisors need to give attention to a plan for professional development so that their supervisory work may be refined. To define and/or refine the supervisory role, a prospective supervisor should, at least, work through Campbell's workbook on clinical supervision (Campbell, 2000). Her workbook is an excellent and readily available resource that can assist prospective supervisors in their training for supervision. Another of Campbell's books, *Essentials of Clinical Supervision*, is also an excellent resource for helping supervisors to understand their role (Campbell, 2006).

Here are some questions that a supervisor may want to answer, in trying to understand the supervisory role: Is a good supervisor one who answers all the questions for the supervisee or one who provides options for the supervisee to "try on" in his or her clinical situation? Does the supervisor see self as the "expert" or a "fellow traveler" on the counseling journey with the supervisee?

How does the supervisor maintain availability for the supervisee? Does the supervisor want to be approachable, dialogical, and disclosing, or does he or she prefer not to disclose self to the supervisee? Does the supervisor want the supervisee to be disclosing of personal issues, or does she or he protect the supervisee from a fear of rejection or ridicule?

Generally, supervisors must draw on their own experience and sense of self to reach thoughtful conclusions about their way of conceptualizing the supervisory role. However, this needs to be done in a manner that is more transformative than summative, more integrative than conclusive, and more growth-oriented than status-affirming. The composition of these conclusions adds to an individual's philosophy of clinical supervision.

Supervisory Interventions

Just as in clinical work, the list of clinical interventions grows to an almost interminably long one, mainly because there are so very many of them and because clinical work requires that mental health care providers continue to add to them as they practice, knowing that their repertoire of skills and interventions is never complete. Therefore, instead of listing all possible interventions that a supervisor may utilize, a description of several types of interventions may be useful. Each of the following types of interventions can be a freestanding one or utilized in combinations with others. Also, none of these types is an intervention that should be utilized simply because it is a favorite one of the clinical supervisor. Instead of thinking in terms of preferred interventions and before utilizing any of the interventions, a clinical supervisor should have completed training in clinical supervision, including training in each of the interventions.

The major types of supervisory interventions include the following:

Didactic	Conceptual
Informational	Confrontational
Directive	Supportive
Experiential	Relational
Questioning	Supervisor disclosure
Supervisor modeling	

Didactic

This type of intervention places the supervisor in the role of a teacher who instructs the supervisee. Usually, opportunities to teach appear in response to a supervisee's needs and express the experiential and intellectual assets of the supervisor. For example, the teaching role may be required in response to a supervisee's needed understanding of adolescent self-harming behaviors as an expression of reactive attachment. The idea is that the supervisee needs to "catch on" so that she or he may provide professional care to an adolescent client more effectively.

Conceptual

A common struggle with supervisees involves an inability to make sense of a client. Presumably, the supervisee has sufficient clinical information about the client but stumbles in integrating the information into a useable conceptualization that may be translated into clinically appropriate actions. In response to the supervisee, the clinical supervisor engages the supervisee in a process of conceptualizing the experience of the client. In some situations, the need for conceptualization may be channeled into helping a supervisee to reach a diagnostic conclusion – or a diagnostic conceptualization – about a client.

Informational

This intervention refers to the fact that, at times, a supervisor holds information that a supervisee needs. In contrast with teaching or conceptualizing, this involves passing needed information to the supervisee. This may be as simple as reporting that a specific book contains information about which the supervisee has asked. It may be a referral of a supervisee to a resource on PTSD, such as PTSD.va.gov/consult, a website that includes numerous expert video presentations on various aspects of PTSD.

Confrontation

This intervention may take multiple forms, including high-intensity or low-intensity ones. Usually, confrontation with supervisees appears as a gentle but clear and firm requirement that a supervisee engage in struggle with barriers to clinical effectiveness. For example, a supervisor may observe that the supervisee evades her or his clients' anger. With this observation, the supervisor may need to do little more than ask, "The client seemed to be pretty angry. Do you have some thoughts about how you handled this?"

Directive

Because of the pre-eminent importance of client welfare, a supervisor may need to direct a supervisee to take a specific action or to cease taking an inappropriate action. For example, a supervisee may show aggressive probing with a highly agitated, PTSD client and, in this process, be re-traumatizing the client. In response, the supervisor may be obligated to direct the supervisee to cease such aggressive probing.

Supportive

Supervisees sometimes fail their clients, even when they perform entirely appropriate clinical services. Or, sometimes, supervisees heroically struggle in quite normative ways and feel frustrated with their efforts. In response to this, a supervisor may want to offer encouragement, maybe, through normalizing the supervisee's struggle. For example, depending on the circumstances and needs of a supervisee, in response to such struggling by a supervisee, a supervisor may say, "I really appreciate your struggle. As difficult as it is, you continue to provide good care for this client. I admire this."

Experiential

All clinicians understand that they sometimes misconstrue their own experience of a clinical encounter. So, if they are clinical supervisors, they are not at all surprised to receive and/or observe such a misconstrued report from their supervisees. When this happens, the supervisor may need to engage the supervisee in a process of experiencing herself or himself. This often comes with questions such as "Can you give me an idea of what it's like for you to experience the client?" or "What's happening with you as you sit with this client?"

Relational

This intervention refers to the need for a supervisor to clarify and enhance her or his relationship with the supervisee. While this may be necessitated by any number of relational and clinical issues, it usually involves some sort of transference issue that the supervisee brings to the supervisory relationship. "When we talk about your clients, you seem to be okay. When we talk about you being with your clients, you seem to be distressed. Is this right?"

Questioning

Generally, supervisees bring reports about their clinical work to their clinical supervisors. Likewise, generally, in response to these reports, supervisors ask questions. In a manner that is similar to conducting a clinical session with a client, much of the work of supervision is asking questions. Some of the interventions described earlier involve asking questions. Questioning itself, though, is another intervention. It refers to engaging the supervisee in reflecting on her or his clinical work and gaining insight and skill in conducting her or his work through this process.

Supervisor Disclosure

The rationale for self-disclosure from clinical supervisors is simple: In contrast with self-disclosure from therapists to clients, self-disclosure from clinical supervisors assumes that the supervisor and the supervisee will become co-equals in their profession. From this assumption, self-disclosure from the clinical supervisor facilitates the process through which the one to whom the disclosure is given successfully enters the profession. Experienced clinical supervisors have probably disclosed both some of their clinical successes and some of their failures. Such disclosures are almost inevitable as ways to teach encourage, and provide practical guidance.

Supervisor Modeling

While modeling appears to be a passive intervention, if there is such a thing, it may be critically important as an intervention. This is to say that many different professional attitudes, habits, and concerns about clients and supervisees; procedures for analyzing and treating clients' problems; and others offer supervisees real, living ways to think about and engage clients and to act in ethical and legally appropriate ways and a view of an effective mental health care provider whom supervisees should want to identify with and to emulate.

Some of the self-disclosures are inadvertent but often critically important. They fall into the category of "modeling." Clearly, clinical supervisors provide models of many different features of the work of clinicians and supervisors. They model attitudes toward client, the enjoyment of being a clinician, enacting clinical strategies, how to handle failure in clinical work, thinking about clinical problem-solving, and many other features of conducting clinical work.

Clinical supervisors tell stories from their work as clinicians. Their stories serve multiple purposes. A story of overcoming failure with a client may be disclosed as a way of encouraging supervisees. Another story may be designed to instruct a supervisee in clinical techniques. And another story may provide the supervisee with new ways to think about the role of clinician. Depending on the supervisors' discernment of the needs of their supervisees, their stories may be intended to serve any of multiple purposes.

More broadly than stories, self-disclosure may fall into any of the categories of interventions that are described here. The disclosure may be relational, for example, with the intention of enhancing the relationship between the supervisor and supervisee. This may be a reflection on the way that the supervisor understands their relationship. The supervisor may offer an invitation to dialogue, such as "I want to make sure that our relationship is working for you. I can tell you that as your supervisor, I like meeting with you. I believe that we may be making good progress, but that does not mean that you believe we are making progress. So, just to be sure that we are working well together, may we talk about our relationship? Let's think about what's good about it and what may not be good about it."

Or, it may be didactic, with specific goals of instructing the supervisee about a specific clinical issue. Given the complexity of what counselors/psychotherapists do, didactic interventions could be almost anything. As just one example from numerous possibilities, a supervisor may need to give a brief lesson on how to complete release-of-information forms. Experienced therapists may find such a lesson to be dull, just because they have completed such forms many times, but a novice counselor/psychotherapist who faces the daunting task of composing a release of information form for the first time may need help. The novice may need to know about the specific expectations that a release-of-information form must meet. Maybe, the novice needs to know that a release of information should be dated and time limited, include client identifiers and reliable information about the person/agency to whom information is to be released, and so on.

Or the disclosure may be supportive, showing an obvious and unambiguous commitment to the well-being of the supervisee. "I know how challenging it is for me to raise these questions. I wonder how you experience the questions and how I may be more useful for you? I ask this because I really believe that you not only can handle the questions but that you provide solid answers and show me that you have the potential of becoming a very effective therapist. The struggle you feel right now is a good sign, even if it is uncomfortable."

All of these interventions contribute to defining the role of the supervisor. With regard to individual supervisors, the utilization of these interventions expresses how she or he defines her or his role. For example, if one supervisor emphasizes didactic intervention more than others, she or he may be defining herself or himself primarily as teacher. Expanding this idea, the major theoretical orientations to mental health care will likely utilize these interventions as expressions of their respective theoretical orientations. For example, a person-centered supervisor is less likely to utilize directive interventions than a reality/choice therapist.

The Role of the Supervisee

Just as the role of the supervisor evolves through the process of providing clinical supervision, the role of the supervisee evolves, too. Similar to the adjustments that clinicians and clients make as they work together, supervisors and supervisees make adjustments. As Martin and Cannon (2010) observe,

> *The supervisee will come to supervision with his or her own ideas about supervision. This will help to define the role of the supervisor. Still, the role of the supervisor and the supervisee should be largely defined by the supervisor, while making the role of the supervisee as much of mutual discovery as possible. The risk of the supervisor taking appropriate authority as a senior member of the profession is that supervisees may take on the role that they feel has been "assigned" by the supervisor, instead of believing that they can discover their own role in the supervision process. Again, while supervisees must define their own respective roles, the conception the supervisor holds of the supervisory process will substantially contribute to supervisees' definition of and selection of their preferred roles.*
>
> (p. 5)

Beyond their ways of thinking about their roles, the clinical supervisor carries significant accountability for the work of the supervisee. For example, the legal doctrine of *respondeat superior* dictates that the "superior" in many professional relationships is the one who is accountable for the actions of the "inferior" or subordinate. In clinical supervision, this doctrine says that the member of the relationship who carries primary accountability for the mental health care that the supervisee delivers is the supervisor. Therefore, the supervisor will need to define their respective roles. One of the methods for achieving this is ensuring informed consent for the supervisee. Inexperienced supervisors may ask, "Informed consent? About what?" An answer is that, just as informed consent in counseling seeks to make sure that a client understands everything about the treatment process, informed consent in supervision seeks the same kind of goal. In the supervision process, informed consent orients supervisees to the supervision process, aids in creating mutual understanding with the supervisor, and explains the expectations and tasks of the supervision process. As indicated in the following, a contract between a supervisor and a supervisee may include important components of informed consent.

Another important responsibility is to complete a contract with supervisees. A clear and thorough contract is a method that contributes structure and important rules for the process of supervision. What should be in the contract? In short, everything of consequence that defines the supervisory relationship should be in the contract. However, more specifically than this, a good supervision contract includes, but is not limited to, the following items:

- Detailed information about the supervisor
- Supervisor's understanding of and philosophy of supervision
- Information about the supervision process
- Days and times of meeting, number of meetings for each week/month
- How to contact each other in case of emergency
- Paperwork to be kept and by whom and payment issues, if a paid process
- Discussion of ethical issues and the ethical code that will govern the supervisory process
- Purpose and goals of supervision
- Specific areas of responsibility for the supervisor and the supervisee
- How the supervisory process will be evaluated
- Signature page to formally adopt the process.

A supervisory contract offers clear boundaries about the supervision process. An important by-product of clarifying boundaries is that both the supervisor and the supervisee create safety for themselves. Also, by knowing the boundaries within the supervisory relationship, the supervisee feels empowered, knows what to expect, and more likely commits self to the experience of receiving clinical supervision. Generally, a supervisor-supervisee contract may include agreements about virtually anything about which either party may be reasonably concerned.

Within the context of supervisor accountability for the actions of supervisees and contracting with supervisees, along with other ancillary features of clinical supervision, for what is a supervisee accountable? As an encompassing statement, the role and purpose of supervisees are to claim their individual professional identity and to demonstrate their commensurate professional competence. Following this statement, more narrowly framed descriptions of supervisees' accountability necessarily may be expressed. For example, according to Pearson

(2004), supervisees should prepare for clinical supervision by identifying topics with which help is needed and forming an agenda for supervision meetings (p. 366). During supervision meetings, supervisees should actively participate in the supervision process, take initiative to effectuate appropriate clinical care and to receive feedback, and monitor themselves with regard to competence and related clinical issues, such as evaluation anxiety and performance anxiety (pp. 368–369). Expanding the frame of reference to include additional features of the role of supervisees, the following may be included:

> *A clinical supervisee should demonstrate a readiness to change toward claiming a professional identity and professional competence. The readiness to change may be identified in several ways. These include expressed and active interest in their own learning, particularly with reference to new clinical demands and discoveries about oneself. They include supervisees' developing ability to reflect on their work, as if they are internalizing supervision. The demonstrated ability to reflect on their work stands as an indicator of professionalism for experienced mental health care providers. The clinical supervisor observes and assesses the development of this ability in supervisees.*
>
> *Supervisees receive feedback, process it in a professionally accountable manner, and apply it to their work with clients. While this may be an obvious feature of clinical supervision, its importance transcends receiving feedback and applying it. It involves the presentation of their clinical work in an open and honest manner. It involves building partnerships with supervisors and others. It involves claiming peership with other mental health care professionals.*
>
> *Supervisees seek to gain awareness of the importance of their work. Again, while this may be obvious, it involves more than understanding their potential impact on their clients. As they gain awareness of the importance of their work, supervisees' performance anxiety and the lack of clarity about their potential competence decline and, in the place of these inhibitions, they see, experience, and utilize their appropriate influence toward clients with heightened intentionality. Thus, they learn to place client welfare above their own.*
>
> *Supervisees demonstrate improving skill in utilizing supervisors, supervisors' time, and other supervision-related resources. Reflecting their evolving accountability, supervisees practice discipline in their work with other professionals. They become cognizant of their rising accountability for clients and other stakeholders, such as the agency where they provide services to clients, as a contributing member of the professional community.*
>
> *Supervisees continually expand their awareness of and skill in managing their ethical and legal accountability. They become increasingly intentional in their actions, instead of succumbing to the infrequent but real and sometimes inappropriate demands from clients or others. They gain respect for their appropriate accountability for influencing others in ethically and legally stressful situations and environments.*

An important feature of the role of supervisees is supervisee development. Supervisee development is covered in Chapter 12.

Conclusion

Ultimately, the role of the supervisee is discovered through the process of supervision. Unlike the supervisor's role, the supervisee's role cannot be known by the supervisee in advance of receiving supervision. Knowing this should enable supervisors to facilitate the supervisees' discovery of their respective roles. While each new supervisee discovers and constructs a role during the process of supervision, several features of the role are fairly common. They include functioning as counselor/psychotherapist, conducting clinical work, identifying and seeking to achieve professional development goals, claiming professional identity and the several functions that inhere in such an identity; self-directed and self-evaluating consultee and consultant; and supporter of the profession as a professional peer. In short, the primary roles of clinical supervisees are therapist, learner, consultant-consultee, and professional peer.

As noted earlier, the role and purpose of supervisees are to claim their individual professional identity and to demonstrate their commensurate professional competence. This also defines the role and purpose of clinical supervisors. They function in such ways that enhance the likelihood that their supervisees will claim their rightful professional identity and demonstrate their professional competence.

7

HOW DO I DEFINE A GOOD CLINICAL SUPERVISOR?

At least in a tacit and experiential manner, supervisors hold ideas about what good clinical supervision is. Currently, several groups, such as the Association for Counselor Education and Supervision, define best practices in clinical supervision. However, much of what may constitute best practices is left to supervisors to determine. The context in which supervision is delivered determines many of the possible ways that clinical supervision defines the role of the supervisor. For example, how may the role of the clinical supervisor be defined differently in these settings: a university counseling center, a youth-serving agency that primarily treats abused children, an outpatient or inpatient alcohol and drug addiction program, a small group private practice, a suicide prevention hotline, or an academic training program for mental health care providers? In addition, the philosophy of therapy and supervision held by the supervisor determines the role of the supervisor.

Allowing for the limitations that may be imposed by the context in which supervision is delivered and the philosophy of therapy and supervision held by the supervisor, the following information is an attempt to express many of the features that define "the good clinical supervisor." In this attempt, several statements from practicing clinical supervisors have been gathered. Generally, they see these statements as understandings that have benefited them, insofar as they offer specific and practical guidelines for their work as clinical supervisors. The reason for citing them here is that they may be useful to others who wish to define their view of the good supervisor for themselves. Others are encouraged to borrow and modify these statements for themselves, as needed. Adapted from Martin and Cannon (2010), here are some statements that define "the good clinical supervisor."

Good supervisors genuinely like providing clinical services to clients.

Good supervisors understand and practice good therapy, because they have practiced good therapy.

Good supervisors understand and affirm the power differential between themselves and their supervisees.

Good supervisors unambiguously support their supervisees in forming clear goals for their supervision so that they gain self-awareness and skill in progress toward being effective practitioners.

Good supervisors should be willing to demonstrate their clinical skill for their supervisees. (The assumption here is that master therapists ought to be able to demonstrate their clinical prowess, as needed, for their supervisees.)

Good supervisors know that their supervision exists in the real world, where human lives are seriously impacted by their supervision, instead of contemplating their supervisory role only as an academic or intellectual exercise. While supervision may have academic components and times for intellectual exploration, it is essentially a clinical process. As such, among many other things, it requires supervisors to confront substandard clinical work, on the experiential base of knowing what good clinical work is.

Good supervisors ask good questions of those whom they supervise and help the supervisee to experience the worth of the struggle to serve clients in a positive fashion. They help supervisees to discover that therapy is more a way of being than a way of doing.

Good supervisors empower supervisees to confidently conduct clinical work, by confronting supervisee's inadequacies, but, moreover, by affirming their struggle to succeed and their consequent successes. They stay alert to opportunities for helping supervisees to improve their clinical judgment.

Good supervisors respect the boundary between clinical supervision and the supervisee's possible need for personal therapy.

Good supervisors understand that their way of responding to clinical situations is likely one among many clinically appropriate ways of responding.

Good supervisors seek to nurture professional identity in their supervisees.

Good supervisors know that clients' needs take precedence over supervisors' and supervisees' needs.

Good supervisors remain cognizant of advancing the profession of counseling and psychotherapy, along with nurturing supervisees' development.

Good supervisors understand that supervision is a process, not an event or a technique. As such, the process involves a quest for meaning, satisfaction, and personal fulfillment as a supervisor. Similarly, the process is perpetual, ever dependent on the need of supervisors and supervisees to improve the delivery of clinical services.

Good supervisors commit to spontaneity, experimentation, inventiveness, and other existential necessities, knowing that their self-discipline is indeed disciplined and well informed. This means that good supervisors are accountable for the process of growth for themselves and their supervisees and, paradoxically, subordinate to it.

Good supervisors know that their conjoint and occasional incapacity to help clients provides opportunities for growth. Further, a great deal may be learned from the experience of failure.

Good supervisors understand that a professional working alliance with supervisees is necessary and mutual.

Good supervisors increase supervisees' awareness of transference and counter-transference issues in therapy, but also in supervision.
Good supervisors establish plans for their own professional development.
Good supervisors remain cognizant of the potential threats that sometimes attend growth toward healthy and effective therapeutic functioning by their supervisees. This is to say that good therapy sometimes upsets individuals and the institutional political systems in which they function.
Good supervisors know that confrontation – along with its consequent stress – is necessary in the conduct of clinical supervision but that tenderness and support are necessary, too.
Good supervisors appreciate empirical research in counseling and psychotherapy and self-consciously integrate findings into the process of supervision.

In the chapter, "Practices Helpful to Developing a Philosophy of Clinical Supervision," the qualities of a good supervisor are converted into professional development exercises.

The self-defined role of the supervisor and the expectations that arise from such a definition form the bases upon which the good supervisor functions. Among other conclusions, one of the operative ones here is that the supervisor's approach to conducting mental health care should not be viewed by the supervisor as a sufficient basis for formulating a conceptualization of the role of the clinical supervisor. The differences in these roles – therapist and clinical supervisor – are significant. Chart 7–1, "A Comparison of Features in the Therapeutic Relationship and the Supervisory Relationship" emphasizes some of these differences:

Chart 7–1 A Comparison of Features in the Therapeutic Relationship and the Supervisory Relationship

Therapeutic Relationship	Supervisory Relationship
Mental/emotional disturbance	Functioning therapist
Relational distress	Professional developmental needs
Very limited therapist disclosure	Larger volume of supervisor disclosure
Critically important boundaries	Boundaries and many shared obligations
Numerous legal protections	Relatively few legal protections
Significantly different histories	Shared professional histories
Therapist accountable for power	Shared understanding of power/authority and authority differential
Focus on clinical relationship	Focus on supervisee's relationship with client

As inherent features of these relationships, clinical supervisors should understand them and account for them in their practice of clinical supervision. Analogous to other roles, such as the differences that may inhere in the respective roles of adult partners or in the roles of parents and their children, the differences among individuals who fill their roles substantially contribute to their individual ways of defining what makes them good at what they do. Individual uniqueness is unavoidably integrated into professional functioning. The effective management of this uniqueness is what differentiates a truly professional clinician or clinical supervisor from others, particularly when the practices and generally agreed upon evidence is blended with individual uniqueness.

Conclusion

Effective mental health care somewhat naturally expresses the aspirational thinking and deeply felt goodwill of its providers. Genuinely, counselors and psychotherapists aspire to improve the lives of their clients. No doubt, it is their aspirational thinking and goodwill that commonly communicates to clients and becomes a source of encouragement for their clients. Moreover, their aspirational thinking also contributes to their desire to improve themselves as mental health care providers. Likewise, when they oversee the counseling and psychotherapy of their supervisees, clinical supervisors somewhat naturally express their aspirational thinking, deeply felt goodwill, and collegial interest in their supervisees and the profession in which they are members. Obviously, these personal and professional assets are reassuring for their supervisees. Moreover, these assets evoke their recognition of needing to be better supervisors than they are and energize them toward improving themselves as clinical supervisors. This is the importance of reflecting on how clinical supervisors define the good clinical supervisor.

SECTION III

Contextual Issues in Clinical Supervision

8

PROFESSIONAL ETHICS AND CLINICAL SUPERVISION

Clinical supervisors define much of what they want for themselves and their supervisees. However, minimally well-informed clinical supervisors know that their individual preferences may or may not be feasible ones, given their ethical and legal obligations. This is to say that ethical and legal obligations pose constraints and limits within which clinical supervisors provide their professional services. The review of these obligations in this chapter is intended to introduce several of the ethical constraints and limits about which clinical supervisors should know.

As a foundation for understanding their ethical and legal accountability, several primary obligations appear consistently in professional associations and in most state laws and regulations. One is that all major codes of ethics, including the American Counseling Association (ACA), the National Association of Social Workers (NASW), the American Psychological Association (APA), and the American Association of Marriage and Family Therapy (AAMFT), place client welfare at the top of the priorities and obligations that clinical supervisors and supervisees carry. For example, the APA ethical principles state that the ethics code "has as its goals the welfare and protection of the individuals and groups with whom psychologists work and the education of members, students and the public regarding ethical standards of discipline" (American Psychological Association, 2017, p. 3). Somewhat more explicitly, in its first standard (i.e., A.1a), the ACA *Code of Ethics* states, "The primary responsibility of counselors is to respect the dignity and promote the welfare of clients" (American Counseling Association, 2014, p. 4). Also, in its first ethical standard, NASW, says, "Social workers' primary responsibility is to promote the well-being of clients" (National Association of Social Workers, 2017, p. 7). In virtually all counseling and psychotherapy codes of ethics, the fundamentally important commitment to the welfare of clients is clear and universal.

From the commitment to client welfare, many practical implications arise. This includes implications for clinical supervisors. For example, no doubt, supervisors prefer that their supervisees receive support and encouragement from their supervision. Similar to the universality of the priority placed on client welfare, this preference is virtually universal, too. However, as much as support and encouragement are needed from clinical supervisors and for supervisees, they should be provided in ways that place the welfare of the supervisee's clients ahead of the supervisee's welfare.

Another common commitment in all major codes of professional ethics for mental health care providers require that those who serve within the constraints of these ethics function within the boundaries of their individual competence. In the current environment in which professional competence continues to decline among mental health care providers (e.g., Goldberg et al., 2016; Spengler & Pilipis, 2015), the critical importance of competent professional functioning cannot be overestimated. Also, given the necessarily high priority placed on client welfare, virtually all codes of ethics emphasize the centrality of competence in the work of mental health care providers. For example, in its *Code of Ethics*, NASW includes ethical standard, 1.04, "Social workers should provide services and represent themselves as competent only within the boundaries of their education, training, license, certification, consultation received, supervised experience, or other relevant professional experience" (National Association of Social Workers, 2017, p. 9). The other major mental health care associations express their commitment to professional competence in language and emphasis that is remarkably similar. For example, APA says, "Psychologists provide services, teach and conduct research with populations and in areas only within the boundaries of their competence, based on their education, training, supervised experience, consultation, study, or professional experience" (American Psychological Association, 2017, p. 5).

While the major codes of ethics include other areas of agreement, the purpose of emphasizing client welfare and professional competence is to express the importance of these ethical priorities as necessary ones for clinical supervisors. Clinical supervisors place high priority on client welfare and professional competence. Thus, competence as a clinical supervisor is a requisite obligation. The need for clinical supervisors to be clear about these priorities is surely tested by their supervisees, often inadvertently. For example, when their supervisees serve a clientele that the supervisor has not served or utilize a treatment modality with which the supervisor is not familiar, clinical supervisors may need to consider their supervisory judgments with reference to client welfare and professional competence.

A clinical supervisor who provides supervision services under the aegis of one of the major codes of ethics should carefully study all of the standards in her or his respective code. The importance of this is that, quite apart from the standards that specifically refer to clinical supervision, many other standards in each of these codes add to the obligations of both supervisors and supervisees. For example, in various ways, these codes refer to client welfare, client rights, competence, avoiding harm to clients, professional boundaries, confidentiality, and much more. Mastery of these standards elevates the level of effectiveness in clinical work, but it also helps to ensure that supervisors and supervisees practice their respective roles in ethically appropriate ways.

To ensure that supervisors and supervisees practice in ethically appropriate ways, several features of initiating supervision should be carefully covered by the prospective clinical supervisor. These features begin with informed consent but include contracting and agreements about scheduling, handling emergencies, and more. For a detailed discussion of the administrative tasks of clinical supervisors, refer to the chapter on "The Administrative Tasks of Clinical Supervisors." For now, as a statement about informed consent, Thomas (2010) recommends that the following items be included in an informed consent document: supervisory methods, confidentiality, financial issues, documentation, risks and benefits, evaluation criteria/procedures, complaint procedures, termination criteria, supervisor's responsibilities, supervision sessions content, supervisory accessibility, supervisee responsibility, informing the supervisor, and professional development goals. To Thomas's list, we would add supervisor qualifications, including relevant clinical experience and preparation for providing clinical supervision.

A major development in ethical and legal issues in clinical supervision has been the evolving commitment to diversity. Along with the codes of ethics from all of the major mental health care provider associations (i.e., ACA, NASW, APA, and AAMFT), all of the major models of clinical supervision include an emphasis on diversity. "In all models of supervision, it is helpful to identify culturally or contextually centered models or approaches and find ways of tailoring the models to specific cultural and diversity factors" (Center for Substance Abuse Treatment. (2009, p. 8). The Center for Substance Abuse Treatment (2009) adds that the diversity issues to consider are as follows:

> Explicitly addressing diversity of supervisees (e.g., race, ethnicity, gender, age, sexual orientation) and the specific factors associated with these types of diversity;
>
> Explicitly involving supervisees' concerns related to particular client diversity (e.g., those whose culture, gender, sexual orientation, and other attributes differ from those of the supervisee) and addressing specific factors associated with these types of diversity; and
>
> Explicitly addressing supervisees' issues related to effectively navigating services in intercultural communities and effectively networking with agencies and institutions.
>
> (pp. 8–9)

Usually, a discussion of professional ethics includes giving attention to specific standards and obligations of mental health care providers. This is necessary and important. Also, knowing that ethical and unethical behavior is enacted by individuals, another necessary and important topic that compels attention is the individuals who act unethically. This is to ask, "Who are these individuals? Who is unethical?"

Who Is Unethical?

The discussion of who is unethical refers both to mental health care providers in general and to clinical supervisors in particular. To begin, who are the individuals among mental health care providers in general who violate professional ethics?

In their book, *Psychology and the Mental Health Professions: Standards and Cases*, Koocher and Keith-Spiegel (2008, 2016) provide a comprehensive and detailed examination of the ethical challenges with which mental health care providers are confronted and the unethical actions that they sometimes perpetrate. More than providing a careful analysis of ethical standards and the lapses in compliance with ethical standards, Koocher and Keith-Spiegel present illustrations that make their book a helpful and readable blend of academic and intellectual analysis as well as a readily recognizable story of the sometimes hazardous challenges and blunders in clinical life. Of particular importance for clinical supervisors, they provide a typology of who violates professional ethics. Koocher and Keith-Spiegel's typology is important for clinical supervisors because it offers supervisors ways to consider some of the salient personal issues that their supervisees may exhibit when they provide clinical services to clients.

Supervisors' consideration of Koocher and Keith-Spiegel's typology needs to be placed in a broader range of consideration than the typology alone. Those who violate professional ethics may be snared into an ethically compromising situation that is not of their own making. For example, a counselor provided treatment for a married, heterosexual couple who came to therapy because both of them engaged in sexual intimacy with partners outside of the marriage. The counselor treated their anger, estrangement, guilt, excessive neediness, and much more, with the general result of enabling the couple to find honesty, desire, affection, and problem-solving skills, among other things. The therapeutic relationship ended. Several months later, though, the same counselor treated an adult male who had betrayed his partner with whom he was married, when he developed an intimate sexual relationship with a woman outside of the boundaries of his marriage. As the counselor treated the man, his story seemed eerily familiar. The counselor recognized the possibility that he had earlier treated the woman with whom his current client had had an illicit affair and that this same woman was a partner in the couple who had been successfully treated. This posed an ethical dilemma that could not have been predicted or reasonably expected by the counselor.

Unforeseen ethical dilemmas may be nearly inevitable for counselors and psychotherapists and their clinical supervisors. An example of an unforeseen ethical dilemma for a clinical supervisor is likely to be readily available for reporting by most experienced clinical supervisors. One such example involved a supervisor and a supervisee who provided services in a private practice that included twelve counselors and psychotherapists. The same private practice served as a training site for supervisees who sought licensing in the state. Unbeknownst to the clinical supervisor, the supervisee began psychotherapy with a young woman who suffered PTSD as a result of an automobile crash that resulted in major injuries, including the loss of one of the young woman's arms. As the supervisee processed the case of the crash victim–young woman with the supervisor, the supervisor realized that the supervisee's client had recently been a student in one of the clinical supervisor's college courses and would possibly be enrolled in future courses. The inappropriate duality of the relationship between the supervisor and the supervisee's client immediately became an ethical situation that required attention. Obviously, the situation was an unforeseen dilemma.

A truism that emerges from considering unavoidable and unforeseen ethical dilemmas is that they almost inevitably occur, although infrequently. Among other important facts about providing mental health care is the fact that neither supervisors nor supervisees can impose control over all circumstances. At times, others will act in such ways that their actions pose ethical challenges for supervisors and supervisees. Nevertheless, in such circumstances, supervisors and supervisees may be liable for the potentially adverse outcomes from the circumstances. For example, an adult individual comes to the mental health clinic for a therapy session. Before joining the counselor for a session, the client goes to the restroom. After returning to the clinic waiting room, the client reports, "I fell in the bathroom." Clearly, the client was in physical pain as a result of the fall. While neither the counselor nor the supervisor acted in any way to create dangerous conditions for the client, they were liable for the injuries that the client suffered. In this situation, the client reasonably expected the clinic to cover medical expenses that resulted from injuries.

Allowing for unavoidable and unforeseen ethical dilemmas that may arise, who are the mental health care providers who may violate professional ethics? Generally, they are individuals who are excessively needy or who are clumsily ill-prepared. In their typology of mental health professionals who violate professional ethics, Koocher and Keith-Spiegel make this clear (2008, pp. 1–17, 2016, pp. 1–17). Their characterizations of these individuals are expressed in titles for each of the types that they discuss. For example, they identify one of the types as "The Unaware and Misinformed." They explain that the individuals in this category lack information about their profession or the standards of ethics. Adapted from the third and fourth editions of their book, the other nine types that they discuss include the following:

The Incompetent or Undertrained – generally, these individuals lack skill and/or preparation for the services that they are attempting to deliver.

The Insensitive – these individuals fail to account for the needs, feelings, and autonomy of others, with particular reference to their clients.

The Exploitive – these individuals take advantage of others in a planned or premeditated manner, giving deference to their needs and not the needs of their clients.

The Irresponsible – These individuals presume to know what they need to do and to hold skills that they do not have, exhibiting unwarranted satisfaction with their clinical skill and effectiveness.

The Vengeful – these individuals suffer disappointment in their service to clients, become angry, and seek to get even.

The Rationalizers – these individuals possess unrecognized confusion about their role of therapist, succumbing to the temptation to believe that they are truly good and worthy of any particular reward or benefit that they can receive from their clients.

The Therapists without Boundaries – these individuals demonstrate their neediness beyond the normative limits of the role of psychotherapists, elevating their vulnerability to making friends, lovers, or otherwise attempting to form other inappropriate connections with their clients.

The Burned-out – these individual have attempted too much for too long and, as a result, have allowed their exhaustion to compromise their clinical judgment.

The Therapist Who Momentarily Slips – these individuals fail to give sufficient attention to a specific set of circumstances and allow themselves to be momentarily compromised. The consequences of such compromises, though, usually extend well beyond the moment.

To Koocher and Keith-Spiegel's list of those who violate professional ethics, we add another category. These are individuals who may be labelled as "The Ideologically-Driven and Self-Interested Therapist." These individuals have committed to an ideology that holds more importance in their clinical work than the needs of their clients. The ideology may be almost anything to which individuals may be strongly committed. Typically, though, these ideologies may be reduced to two kinds. One is a clinical ideology. This is an ideology such as contemplative psychotherapy or cognitive behavior therapy that is held so strongly that it narrows the clinical thinking of the therapist to rigid responses to their clients. These therapists defy one of the necessary qualities of effective therapists: adaptability. Similarly, the other kind of ideology is commonly and specifically religious. This is a religious commitment that is held so strongly that, again, the needs of clients are not taken sufficiently into account. For example, this is seen in therapists who promote their belief that their purpose is "to bring you into a loving relationship with Jesus Christ." As a personal value, such a purpose may be entirely wholesome. As a clinical priority, it lacks sufficiency and to some may be harmful. At least, ideologically driven therapists circumvent some of the fundamentally important values upon which counseling and psychotherapy stand, such as client autonomy and professional integrity.

Clinical supervisors need to be aware of all of these types of individuals and to be alert to the potential of unethical actions by their supervisees and possibly in themselves. Generally, the less accurate self-awareness is among supervisees, the more likely they are to engage in unethical decision-making and actions. Their lack of awareness conceals unmet needs that find expression in their relationship with clients. For example, despite how well they may appear to be functioning as therapists, they may carry within them a deeply held belief in their inadequacy. Therefore, as they relate with clients, they are seeking approval and support, maybe, through flattery or romantic intimacy or other forms of expression from clients, and, consequently, they falsely believe that they may be acceptable and adequate, when they receive approval and support from their clients. The dynamic importance of unmet needs calls for attention by clinical supervisors, lest they, too, elevate their vulnerability to unethical actions.

Turning to clinical supervisors, who are the unethical ones? Just as the conclusions about unethical clinicians are not settled, the conclusions about unethical clinical supervisors are even less settled. As an emerging specialization within counseling and psychotherapy, clinical supervision continues to challenge its practitioners with unanswered questions. For example, the question, "Which model of clinical supervision rises above the others in effectiveness?" remains unanswered. The best answer is that no one knows. Further, despite claims about the efficacy of their preferred model of clinical supervision, analyses of models have not established that any of a large number of models of clinical supervision have good evidence to support them. "Unfortunately, although most models cited empirical research, none were directly based on an empirical study. Nor had any been tested fully, making it difficult to know whether we have a model that works," according to Simpson-Southward, Waller, and Hardy (2017, p. 1242), based on their examination of fifty-two models. Their conclusion is that models "lack consistency and therefore reliability" (p. 1242).

The emerging status of clinical supervision suggests that the ethical standards may be emerging, too, and similarly lack consistency and therefore reliability. While simplistic, the condition of clinical supervision may be implied by the number of specific ethics standards in some of the major codes of ethics. The American Counseling Association *Code of Ethics* (2014) includes twenty-two (22) standards related to education, training, and supervision, while the National Association of Social Workers and the American Psychological Association have ten each, and the American Association of Marriage and Family Therapy has nine. Quite apart from the number of specific standards, these major mental health care associations agree about their ethical commitments, with regard to several issues. All of them emphasize the importance of preparation for teaching and clinical supervision, objective and clear evaluations and endorsements of their supervisees, and prohibitions of sexual relations between supervisors and their supervisees. Clearly, these professional associations hold clear and high standards for their respective clinical supervisors.

Despite the clear and high standards for clinical supervisors, approximately one-half of clinical supervisors fail to comply with these standards (Crall, 2011, p. 3). Their vulnerability stems from several professional issues that arise in clinical supervision. A large but precisely unknown proportion of these involve the uniquely personal issues that inhere in most human relationships, including transference-countertransference issues (Pakdaman, Shafranske, & Falender, 2015) and boundary crossings or violations (Kozlowski et al., 2014). However, assessing these somewhat limited topics may not provide a large enough picture of the ethics of clinical supervision. Crall (2011, pp. 39–47) has delineated the significance of each of the major ethical violations of clinical supervisors. The categories of such violations and the frequency of their occurrence as proportions of supervisees who reported violations are listed in Chart 8–1: Common Ethical Lapses among Clinical Supervisors

Chart 8–1 Common Ethical Lapses Among Clinical Supervisors

Type	Frequency
Performance evaluation and monitoring of supervisee activities	20%
Session boundaries and respectful treatment	10%
Able to work with alternate perspectives	10%
Modeling ethical behavior and responding to ethical concerns	10%
Multi-cultural sensitivity toward supervisee	10%
Expertise/competency issues	6%
Termination [of clinical work with clients] and follow-up issues	6%
Differentiating supervision from psychotherapy/counseling	6%
Orientation to professional roles and monitoring site standards	5%
Dual roles	5%
Sexual issues	2.6%
Crisis coverage and intervention	3%
Confidentiality issues in supervision	2%

At least, this list of ethical violations should alert clinical supervisors to their professional vulnerabilities. More than alertness, though, the remaining question is "Who are the clinical supervisors who violate professional ethics?" The question is clearly an important one that has not been sufficiently researched. For now, this is a serious limitation for this discussion. Allowing for this limitation, Cimino, Rorke, and Adams (2013) provide a partial answer to the question. They identify six types of "supervisors behaving badly." One, "The Alcoholic" (p. 51) drinks too much, and at times, that leads to impaired professional functioning. This type may be reasonably enlarged to include all forms of impairment that come from substance abuse. Two, "The Bully" (p. 52) scolds and corrects supervisees with the apparent aims of humiliating them and requiring compliance with the supervisor's dubious expectations. Three, "The Romeo" (p. 52) seeks to inappropriately involve himself or herself with his or her supervisees and/or their clients, with apparent interest in romance. Four, "The Three Profiteers" (p. 53) refers to three supervisees who reported that their supervisors placed a value on the financial interests in clients that took priority over clinical interests. Five, "The Misguided" (p. 53) seems unable to take actions that place appropriate priority on the best interests of clients. And, six, "The Unjust" demonstrates insensitivity around multicultural competence and unduly discriminates against individuals because of insensitivity. Recognizing the obvious risks for supervisees in confronting supervisor-instigated ethical dilemmas, Cimino, Rorke, and Adams (2013) recommend "honest and open discussions during supervision" sessions (p. 54). Moreover, they offer the idea that others can and should gain productive insights from studying supervisor-instigated ethical dilemmas (p. 56).

Ethical Decision Making for Clinical Supervisors

Ethical decision-making procedures and models emerge from professional ethics. Insofar as professional ethics call for disciplined commitment to client welfare, professional competence, compliance with professional ethics, and other priorities, decision making about ethically demanding situations stands on professional ethics. Indeed, decision making itself is an ethical issue. For example, the *Code of Ethics* of the American Counseling Association (2014) says,

> **I.1.b. Ethical Decision Making**
>
> *When counselors are faced with an ethical dilemma, they use and document, as appropriate, an ethical decision-making model that may include, but is not limited to, consultation; consideration of relevant ethical standards, principles, and laws; generation of potential courses of action; deliberation of risks and benefits; and selection of an objective decision based on the circumstances and welfare of all involved.*
>
> (p. 18)

While published codes of ethics provide important standards and guidance for clinical supervisors who must sometimes make decisions about difficult ethical situations, they are incomplete sources of guidance when ethically challenging situations call for decisions. This heightens the importance of having a model for ethical decision making, in anticipation of such situations. At this time, numerous models may easily be located. Some examples are the counselor values-based conflict model (Kocet & Herlihy, 2014), a social constructivism model (Cottone, 2001), a transcultural integrative model (Garcia et al., 2003), the ETHICS model (Ling & Hauck, 2016), and an intercultural model (Luke, Goodrich, & Gilbride, 2013). However, regardless of the number of models that may be available, models do not decide what to do when an ethical decision is required. Individual clinical supervisors make decisions. Recognizing this, all clinical supervisors should review as many models as they may find necessary to construct a model of their own. Toward constructing such a model, the following recommendations may be useful.

One, review all relevant codes of ethics. The importance of this is that it accounts for the standards with which supervisors and their supervisees should be expected to comply. No doubt, in some supervisory relationships, this will be a relatively simple matter, such as when both the supervisor and the supervisee must comply with only one code of ethics. In other relationships, though, one or both of the individuals in the supervisory relationship must comply with more than one code of ethics. For example, if the clinical supervisor is a registered play therapist, a member of the American Association of Marriage and Family Therapists, and a certified approved clinical supervisor, the supervisor must comply with three codes of ethics.

Two, review all relevant laws and regulations within the jurisdiction where clinical supervision occurs. While this is necessary as a stand-alone activity, it also contributes to the adequacy of ethical decision making or, in some situations, complicates ethical decision making. For example, mandated reporting of child abuse is a near universal legal requirement but may pose an ethical challenge when the presumed reporter concludes that reporting child abuse may harm the already victimized child.

Three, establish personal clarity about the values of the profession in which membership is held and the personal values that guide clinical supervision. For this purpose, virtually all of the major professional associations include values orientations in their codes of ethics. For example, the National Association of Social Workers' *Code of Ethics* states,

> *The mission of the social work profession is rooted in a set of core values. These core values . . . are the foundation of social work's unique purpose and perspective: service, social justice, dignity and worth of the person, importance of human relationships, integrity, and competence.*
>
> (p. 1)

In addition to the profession's code of ethics, individual clinical supervisors should attempt to clarify their personal values, with emphasis on those that influence their work as supervisors. For example, an individual clinical supervisor may place a high value on distributive or democratic decision making. As a consequence of this value, the supervisor will place a high value on the collaborative role of supervisees and the autonomy of supervisees and recognize that this contributes to defining the respective roles of supervisors and supervisees.

Four, establish specific steps for managing ethical decision making. While the prevailing circumstances of each ethical dilemma may dictate what is possible, with regard to decision making, having specific steps for such decisions likely makes the process much easier than it would be without them. In response to a challenging ethics situation, the specific steps may include the following:

- Gather the best, most relevant evidence about the challenging situation.
- Identify the relevant standards in the code(s) of ethics that apply to the situation.
- Carefully define the ethics problem.
- For clarification, guidance, and support, consult with others.
- Answer the question, "Who needs to know about this situation?" and inform them.
- Determine specific courses of action that comply reasonably well with identified ethical standards, law and regulations, agency or institutional policies, or other requirements for compliance.
- Anticipate the likely immediate and long-term consequences of taking any particular course of action.
- Select a course of action, anticipating that a course of action may require adjustments as it is implemented.
- Implement the selected course(s) of action.
- With the assistance of trusted and competent others, evaluate the decision making and its consequences.

Generally, all of these steps require consideration of what may be in the best interest of clients, when the situation involves clients. The steps require consideration of what may be in the best interest of supervisees and supervisors, when either is involved in the situation. Finally, the steps require consideration of what may be in the best interest of the profession in which the clinical supervisor holds membership.

An Exploration of Supervision Ethics

Before concluding this discussion of ethical issues in clinical supervision, a brief review of the vignettes at the beginning of this book may be helpful, with emphasis on asking you – the reader and prospective clinical supervisor – some questions about these vignettes. The case of Franklin and Charles and the case of Kaitlyn and Rachel pose serious challenges for supervisors who may be supervising Franklin or Rachel.

After re-reading these vignettes, reflect on the following questions. With regard to the case of Franklin and Charles, how would you respond to the following questions:

Which specific professional standards for clinical supervisors may Charles not have exercised appropriately?

Which specific ethical standards, if any, may Charles have violated?

Based on your reading of the case, do either Franklin or Charles possibly face ethics complaints against them?

If you were examining this case as a member of an ethics committee, what issues, if any, would you consider addressing with Franklin and/or Charles?

Based on your reading of the case, do either Franklin or Charles possibly face legal complaints against them?

Do you conclude that bartering for clinical supervision services is a professionally accountable thing to do?

Did Charles fail to supervise Franklin in appropriate ways? May Franklin make an ethical or legal case against Charles? If so, what would such a case claim?

Clearly, more questions than these may be raised. For example, among the questions raised at the beginning of this book, there was one that referred to Charles's failure to execute a supervision contract with Franklin. This is significant, inasmuch as a contract seeks to make explicit the accountability that each of these individuals has in the supervisory relationship. Added discussion of contracts in supervision appears later.

The vignette about Kaitlyn and Rachel poses a very different set of issues for Rachel and her clinical supervisor. In short, Rachel reports to her clinical supervisor about her transparently inappropriate responses to her client, Kaitlyn. Based on this, consider the following questions:

Did Rachel do damage to Kaitlyn? If so, what actions, if any, may be needed by either Rachel or her supervisor? Also, if so, how would you identify and explain the damage to Kaitlyn?

As you review this case and the ethical standards presented earlier, which standards, if any, may be useful in guiding your understanding and responses to Rachel?

Which specific ethical principles and/or laws may apply to this situation?

Insofar as clinical supervisors are ethically accountable for the professional behavior of their supervisees, what is your specific ethical accountability in this situation?

In response to Rachel's report about her inappropriate "intervention" with Kaitlyn, how may your actions define or re-define your role as her clinical supervisor?

If you continue to supervise Rachel's clinical work, following her way of "treating" Kaitlyn, what new understandings may you want to establish with Rachel?

The cases of Franklin and Charles and of Kaitlyn raise challenges for clinical supervisors. Surely, they raise the challenge of how to assist Franklin and Rachel in their respective professional development. Also, they raise the challenge of whether Charles's and Rachel's supervisors may be ethically and legally liable for the actions of their supervisees. These challenges point to the high obligation of clinical supervisors to understand and practice within the boundaries of their professional competencies and within the scope of professional ethics and relevant laws.

With regard to the two vignettes presented in the Introduction to this book and the added consideration of ethics in this chapter, an experiment in learning about supervision ethics may be helpful. The experiment is simple. Re-read the vignettes, and then review the ethical decision-making steps in this chapter and apply them to the vignettes.

The following chapter offers a discussion of law-related issues in clinical supervision. For now, in the context of this discussion about ethics issues in clinical supervision, a comment about the place of legal considerations may be needed. In short, all clinical supervisors should function within the constraints of relevant laws. While this may seem to be a self-evident obligation for clinical supervisors, the specific ways of meeting the expectations of this obligation may not be quite so obvious. For example, laws vary from state to state, with respect to many aspects of clinical work and clinical supervision. Such variation may be seen in laws that mandate reporting for child abuse, elder abuse, the minimum age of consent for services, the length of time that records must be maintained, the specific information that must be contained in clinical records, and many others. In addition, as another example, from one state to another, laws and regulations may be quite lengthy and explicit about advertising for clinical service, or they may not exist. The relevance of this is that clinical supervisors generally carry legal accountability – vicarious liability – for all of the professional functioning of their supervisees, including their supervisees' advertising. The supervisor may quite unexpectedly be expected to defend providing supervision for a supervisee's advertising for, say, offering equine therapy, although the supervisor has no knowledge of or experience with equine therapy.

Conclusion

Studying the sections of the major codes of ethics that include the ethical standards for clinical supervisors may be a requisite activity for clinical supervisors. The codes of ethics for the four major American mental health care associations are readily available online. They include the American Counseling Association's *Code of Ethics* (ACA, 2014, pp. 12–14), the National Association of Social Workers' *Code of Ethics* (NASW, 2017, pp. 19–20), the American Psychological Association's *Ethical Principles of Psychologists and Code of Conduct* (APA, 2017, pp. 10), and the American Association of Marriage and Family Therapy's *Code of Ethics* (AAMFT, 2015, p. 3). In addition to these codes of ethics, codes of ethics have been composed exclusively for clinical supervisors. Two instructive and valuable examples are AAMFT's *Responsibilities and Guidelines for AAMFT Approved Supervisors and Supervisor Candidates* (AAMFT, 2019) and the Approved Clinical Supervisor (ACS) *Code of Ethics* (Center for Credentialing and Education, 2008).

No doubt, clinical supervisors should maintain vigilance with regard to ethical concerns and potentially compromising ethical situations, just as practicing counselors and psychotherapists maintain vigilance in their treatment of clients. However, such vigilance ought not to be contaminated by fear. Instead of fear, vigilance elevates the likelihood that clients' needs will be met and that supervision will achieve its intended goals and purposes.

9

LAW-RELATED ISSUES IN CLINICAL SUPERVISION

Generally, law tells practicing mental health care providers what they can do or cannot do, usually based on the scope of practice and related statutes and regulations within each state. While these directives establish commonly accepted standards of practice for almost all clinicians in almost all situations, nothing like this may be said about laws, scopes of practice, or regulations for clinical supervisors. At this time, the variability among states is extreme, with some states having comprehensive and detailed laws and regulations and other states having virtually nothing. Despite this, commonly accepted professional standards have emerged from the practice of clinical supervision, laws and regulation, and case law.

The various forms of regulations may be viewed as ways to hold clinical supervisors accountable for their practice of clinical supervision. Equally, though, they may be viewed as providing protection for clinical supervisors. In other words, they increase the level of clarity and certainty about the practice of clinical supervision that assures supervisors that they know what to do and what not to do in their practices.

Basic Legal Concepts

Several key concepts and legal obligations may help new supervisors to find direction toward practicing safely and wisely but also toward developing a philosophy of clinical supervision. Among them, the following may be necessary considerations:

Standard of care
Duty to the supervisee and client
Vicarious liability
Direct liability
Statutory liability
Competence
Evaluation of supervisees
Records

Standard of care: In short, a standard of care determines what is or is not an acceptable practice in clinical treatment or clinical supervision. A standard of care is what a profession says that it is. In clinical treatment, an example of a normative standard of care that almost all clinicians would endorse is cognitive behavioral therapy (CBT). In contrast, only a miniscule minority would endorse Vedic astrology or power animal retrieval as interventions that would fall within a normative standard of care. If legal action were taken against a clinician and she or he were required to defend the practice of CBT, this would be relatively easy, insofar as numerous clinicians and other experts would readily testify on behalf of the defending clinician. In contrast, if a legal action required a clinician to defend Vedic astrology or power animal retrieval, finding clinicians and other experts to testify on behalf of the defending clinician would be highly improbable.

Similarly, clinical supervisors must comply with a normative standard of care – as almost all of them surely do. If a normative standard of care is interpreted somewhat broadly, it includes almost everything that a supervisor may do. For example, does the clinical supervisor keep appointments with supervisees? If not, the supervisor may fail to maintain a normative standard of care. Or if a clinical supervisor falls asleep during supervision sessions, she or he may fail to provide a normative standard of care.

Extending the discussion of a standard of care, the concept of negligence should be mentioned. If a clinical supervisor holds supervision meetings, say, once every two or three months, the charge of negligence may justifiably arise. Or if a clinical supervisor keeps no records about her or his practice of supervision, a charge of negligence may arise. At least, in these kinds of situations, a supervisee may initiate a complaint about the supervisor. Also, the demonstration of negligence may abet a successful complaint that has no relation to negligence but that – even when the other complaint has no basis in fact – confirms inadequate and/or unprofessional clinical supervision.

Duty to the supervisee and client: In short, if there is no duty, there is no problem – no vulnerability. However, clinical supervisors and their supervisees should know when there is a duty and when there is no duty. So, how may a duty to a supervisee be confirmed? The list of possible confirmations includes numerous items, such as a cancelled check for payment for supervision, names and times in appointment books, telephone records, notes from meetings, and so on.

The significance of establishing a duty to the supervisee is that it also establishes accountability for compliance with relevant laws, regulations, professional ethics, and normative standards of care, among other things. Extending this, if a duty is established, all other relevant issues come into consideration. For example, when duty is established and when a supervisee or client suffers damage as a result of a supervisee's poor care, the supervisor's liability may be established, too. However, in most cases of liability, the legal procedures are more complicated than this short discussion captures.

Vicarious liability: Vicarious liability may be regarded as indirect liability for clinical supervisors. This is to say that a clinical supervisor is accountable for almost every professional action of a supervisee, including those actions of which the supervisor has no direct knowledge. Such actions include interactions between the supervisee and a client, extra-clinical contact between a supervisee and a client, clinical modalities with which the supervisor may have no familiarity, advertising and other promotions by the supervisee, and more. If a clinical supervisor compiles a list of all professional actions of a supervisee and of which the supervisor has no direct knowledge, including maintaining clinical records, practicing outside of the supervisee's competence, badly mishandling a suicidal crisis, and other possibilities, the supervisor is accountable for these actions. This is vicarious liability. Presumably, the clinical supervisor either knew or should have known about the supervisee's actions.

Direct liability: Direct liability refers to the legal accountability of the supervisory actions of a clinical supervisor. It encompasses fraudulent, misleading, erroneous, improper, unethical, and illegal actions and omissions of a clinical supervisor. It is a dereliction of duty in carrying out the responsibilities of a clinical supervisor. For example, if a supervisor gives ill-informed and damaging clinical directions to a supervisee, this is direct liability. Or if a clinical supervisor fails to monitor the caseload of a supervisee, this is direct liability. Other examples include failure to provide or arrange for emergency coverage of clients' crises, failure to evaluate a supervisee's professional functioning, allowing a supervisee to practice outside of her or his scope of practice or areas of normative expertise, failure to listen to or receive a supervisee's report about a client's needs and therefore failing to comprehend and respond appropriately to a client's needs, and much more. Direct liability also includes actions toward a supervisee, such as taking payment for services that were not delivered or making romantic advances toward a supervisee.

Statutory liability: Statutory liability comes with a clinical supervisor's obligation to comply with laws and regulations. For example, practicing clinicians and clinical supervisors should know about the legally defined obligations to report child abuse. Whether the clinician or the clinical supervisor wants to do this or not, the obligation to report child abuse to state-designated authorities is statutory. It is mandated by law. Failure to do this incurs liability.

Competence: Practicing professional competence appears as a standard of ethics in all codes of professional associations, including the ones mentioned earlier (ACA, NASW, APA, and AAMFT). The expectation of practicing competently applies to clinical supervisors. The standards of competence for clinical supervisors continue to develop. While the standards may not be entirely clear at this time, all practicing clinical supervisors should know what competent clinical supervision is, in quite specific and detailed ways. The details that a competent clinical supervisor should know require more space than this book allows.

However, resources are easily available for clinical supervisors and prospective clinical supervisors. Albeit quite limited, here is a list of some of these resources:

American Psychological Association. (2014). *APA guidelines for clinical supervision in health service psychology*. Retrieved from http://apa.org/about/policy/guidelines-supervision.pdf

Association of Counselor Education and Supervision. (2011). *Best practices in clinical supervision – 2011*. Retrieved from: https://acesonline.net/wp content/uploads/2018/11/ACES-Best-Practices-in-Clinical-Supervision-2011.pdf

Brown, H. (2013, March 25). *Looking for evidence that therapy works*. Retrieved from http://well.blogs.nytimes.com/2013/03/25/looking-for-evidence-that-therapy-works/?r=

Center for Substance Abuse Treatment. (2007). *Competencies for substance abuse treatment clinical supervisors*. Technical Assistance Publication (TAP) Series 21-A. HHS Publication No. (SMA) 12-4243. Rockville, MD: Substance Abuse and Mental Health Services Administration.

Falender, C. A., Shafranske, E. P., & Ofek, A. (2014). Competent clinical supervision: Emerging effective practices. *Counselling Psychology Quarterly*, 27(4), 393–408.

Genuchi, M. C., Rings, J. A., Germek, M. D., & Cornish, J. A. E. (2015, February). Clinical supervisors' perceptions of the clarity and comprehensiveness of the supervision competencies framework. *Training and Education in Professional Psychology*. *9*(1), 68–76.

McMahan, E. H. (2014). Supervision: A Non-Elusive component of deliberate practice toward expertise. *The American Psychologist*. *69*(3).

Six, T. (2014). *Characteristics of highly effective therapists*. Master's Thesis. Gent University. Retrieved from http://lib.ugent.be/fulltxt/RUG01/002/166/096/ RUG01-0021660962014_0001_AC.pdf

Storm, C. I., and Todd, T. C. (2002). *The reasonably complete systematic supervisor resource guide*. New York, NY: Authors Choice Press.

This very brief list of resources suggests only that helpful resources are readily available, if a clinical supervisor or a prospective clinical supervisor needs and wishes to utilize them.

Evaluation of supervisees: One of the most common failures of clinical supervisors is that they do not evaluate their supervisees. Usually, this is not a complicated task, although it can be an uncomfortable one. Comfortable or not, though, it is an essential obligation of clinical supervisors. The question that evaluation seeks to answer may be stated somewhat simply: Is the supervisee functioning within normative professional standards and improving her or his skills and abilities to deliver effective clinical services?

Naturally, this question leads to additional questions, such as "How does a supervisor evaluate supervisees?" This question, too, may be answered in a relatively simple manner. The answer is that numerous evaluation tools (i.e., form and procedures) are readily available. For example, one of the references at the end of this book is this one:

> Center for Substance Abuse Treatment. (2009). Clinical supervision and professional development of the substance abuse counselor. Treatment Improvement Protocol (TIP) Series 52. HHS Publication No. (SMA) 14–4435. Rockville, MD: Substance Abuse and Mental Health Services Administration.

This book may be ordered and received at no cost from SAMHSA. It may be downloaded and used by clinical supervisors. It is referenced here because it includes forms for evaluating supervisees, including the form, "Evaluating Counselors and Supervisors." Also, virtually all of the training programs that prepare individuals for licensing as professional counselors, mental health counselors, psychologists, social workers, and marriage and family therapists have forms and procedures for evaluating their trainees. Many of these documents appear online. Also, based on the competence-oriented model of clinical supervision (COMCS) provided in this book, an evaluation form appears in the Appendix.

Malpractice in Clinical Supervision

Malpractice may occur in many different forms. Experienced clinical supervisors usually hold knowledge of the many possibilities. Without attempting to offer a complete list of the possibilities, a list of malpractice occurrences that carry potential liability for clinical supervisors includes directing or encouraging inappropriate client care (e.g., advising a supervisee to deliver a form of care of which the supervisee is incapable), lapses in normative supervisor accountability (e.g., failing to attend scheduled meetings with supervisees or failing to assess a supervisee's skills), direct harm (e.g., sexual intimacy with a supervisee), or violation of laws or regulations (e.g., neglecting to make a state-mandated report, say, of the sexual victimization of a child). Malpractice claims against supervisors and clinicians succeed because the supervisee or client suffered damages and the damages meet the standards for a successful claim in legal proceedings.

Generally, a claim against a supervisor begins with a normative and demonstrable duty to the supervisee. The fact of a duty to the supervisee – and, therefore, the client who may be treated by the supervisee – may be established in many different ways. Usually, the fact of a duty to the supervisee is not contested. However, where the fact of duty is contested, it may be established through many different kinds of evidence. Such evidence includes, but is not limited to, appointment books, electronic appointment schedules, telephone records, cancelled checks, testimony from witnesses, registration in a practicum or internship or other institutional program, documents kept by the supervisee or the supervisor, or others. The importance of establishing a duty to the supervisee is that a malpractice claim cannot proceed without this foundational fact. In short, if there is no duty, there is no claim.

The fact of duty must be established before a successful malpractice complaint can proceed. Generally, three additional criteria must be met. If establishing duty is the first, the second is that there must be a breach of duty. Such a breach, as indicated earlier, may take many different forms. It may be that the supervisor gave poor advice, came to a meeting reeking of alcohol or another substance, used meetings to plan publications, solicited services from a supervisee that violated normative standards of supervision, pursued romantic interests in the supervisee, and so on.

The third criterion is that the supervisee – or, possibly, the client – suffered damages as a result of the actions of the supervisor or the supervisor failed to take appropriate actions. The meaning of damages often eludes mental health care providers, because they engage with damaged persons in much of their clinical work and sometimes take for granted that such things occur without consequences for those who cause damages. This is to say that their professional efforts are oriented toward remediation of damages and not prosecuting those who cause damages. Unfortunately, this sometimes causes supervisors to minimize their potential for being the source of damage to supervisees or clients. Allowing for this, the supervisee who alleges that she or he suffered damages carries the burden of establishing the fact of damages. In many cases in which damages are alleged, the facts are relatively easily established. For example, if documentation indicates that a supervisor directed a supervisee to provide care for a client that 1) was inappropriate for the supervisee or the client; 2) was clearly beyond the supervisee's capabilities; 3) posed somewhat predictable risks for the supervisee or client; or 4) violated the law, regulations, or policies of an employing agency, or other indicators of poor supervision, and if, say, a supervisee lost her or his employment or internship because of the supervisor's actions, a case for damages may be made somewhat easily.

Finally, the allegations against a supervisor must establish that there was causation between the breach of duty and the damages that the supervisee suffered. For example, if a supervisor gave poor advice and direction to a supervisee and the supervisee suffered the loss of employment or an internship, the necessary question is whether these two facts are connected by cause and outcome. Conceivably, the supervisee lost her or his employment or internship for reasons that had no connection with the supervisor's actions.

Conclusion

This discussion of legal issues in clinical supervision is far from complete. Instead of attempting to be complete, it is intended to enable clinical supervisors and prospective clinical supervisors to continue or to sustain their work with an awareness of and orientation to some of the basic legal issues in clinical supervision. Quite probably, a single resource, such as this book, cannot provide all that needs to be known and understood about the legal issues in clinical supervision. An easy illustration of this is that state laws and regulations of clinical supervision continue to evolve somewhat rapidly. They look very different from the way they did ten years ago. More important, even if they are well understood today, they will look very different from this over the next ten years. They will continue to evolve.

Competent clinical supervisors understand and comply with the normative standards of clinical supervision and clinical performance, professional ethics, and the laws and regulations of the jurisdiction within which they provide their professional services. This chapter has emphasized the importance of compliance with laws and regulations. When this topic arises among clinical supervisors, it usually becomes attached to considerations of contracting, vicarious, and direct liability; mandated reporting; duty to warn; lawsuits; and other specifically law-related topics. Frequently, these topics also become associated with apprehension about the vulnerability and risks of providing clinical supervision. No doubt, the vulnerability and risks are real. However, they rarely define or provide guidance for a supervisory relationship. Giving undue attention to vulnerability and risk, instead of the almost immeasurable potential of shaping the clinical futures of supervisees and their profession and the rightful fulfillment that attends success as a clinical supervisor, may obscure their importance for clinical supervisors. Thus, instead of succumbing to dire forecasts based on laws and regulations, clinical supervisors may view laws and regulations as tools to use as they build their approach to supervision, with the desired outcomes of transcending mere compliance and achieving the best possible clinical supervision.

10

TRAINING, ACCREDITATION, LICENSING, AND PRACTICE AMONG SUPERVISEES

Adding to the contextual issues for which clinical supervisors may need to account when they provide clinical supervision, this chapter discusses the size of training programs of prospective supervisees, licensing differences among prospective supervisees, the character of training programs, and practice issues among supervisees. The emphasis is that the training and preparation of prospective supervisees places prospective supervisors in the position of having to assess the training and preparation of supervisees, instead of assuming that, for example, a supervisee is prepared to engage in continued professional development, based on familiar markers of readiness, such as the completion of internships and/or degrees. This implies and means that the training, licensing, training programs, and type or quality of practice of one supervisee may bear almost no resemblance to those of another supervisee.

With reference to their training, what may be some of the important differences between and among clinical social workers, psychologists, professional counselors, and marriage and family therapists – the major types of licensees among non-medical mental health care providers? Who or what ensures that the training of these types of mental health care providers is minimally adequate? And, if a clinical supervisor holds one of these types of licenses, does she/he understand the training of the others and their normative expectations from clinical supervision?

The full answers to these questions expand the discussion beyond the scope of this book. However, toward answering these questions, a clinical supervisor who holds a license as a professional counselor, psychologist, social worker, or marriage and family therapist, should consider several relevant facts, in anticipation of providing clinical supervision for a prospective supervisee. The relevant facts may be clustered into four categories: the size of training programs, the accreditation status of programs that lead to licensing, the character of the academic/training program and the clinical practice that comes with the license of the clinical supervisor, and the scope of practice of the license that a supervisee is pursuing. Taken together, these four categories provide clinical supervisors or prospective clinical supervisors with a large informational context from which they may gain a clearer orientation to their supervisees.

With near unanimity among states, the licenses that are issued to individuals who have completed training in professional counseling, psychology, social work, or marriage and family therapy have many features in common. Generally, the training programs that prepare them and the states that issue licenses to them expect and authorize licensees to diagnose and treat mental disorders and to practice independently. However, as common as this general orientation to practice may be, the differences in the size of training programs, the accreditation status of training programs, the character of training programs and the clinical practice that comes with a license, and huge differences among these primary types of licensees may be easily found.

Size of Programs for Supervisees

In this discussion, "size" refers to the number of credit hours of a program that prepares its students for licensing as mental health care professionals. Why is the size of a training program a factor to consider, when clinical supervision is offered? While the answer may be complicated, due to a variety of requirements for the size of training programs from one state to another, the size of the program points only to the considerable differential among programs that prepare students for licensing.

At this time, with regard to the number of semester hours required for a professional counselor or a marriage and family therapist, the low number is forty-eight graduate semester hours, although almost all programs of this kind require considerably more than forty-eight semester hours. Although the number of states that require only forty-eight semester hours for licensing continues to decline, those that require only forty-eight semester hours may be easily located. For example, Alabama, Oregon, and South Dakota require only forty-eight semester hours of graduate studies for individuals who aspire to be licensed as marriage and family therapists (MFT license requirements in Alabama, n.d.; Oregon, 2018b; South Dakota, 2018b) or as professional counselors (Alabama Board of Examiners in Counseling, n.d.; Oregon Board of Licensed Professional Counselors and Therapists, 2018; South Dakota, 2018).

The lowest number of semester hours at forty-eight may be misleading, because the number of graduate semester hours for social workers may not be precise or clear, due to the practice in most states of accepting the accrual of undergraduate semester hours that may be counted toward the completion of a master's degree in social work. For example,

> *In the state of North Carolina, an MSW is the minimum educational degree required for any position higher than that of a CSW. A bachelor's degree in any field is necessary to obtain an MSW; however, if a BSW has already been completed, students may be eligible for an "advanced standing" status, which will allow them to complete the program in an expedited term of one year rather than two.*
>
> (North Carolina, 2018)

Generally, the practice of most states is that an individual who completes an undergraduate degree in a program that is accredited by the Council on Social Work Education (CSWE) is required to complete only one of two years of graduate studies in a CSWE-accredited program. The result of this is that an individual may complete a master's degree in social work in either approximately thirty (30) graduate semester hours or approximately sixty (60) graduate semester hours. Whether the licensed clinical social worker completes thirty graduate semester hours or as many as sixty graduate semester hours, the requirements for the licensing of a social worker adds to quite unnecessary chaos in the licensing of mental health care providers. For example, the University of Tennessee School of Social Work includes the following statement in the description of its master of science in social work, for prospective students:

> *The Advanced Standing program is designed for students who have a BSW or BSSW degree from a school of social work accredited by the CSWE, and can be completed in one year as a full time student or two years as a part time student.*
>
> (University of Tennessee School of Social Work, 2018)

Similar to social work students at the University of Tennessee, social work students at Loyola University Chicago may complete as few as twenty-eight (28) graduate semester hours as a basis for receiving a license (Loyola University Chicago, 2019a).

In contrast with these requirements, licensing for psychologists in the same three states described earlier include the requirement of 120 graduate semester hours or more (How to become a licensed psychologist in Alabama, n.d.; Oregon, 2018a; South Dakota, 2018a). Obviously, while the authorization to practice clinical work in these three states is very similar among counselors, psychologists, and marriage and family therapists, the sizes of the degree programs that they complete show extraordinary differences. Maybe, fair and important questions are these: Are those who receive licenses as counselors and marriage and family therapists receiving much too little training? Are those who receive licenses as psychologists receiving much too much training? From a public policy point of view, along with a presumed commitment to protect the citizens of their respective states, what, if any, reasonable sense may be made of the extraordinary differences among the requirements for licensing of these mental health care providers?

The large differential in the sizes of training programs raises the likelihood of large, potential differentials between supervisors and supervisees. Although their respective licenses qualify them to provide many of the same services, the differential in their preparation for providing these services may cause inadvertent dissonance between them, when one of them provides clinical supervision for one of the others. Obviously, as described already, the differential in the size of training programs likely contributes to inadvertent dissonance. In addition, as another example, because the doctoral degree has long stood as a requirement for licensing in psychology, those who pursue licensing as psychologists will necessarily have completed a dissertation, along with approximately one hundred graduate semester hours. In contrast, a master's degree is the most common educational requirement for those who pursue licensing as professional counselors, social workers, and marriage and family therapists. These degree programs almost never require a dissertation or as many semester hours as psychologists' training programs. Presumably, the differential of completing a dissertation or not means that psychologists who provide supervision for supervisees who anticipate receiving one of the other licenses will more likely understand and utilize relevant clinical research in their clinical work than their supervisees. This may not be either inevitable or important, but it may lead to inadvertent dissonance between them.

More broadly, the numerous differences among the training and preparation of licensees as professional counselors, social workers, psychologists, and marriage and family therapists raises difficult but necessary questions. Insofar as these licensees prepare practitioners to provide counseling and psychotherapy, are some of them required to complete far too much preparation or far too little preparation? If, say, a professional counselor and a psychologist receive their respective licenses in South Dakota, with one holding a forty-eight-semester-hour graduate degree and the other holding a one-hundred-six-semester-hour – or more – graduate degree (University of South Dakota, 2019), is one required to prepare too much and one required to prepare too little? From too little preparation for clinical practice or from excessive demands on prospective licensees, are professional ethics compromised? Are recipients of clinical services going to receive inadequate services or pay too much, as a consequence of their therapists' inadequately small training or excessively long and expensive training? From the views of public policy, professional accountability, and normative professional ethics, how may this difference be justifiable? And, in the context of a supervisor-supervisee professional relationship, what, if any, difference does this make?

With regard to clinical training, the requirements for the various mental health care licenses share relatively little in common. This is to say that the amount and kind of specific clinical services in which a prospective licensee must demonstrate competence varies extremely among prospective licensees. For example, social workers will likely utilize clinical interviews as their primary means of assessing the needs of clients, while clinical psychologists will utilize clinical interviews and psychological assessment tools, such as a personality test, an intelligence test, or an occupational test. In most states, social workers are not authorized to utilize such tests, while psychologists routinely utilize them. This kind of difference does not necessarily predict the level of clinical effectiveness of these two types of licensees. It likely predicts that if one is providing clinical supervision for the other one, significant differences in their understanding of their respective clinical work will emerge. This kind of difference is a product of the size of a training program but also, because of the difference in sizes, a difference in the content of training. In short, the larger the program, the more encompassing and expansive the content, or the smaller the program, the smaller the content.

Accreditation of Training Programs

Generally, clinical supervision rests on the reasonable assumption that both supervisors and supervisees come to clinical supervision prepared to engage in the process of supervision. However, one of the mitigating factors that either or both of them may bring to pre-degree supervision or post-degree supervision is the quality of their training and preparation for delivering clinical services and overseeing the clinical work of others. These mitigating factors may be credibly reassuring ones, when the accreditation status of the training programs of the prospective supervisee is known and understood.

For the purpose of illustrating the significance of the accreditation of programs that prepare counselors and psychotherapists, the next few paragraphs provide a profile of accreditation in the state of Tennessee.

At this time, within the State of Tennessee, nine psychology programs prepare individuals for licensing as psychologists. All of them are APA-accredited programs in five universities (American Psychological Association, 2017). These universities include East Tennessee State University, Tennessee State University, University of Memphis, University of Tennessee-Knoxville, and Vanderbilt University. Because APA-approved programs in Tennessee and every other state are usually mandated prerequisites for licensing, the fact of accreditation is important. These nine programs admit a combined total of less than one hundred students each year, according to their online reports, with an approximate annual average of eighty-five. These facts alone may have relatively little meaning. However, in the context of providing clinical supervision for completers of these programs and completers of other licensing preparation programs, these facts may take elevated and unexpected meaning. At least, the graduates of these psychology programs will have fulfilled the requisite expectations – that is, met minimal professional standards – that the profession of psychology has established and maintained through its accreditation agency, the American Psychology Association Commission on Accreditation (APA-CoA) (American Psychological Association, 2018).

In contrast with the accreditation picture of psychologist preparation programs, at this time, an unknown number of graduate programs – but a number that is larger than forty – prepare students for licensing as professional counselors in Tennessee. The license is licensed professional counselor – mental health service provider (LPC-MHSP). The unknown number arises from the fact that preparation programs are not required to hold any form of professional endorsement or accreditation. If a college, university, seminary, academy, or other institution holds only institutional, regional accreditation, it qualifies within the state to offer a counselor preparation program. In contrast with psychology and social work programs, institutional accreditation alone is sufficient as an academic and professional status for programs that prepare individuals to become licensed as professional counselors. Neither professional endorsements nor accreditation is required.

An easy illustration of this situation is Vanderbilt University, Nashville, Tennessee. Vanderbilt University offers a graduate program in professional counseling that is accredited by the Council for the Accreditation of Counseling

Related Educational Programs (CACREP, 2019). CACREP is the accreditation agency of the American Counseling Association. The graduates of this sixty-semester program receive training for licensing as LPC-MHSPs in Tennessee and as equivalent licenses in other states. Vanderbilt University's counselor training program has a long history of major contributions to professional counseling. However, with no relevant professional endorsements, no accreditation, and no visible relation to professional counseling, graduates of other programs at Vanderbilt University may also apply for and receive licenses as professional counselors. The other programs include divinity and nursing. These programs have no accreditation or professional endorsements from mental health care accreditation agencies, such as the Council on Social Work Education (CSWE) or CACREP. At this time, while these programs cannot qualify for accreditation by a mental-health-care-related professional association, their graduates receive licenses from the State of Tennessee as professional counselors. Unlike psychologist training programs, the accreditation status of other counseling and psychotherapy training programs appears to have little significance, with regard to licensing. In contrast with the state-mandated accreditation of psychologist training programs, the state of Tennessee, along with most other states, imposes no demands on programs that train professional counselors and marriage and family therapists.

The importance of this is that, if completers of un-accredited programs cannot assure a prospective clinical supervisor that their training has met minimal professional standards – such as the standards from CSWE or CACREP – should an appropriately credentialed clinical supervisor provide supervision for them?

In almost every state, the authors of this material have found programs that cannot qualify for any professional endorsements – namely, accreditation. Our most recent count of these programs was that two hundred four such counselor preparation programs fall extremely below minimal standards for programs that prepare professional counselors. Locating them is as easy as it is alarming. Within our state, Tennessee, we can easily find graduate programs that prepare counselors for licensing and that have no – this is, none – licensed mental health care providers on their respective faculties. They include state-supported and private institutions. Despite this apparent and serious limitation, their graduates receive licenses as professional counselors. Again, while we are concerned about the status of training programs in our state, we recognize that these programs currently operate in many other states.

The necessary question, therefore, is "What implications may accreditation status have for clinical supervision?" The possible answers to this question may be critically important. Surely, the possible answers include the following:

Prospective supervisors cannot know that their prospective supervisees are prepared to receive clinical supervision. Completers of unaccredited programs are often trained by faculty who have never practiced counseling and psychotherapy or held professional accountability for professional, ethical behaviors. More generally, if those who train prospective clinicians are not themselves clinicians, how effective is the training for their students?

Prospective clinical supervisors may not know whether their prospective supervisees can function appropriately as clinicians. While some prospective supervisees who completed unaccredited programs may function quite appropriately as professional persons, a prospective clinical supervisor has no way to confirm this, insofar as they cannot accurately report that their degree programs complied with minimal professional standards.

Prospective clinical supervisors may not know whether their prospective supervisees may be dangerous for their clients. Our review of numerous unaccredited programs, particularly those that clearly and firmly advocate theological views or other ideologies, also often transparently espouse misogyny, homophobia, conversion/reparative therapy, or other views that may harm clients. In addition, insofar as normative professional ethics, such as those established by the APA, ACA, and NASW, may not be compatible with the ethical standards of other codes of ethics, such as the code of ethics of the American Association of Christian Counselors (AACC), prospective supervisees who affiliate with the AACC should be carefully examined. To suggest that adherents of the AACC Code of Ethics may need to be carefully examined could appear to be judgmental. To be clear about such a suggestion, additional information is needed.

The AACC Code of Ethics states that "this Code defines biblically-based values" (AACC, 2014, p. 10). Likely, most Christians would agree with this idea, endorsing the thought that biblically based values are ones that they support. The code extends the idea of being biblically based to its definition of counseling. It says, "'Counseling' is usually a generic reference to clinical, psychiatric, pastoral, and lay helping" (AACC, 2014, p. 11). It further defines the aim and aspirations of Christian counseling in the following manner: "Christian counseling, at its best, is a Spirit-led process of change, transformation and growth, geared to help others mature in Christ by the skillful synthesis of counselor-assisted spiritual, psychosocial, familial, bio-medical, and environmental interventions" (AACC, 2014, p. 12). Professional clinicians must challenge the idea that counseling and psychotherapy "is a Spirit-led process of change" or that they should aim "to help others mature in Christ." A feature of such a challenge involves the question of whether adherents to the AACC Code of Ethics may violate normative clinical judgment and the ethics of other major mental health care provider associations. Specifically, instead of normative clinical and ethical judgment, the AACC Code of Ethics says, "Christian counselors do not condone or advocate for abortion or the abortion-related activities of clients, especially when the life of the fetus and/or mother are not at risk or in jeopardy" (AACC, 2014, p. 15). Also, specifically, the code says, "Christian counselors do not condone or advocate for the pursuit of or active involvement in homosexual, bisexual or transgendered behaviors and lifestyles" (AACC, 2014, p. 15). Are these "biblically based values" or political positions or socialized orientations that may be neither biblical nor political?

Christians or anyone else should be entitled to hold beliefs that the AACC Code of Ethics espouses, with regard to abortion and homosexuality. Obviously, beliefs about these very sensitive matters involve personal and social values. However, advancing these beliefs as ones that may somehow be "clinical," the code espouses beliefs that are much more political and religious than clinical. They are not clinical. Insofar as they are not clinical, they betray normative clinical judgment and, instead, exploit counseling as a means of religious and political expression. More than exploiting counseling as an abstraction of the real and immediate experience of helping others, they also exploit their clients. Again, whether they come from the AACC or elsewhere, the beliefs about abortion and homosexuality should be respected. They should not be regarded as views to be integrated into clinical practice. The importance of this for clinical supervisors is that the religious, political, and moral views of their supervisees should be respected and that these views should be placed in the context professional accountability.

Prospective clinical supervisors may inadvertently promote and support practices and views with which they seriously disagree. If clinical supervisors provide supervision for supervisees who have completed unaccredited programs, they may be endorsing and promoting misogyny, homophobia, and other unethical attitudes and practices. This problem is discussed further in the following.

Prospective clinical supervisors may open themselves to charges of unethical practices. As discussed in the chapters on "Ethics and Supervision" and "Law and Supervision," clinical supervisors are accountable for the clinical work of their supervisees. Therefore, under the aegis of professional ethics, regulations, and law, clinical supervisors should understand that they are accountable for the actions of their supervisees, including discriminatory actions and any other harmful actions toward their clients.

The significance of providing clinical supervision for completers of unaccredited programs may be easily illustrated. In addition to misogyny and related concerns, the completer of an unaccredited program may pose other legal and ethical concerns of which the clinical supervisor may not be immediately aware. For example, a prospective supervisee may have completed the "mental health counseling program" at a certain state-supported university in Tennessee, a psychology department that alleges to prepare individuals for licensing as professional counselors. The department does not prepare psychologists for licensing. It has no counselors on its faculty. Usually, it has no faculty who hold a mental health care license. A prospective clinical supervisor may reasonably wonder what professional ethics, if any, should a prospective supervisee be expected to know and understand. Should it be the ethics of the American Psychological Association, when the supervisee is seeking licensing as a professional counselor? Should the prospective supervisee be expected to comply with ethics of the ACA that the state's professional counselor licensees must follow? If no one who serves on the faculty of this program has professional accountability under the

ACA ethics – she or he does not have to practice under this authority – what may she or he be reasonably expected to know about them?

No doubt, clinical supervisors carry risks in their role as supervisors. In the context of this discussion, how may they mitigate their risks? These are some of the ways:

When lacking knowledge or having doubt about a prospective supervisee's training program, gather information about the program.

When lacking knowledge or having doubt about a prospective supervisee's knowledge and understanding of professional ethics, ask relevant questions about this and get substantial and conclusive answers.

If clinical supervision is provided in the context of an agency that has policies and procedures, the prospective supervisor and supervisee should study the policies and procedures so that they know and hold in common the institutional obligations with which they must comply.

When lacking knowledge or having doubt about the adequacy of a prospective supervisee's preparation for clinical supervision, seek consultation from those who have useful knowledge of the prospective supervisee.

Carefully document any and all concerns about a prospective supervisee, including any actions that may have been taken.

Establish agreements with the new supervisee about whom the prospective supervisor has doubts, including an informed consent document that both the supervisee and the supervisor sign. Carefully document all supervisory sessions.

Review the supervisee's clinical records.

Protect client welfare. When in doubt about whether clients' interests are being protected by a supervisee, document this and carefully describe all actions taken.

Does the accreditation status of a training program make a significant difference? The short answer is clearly "Yes." Every major mental health association has established minimal training standards for its programs and its prospective licensees. These standards largely define minimally appropriate professional preparation, in contrast with preparation in unaccredited programs that presumably and generally fall below minimal standards. The major mental health associations and their accreditation agencies are these:

Major Association	**Accrediting Agency**
American Counseling Association	Council for the Accreditation of Counseling and Related Educational Programs
American Psychological Association	Commission on Accreditation
American Association of Marriage and Therapists	Commission on Accreditation for Marriage Family and Family Therapy Education
National Association of Social Workers	Council on Social Work Education

The Character of the Academic-Training Program

As already noted, the quality of mental health care from those who complete unaccredited training programs is in doubt. Students, graduates, licensees, and, most important, consumers of mental health services are considerably more likely to receive inadequate, even harmful, services from completers of unaccredited programs. In not yet published research, we found that approximately twenty percent of licensees who graduated from CACREP-accredited programs and approximately twenty-five percent of licensees who graduated from unaccredited programs advertised inappropriate approaches to counseling and psychotherapy (Martin, in press). The inappropriate treatment approaches included alchemy, aromatouch (massage), chiropractic care, craniosacral therapy, earth-based religious, essential oils, feline-assisted therapy, Kundalini yoga, past life regression therapy, past life soul retrieval, power animal retrieval, shamanism, spiritual direction, the power of prayer, time traveling, truth of God's Word, Wicca, Vedic astrology, and numerous others. The differential between supervisees from accredited and unaccredited programs may matter a great deal to clinical supervisors whose license and reputation may be questioned, as a result of providing supervision for individuals who completed un-accredited programs.

Also, as already noted, the risks carried by clinical supervisors of completers of unaccredited programs should be taken into account when such supervision is provided. The risks include significant ethical and legal ones.

Generally, by definition, theological schools that allege to train counselors and psychotherapists usually re-define mental health care as something other than health care. However, attributing such a re-definition to all therapists who are theologically trained would be a mistake. Instead, whether they are theologically trained or not, a virtually countless number of licensed counselors and therapists advertise their services in such ways that indicate a radical and dangerous re-definition of mental health care. At least, they reject a century-long accrual of evidence about the practice and effectiveness of psychotherapy. Worse, instead of practicing mental health care, they view counseling and psychotherapy as expressions of their religious views, separating their understanding and practice of counseling and psychotherapy from health care. The suffusion of religion – any religion – into health care often radically re-defines health care as not health care and as something that distorts mental health care to accommodate the personal interests and needs of "therapists," instead of the interests and needs of clients. One of an almost limitless number of such re-definitions is this one:

> *For Christian psychologists, our worldview must be determined by Scripture. Not only should we see our clients as individuals in need of Jesus Christ, but our understanding of mental illness and disorder should also be based upon a Gospel-oriented worldview. As a result, our therapeutic practice will utilize Scripture to heal our clients and glorify Jesus.*
>
> (Rainer, 2018)

This statement falls into a category of advocacy among those who read about and practice their religion and psychotherapy. Quite apart from this category, another almost limitless number of practicing therapists advertise their services to prospective clients, expressing a very similar and radical re-definition of mental health care. The authors of this book have located thousands of examples of websites on which licensed counselors, psychologists, social workers, and marriage and family therapists have promoted their practice of counseling and psychotherapy as a religious activity and, from the authors' view, a potentially dangerous activity, insofar as it appears to make professionally accountable services for their clients subordinate to personal religious beliefs. Only to illustrate a situation that is much larger than this discussion can adequately cover, the problem may be seen in examples selected from websites of practicing and licensed therapists. Copied and pasted here, these illustrations come from the advertising of each of three professional counselors, psychologists, social workers, and marriage and family therapists.

Licensed Professional Counselors

1 As a Christian, I know some are seeking a Christ-Centered approach. To me, being a Christian is about relationship with our Creator and Savior. My practice is not to exclude those who are not seeking a Christian approach, but to offer help in the most respectful way.

(LPC-1, 2018)

2 God values your family unit and so do I. Unfortunately in today's stressful world disharmony results. If you are willing, together we can work on healing and restoration. Behavioral problems, sexual addiction, and relationship issues are problems I frequently see. Through Biblical counseling I strive to help you see yourself as Christ sees you. You are unique, precious and deeply loved by God. As a Christian, I strive to treat the whole person: body, soul, & spirit. For this, we've created a calming, peaceful environment for relaxation therapy.

(LPC-2, 2018)

3 I also utilize Christian-based Cognitive Behavioral Therapy and Family Systems approaches to therapy. People have become numb in the way they live – detached from God, their marriage, their children, and their purpose. God's desire is to live the fully restored life that He promises in His Word – a life of happiness and joy free from the bondage of sin, addiction, and shame.

(LPC-3, 2018)

Licensed Psychologists

1 My rabbinical services include spiritual, premarital and bereavement counseling and officiation of weddings, funerals, baby-namings and b'nai mitzvah. I am a Temple University psychology professor teaching human development, sexualities and intimate relationships. Extensive study of yoga and

eastern philosophies supports practices and teaching of integrated mind-body awareness.

(Psychologist-1, 2018)

2 I am skilled in NLP, hypnosis and Past Life Regression Therapy.* My practice is located a half a block from the bus line on the northeast end of ________. I am a half a block from beautiful ______ ______ and ______ _______ Road. The office space is calming and private.

(Psychologist-2, 2018)

**Generally, "past life regression" is associated with past lives of a client, of course, but also religious beliefs, such as re-incarnation.*

3 Research has proven that a strong faith helps many people deal with the challenges and complexities of life. Moreover, studies have shown that religious individuals live longer and stay happier in comparison to the average American. This is why we make it a point to integrate Christian beliefs in our Christian clients' counseling sessions. Rest assured that our counseling methods for Christian clients are always Christ-centered and Biblically sound.

(Psychologist-3, 2018)

Marriage and Family Therapists

1 With the help of the Holy Spirit, my goal is to help you understand and acquire new skills to live worry free in God's Grace. Call me and let me pour you a cup of hot tea as we begin the healing process together.

(LMFT-1, 2018)

2 Individuals are encouraged to work toward unlocking their pain and confusion, depression, anxiety, pain, grief, and loss or anything that keeps them stuck from living a Christ filled lifestyle or reaching their ideal goals.

(LMFT-2, 2018)

3 As a deeply committed Christ follower, I integrate biblical principles into the therapy I provide. I believe the foundation of every healthy marriage is rooted in God's written plan. Every effective therapeutic philosophy draws on those principles, whether it is acknowledged or not.

(LMFT-3, 2018)

Licensed Social Workers

1 Harmonious Space – within two medicine wheels, & the guides & guardians of the Directions; I employ Embodied Kabbalah,* reflexology, flower essences, chant & meditation. I am a Spiritual Midwife–Rabbinic Pastor, Interfaith Minister, Spiritual Director. As an activist in environmental,

social, racial, LGBTQ justice in ____________, I bring the inner & outer worlds together.

(LCSW-1, 2018)

**The Kabbalah Center offers this definition of Kabbalah: "Kabbalah is an ancient wisdom that reveals how the universe and life work. On a literal level, the word Kabbalah means 'receiving.' It is the study of how to receive fulfillment in our lives and discover how the universe works and what the meaning of life is" (The Kabbalah Center, 2018). As an ancient Jewish religious-theological assertion, the "receiving" usually emphasizes the dwelling of God in the body of those who believe, similar to many Christians' belief that God was incarnate in Jesus.*

2 I use plant medicines, shamanic healing,* bodytalk, advanced energy healing techniques, and trauma resolution therapy besides traditional counseling. Any issue or any problem, I have a technique that can help. No need to spend years in therapy my approach is fast and effective.

(LCSW-2, 2018)

**Generally, shamanic healing is not regarded as a religion. However, emerging from spiritualistic practices that have endured for many centuries, it is usually regarded as a spiritual practice that is delivered by a spiritual leader or shaman. It includes practices such as soul retrieval therapy, neutralizing unwanted and negative energies, ancestral work, body manipulations, and facilitating the process of helping body-departed souls to find the light, among many others. Therapists who advertise shamanic healing as one of their offerings often also offer energy healing techniques and various physical resources, such as plant medicines or herbal medicines.*

The following two statements come from the LCSW who posted these statements on two websites in which she advertises her professional services. In one, she advocates for "Core Shamanism" – defined, here – and in the other offers "evidence based clinical techniques."

3 Core Shamanism,* developed by Michael Harner of the Foundation for Shamanic Studies, consists of the core practices which are common or near-universal among all shamanic traditions without the specific cultural aspects of any one of them. Core shamanism includes: rhythmic drumming to help change state of consciousness the shamanic journey to make a healing request the gift of wisdom and healing power not accessible in an ordinary state of consciousness relationship with ancestors, teachers, power animals, and other helping spirits the intention to help alleviate pain and suffering.

(LCSW-3, 2018)

> I use a collection of evidenced based clinical techniques in collaboration with gentle somatic release through a healing modality called Reiki. Reiki is a Japanese technique involving light touch for stress reduction and relaxation that promotes health.
>
> (LCSW-3a, 2018)

> **What is core shamanism? According to Michael Harner, the developer of Core Shamanism referred to by the LCSW, core shamanism is defined in the following manner:*

> *Core shamanism consists of the universal, near-universal, and common features of shamanism, together with journeys to other worlds, a distinguishing feature of shamanism. As originated, researched, and developed by Michael Harner, the principles of core shamanism are not bound to any specific cultural group or perspective. Since the West overwhelmingly lost its shamanic knowledge centuries ago due to religious oppression, the Foundation's programs in core shamanism are particularly intended for Westerners to reacquire access to their rightful spiritual heritage through quality workshops and training courses.*
>
> (Harner, 2018)

This brief sampling represents thousands of similar advertisements by licensed mental health care providers. Clearly, they stand outside the normative professionally accountable practice of mental health care. Regardless of how they may be viewed by others in their professional community, the matter of concern in this discussion is whether they have relevance for practicing clinical supervisors who may provide oversight of individuals whose views, such as those expressed in "biblical counseling," should be taken into account.

In the interest of client welfare, at least, a prospective supervisee who completed training in a theological school or who holds strong religious views may cause necessary and heightened concern about client welfare, along with specific ethical and legal concerns. For example, we have found that training in an un-accredited training program in a theological school often involves institution-sanctioned misogyny and/or homophobia. Specifically, as one among many theological schools with such views, the Pentecostal Theological Seminary prepares students to become licensed mental health professionals who must believe in the absolute authority of the Bible, according to the seminary (Pentecostal Theological Seminary, 2017). From the point of view of "the absolute authority of Scripture," what accountability may this impose on a clinical supervisor? If the supervisee holds beliefs that are not homophobic and/or misogynist, as a matter of conscience and ethics – albeit tacit conscience and ethics – should the clinical supervisor respect and/or uphold the supervisee? In fact, The PTS "recognizes homosexuality as an unscriptural lifestyle." Should a clinical supervisor want to know this? This discussion illustrates the challenge of supervising or planning to supervise graduates of un-accredited training programs. At this time, numerous programs that allege to prepare mental health care providers shroud these programs in strongly ideologically driven approaches to mental health care, converting health care into a religious expression and, through this, betraying the interests and needs of clients who may be served by therapists who share and express such ideologies.

If only for self-protection, clinical supervisors should be alert to the vulnerabilities that may befall them, when they provide clinical supervision for individuals who completed their training in theological schools or who hold strong religious views that skew and seriously compromise the integrity of mental health care. In addition, they should carefully monitor all of their supervisees, with reference to the quality of care that their supervisees provide. In this discussion, the particular emphasis is that the quality of care may be seriously impaired by the inadequate academic and clinical preparation and/or by uncompromising religious views that a prospective supervisee brings to supervision. To be clear, the authors hold religious commitments. Martin has published books (Martin, 1975, 1990, 2010) and articles that are specifically religious. Neither he nor any other mental health care provider should deny the importance of sincerely held religious beliefs and commitments. However, they should not be regarded as qualifiers or disqualifiers of competent and professionally accountable mental health care. Nor should they be defenses behind which irresponsible counselors and psychotherapists rationalize their ideology-driven services with arguments about freedom of religion.

Differentials in Scope of Practice in Clinical Supervision

As already noted, specific practice issues may arise in clinical supervision from the size of a training program, the accreditation status of a training program, and the character of a training program. Within this discussion of the scope of practice, attention is given to the need of the clinical supervisor to examine the differences in the scope of practice between supervisors and supervisees. However, regardless of the scope of practice within which a supervisor or supervisee may provide clinical services, the supervisor carries the obligation of accounting for the supervisee's professional functioning. Surely, the supervisor should be alert to the possibility that the supervisee may want to provide un-professional and unethical services, such as those that appear earlier in this chapter but that may include numerous others. To name relatively few of the thousands of so-called "therapy orientations," a supervisee may wish to practice acupuncture-Chinese medicine, ancient wisdom, angel therapy, anthroposophical counseling, astrology, Bach flower therapy, biodynamic craniosacral therapy, chakra balancing, Chassidic spirituality, circus arts therapy, comedy psychotherapy, contemplative Tibetan Buddhist psychology, continuing bond with the deceased, crystal therapy, energy psychology-splanka, enneagram personality system, fairy tale model of therapy, ichthotherapy, Immanuel prayer process, induced communication after death, medicinal aromatherapy, meridian psychotherapy, Mormon/LDS therapy, mud therapy, muscle therapy, near death experience and spiritually, plant spirit medicine, power animal retrieval, quantum healing, reflexology,

Sogyal Rinpoche, soul retrieval therapy, tarot, theophostic therapy, transformational anthropology, universal values therapy, yield therapy, or yin warrior therapy. (All of these approaches to counseling and psychotherapy have been located on the websites of licensed mental health care providers.)

Any of these should raise questions, such as this one: "If you were the clinical supervisor, would you want to be held legally and ethically accountable for overseeing the 'clinical' work of a supervisee who sought to provide services that are based on one or some of these orientations to therapy?" In addition to these approaches to clinical work that are clearly inappropriate, supervisors may also want to examine a supervisee's offerings that may easily be regarded as professionally appropriate but that are inappropriately offered and/or delivered. For example, a supervisee may offer and try to deliver trauma-focused cognitive behavioral therapy (TFCBT) but with little or no training in TFCBT. Similarly, a supervisee may attempt to respond to a client's clinically identified need, with which the supervisee has little or no experience, such as treating obesity/weight loss issues or a client's needs related to terminal illness.

Quite apart from the challenges that may arise from the size of training programs, the accreditation status of a training program, or the character of the training program, the scope of practice differentials among various types of licensed mental health care providers should be taken into account, too. These differentials require that clinical supervisors or prospective clinical supervisors know about the realities of clinical practice for their supervisees. The challenge of this may be understood when a number of questions about clinical practice are asked.

What do licensed clinical social workers who are clinical supervisors know about the professional ethics of the American Association of Marriage and Family Therapists (AAMFT), in a supervisory relationship in which the social worker provides clinical supervision for a prospective licensee as a licensed marriage and family therapist?

What are the licensing requirements for psychologists? If a pastoral therapist is providing clinical supervision for a prospective psychologist, what ought she or he know about licensing requirements? Alternately, if a licensed psychologist is providing clinical supervision for a pastoral therapist, what should the psychologist know and understand about pastoral counseling?

The scope of practice for mental health care licensees is defined by each state in which the licensee holds a license. With regard to scope of practice for professional counselors, marriage and family therapists, psychologists, or social workers, what should a clinical supervisor know about the others' scope of practice? How may this influence the practice of clinical supervision? Based only on a state's definition of the scope of practice, a clinical supervisor may misunderstand the scope of practice of a clinician in another state. For example, in the state of Kentucky, licensed professional counselors receive authorization from the state to administer psychological tests, while in the state of Tennessee, licensed professional counselors are prohibited from administering psychological tests.

With regard to numerous specific client issues, what may be the status of client privilege? In one state, clients of mental health care providers who are also involved in a custody dispute do not have client privilege, while in another state, the client maintains such privilege. In one state, clinical supervisors must submit a supervision contract, a philosophy of clinical supervision, and a detailed plan for clinical supervision to designated state authorities, while in another state no such requirements exist. And, if a supervisor or the supervisee relocates from one of these states to the other state, are these clinical supervision issues? Obviously, the answer is "Yes." They could be significant issues.

This discussion is necessarily incomplete. It is not intended to provide a survey of the multiple issues that inhere in comparisons of training, accreditation, licensing, and clinical practice among supervisees. Instead, its limited purpose is to heighten supervisors' awareness of their obligation to investigate these comparisons so that they may ensure that their supervisees receive the clinical supervision that they need and to protect their professional interests as clinical supervisors.

Quite apart from the specific issues that are addressed in this chapter, all conscientious mental health care providers should be alert to the multiple ways that their profession and, more important, their clients or prospective clients may be compromised. For example, a seminary (Pentecostal Theological Seminary, 2018) that offers a graduate degree program that leads to licensing includes the following statement in its academic catalog: "The Seminary, as part of the Church of God, recognizes homosexuality as an unscriptural lifestyle which precludes church membership, ministerial credentials, and, therefore, participation in this Seminary" (p. 23). While anyone, including those who are connected to this seminary, should be quite free to believe whatever they wish to believe with regard to sexual orientation and practice, the issue here is whether a clinical supervisor may wish to know that a supervisee holds a view such as this and expects to deliver professional services that incorporate this view.

Further, a clinical supervisor may wish to know that a supervisee affiliates with organizations that hold views that are hostile to normative mental health care. For example, the Association for Certified Biblical Counselors (ACBC) is one of these organizations. Membership in this organization means that the supervisee is likely to hold views of counseling that the vast majority of mental health care providers emphatically and with sound ethical, legal, and clinical reasoning reject. For example, the ACBC says,

> *Many fashionable views abound. In particular, numerous voices in our culture embrace, as normal and proper, same-sex desires and behavior, same-sex marriage, transgender identification, and malign – as evidence of ignorance and cruelty – efforts to counsel people away from such behaviors.*
>
> (ACBC, 2017)

Also, it says that its theological position rejects the idea that "homosexual desires, behavior, or marriage is an acceptable or moral lifestyle." At least, a qualified clinical supervisor should examine the risks of providing supervision for a prospective supervisee whose religious views – if such views are expressed as clinical views in working with clients – pose major risks for a supervisor.

Obviously, a discussion that refers to the possibility that a prospective supervisee may hold strongly homophobic views has important implications for clinical supervisors. For example, a clinical supervisor may wish to explore the ethical boundaries with a supervisee who identifies as member of the Church of the Nazarene. The Church of the Nazarene Manual states,

> *Because we believe that it is God's intention for our sexuality to be lived out in the covenantal union between one woman and one man, we believe the practice of same-sex sexual intimacy is contrary to God's will for human sexuality.*
>
> (Church of the Nazarene Manual, 2017, p. 56)

The authors wish to emphasize, again, that diversity of political and religious views should be expected and generally accepted among mental health care providers. As noted, each of us should be free to believe almost anything that we wish to believe. The critical issue for clinical supervisors is not that their supervisees may have religious or political views with which they disagree, but that professionally accountable mental health care is expected, with or without such points of view. Another implication from this discussion is that supervisors should seek to clearly define the ethical and legal dimensions of the clinical work of their supervisees. Additionally and more narrowly, supervisors should carefully review the code of ethics of supervisees, particularly when the supervisee's code of ethics is different from that of the supervisor's. Or, to frame the matter differently, if a licensed psychologist provides clinical supervision for a social worker, whose professional ethics prevail, if there are conflicts between one code of ethics and the other?

As a personal view of mental health care supervision, we believe that professional accountability should allow for considerable diversity in points of view among us. We believe that allowing for considerable diversity among us has promoted the advancement of our profession. Surely, this idea may be seen in all of those who led us to understand advancements in our clinical services that, if left to ourselves, would not have happened. Consider Joseph Wolpe and systematic desensitization. Or consider Carl Rogers and person-centered therapy. Or consider George Kelly and cognitive therapy. Each of them dared to challenge the psychotherapeutic community and made it better than it was. Numerous individuals who are not nearly as well-known as these innovators, including many of the heroic and likely very patient clinical supervisors who helped us, have also helped mental health care to make its slow but inexorable advances. However, our openness to advances should come with a capacity to distinguish between professional accountability that includes both protecting the integrity of mental health care and exhibiting the courage needed to advance it, while denying bigotry and self-serving ideologies that impair the best of what we may be capable of offering. This is a duty of clinical supervisors.

Conclusion

This chapter calls for due diligence in screening candidates into clinical supervision. Specifically, it calls for clinical supervisors to assess the training of prospective supervisees, the accreditation status of their preparation program, and qualifying or disqualifying personal beliefs and attitudes. The importance of assessing these features of prospective supervisees receives confirmation from professional ethics and best practices that have been prepared by most, if not all, major mental health care associations. For example, the *Code of Ethics* of the American Counseling Association (2014) states, "Counselors practice only within the boundaries of their competence, based on their education, training, supervised experience, state and national professional credentials, and appropriate professional experience" (p. 8). The major associations promulgate similar standards for clinical supervisors. Truly, screening is a sensitive matter that holds significant consequences for supervisors and prospective supervisees. While screening is a sensitive matter, sometimes leading to disappointment when candidates for supervision are not accepted as supervisees, it ranks as a critically important and high priority, when placed in the context of providing mental health care for clients.

11

SUPERVISOR DEVELOPMENT

This chapter and the one that follows address supervisor and supervisee development. With focused assumptions described later, the broad-based assumption for now is that every mental health care provider develops. Usually, whether they are supervisors or supervisees, this is understood to mean that they evolve from demonstrable incompetence to demonstrable competence. The current condition of understanding this evolution for supervisors and supervisees is one of incompleteness. As noted elsewhere in this book, presentations of "best practices" in clinical supervision are readily available. Such presentations arise almost exclusively from the accrued wisdom of the practice of clinical supervision and not from a solid evidentiary understanding of clinical supervision. In other words, the research-based evidence that defines clinical supervisor and supervisee development lacks sufficiency, at this time. Despite this insufficiency, supervisors must supervise. And as they practice supervision, they must develop toward increasing effectiveness even when increased effectiveness is defined in terms that are unique to each clinical supervisor or most clinical supervisors.

Supervisor Development

Similar to what most new parents experience, clinical supervisors must supervise others, whether they have grounding in best practices that have evolved from research or not. The need for evidence- and research-based practices is indisputable. The need arises from several demands. The first and most important is the demand to ensure client welfare. In addition, from a time only a decade ago, most states have established new demands, including procedures for approving prospective clinical supervisors. Depending on the state, these procedures call for prospective clinical supervisors to submit a philosophy of clinical supervision, a description of the clinical setting in which the supervisee will practice, the frequency of supervision meetings, a contract between the supervisor and the supervisee, a statement of goals for supervision, and more. The third demand is the tacit and broadening consensus around the belief that clinical supervision must be refined, although the existential immediacy of this belief is not entirely clear. Lacking this kind of clarity, the general situation may be described as one in which clinical supervision has entered another stage of development.

Roughly characterized, clinical supervision began with heavy tutorial and personal-clinical self-examination from emergent psychoanalysis approximately a century ago. After this, competing models – or philosophies – of clinical supervision arose along with the clinical orientations or theories through which they were expressed. Each respective theory of therapy was presumed to contain a necessary approach to clinical supervision. These included person-centered therapy, behavior therapy, reality therapy, and others. As theories began to recede in importance, because of newer forms of competition that arose from research about treatment interventions, approaches to clinical supervision took the shape of a quasi-autonomous discipline that was no longer contained within a theoretical orientation or combinations of theoretical orientations. The fledgling discipline included new applications of longstanding ideas, such as developmental thinking being applied to clinical supervision and a spreading and specifically tactical orientation.

As an important aside, numerous so-called "approaches to counseling and psychotherapy," such as past life soul retrieval therapy, grace therapy, and wisdom-based therapy, simply lack any basis for their respective practice, except the highly individualistic preferences of the practitioner. We have come to refer to these approaches as "theo-rectal" orientations. These "theo-rectal" orientations may be re-shaping counseling and psychotherapy toward becoming something that, as a result, will harm professionally accountable counselors and therapists. Recently, because of somewhat inadvertently locating a small number of "theo-rectal" orientations to counseling and psychotherapy, we decided to look further into this matter. By looking at the websites of practicing licensed mental health professionals, we gathered a list of almost 22,000 orientations to therapy. Depending on how some of them may be judged, approximately 2,000 of these orientations look familiar. They would include

Cognitive-behavioral therapy	Person-centered therapy
Solution-focused therapy	Emotion-focused therapy
Applied behavioral analysis	Psychoanalysis
Family therapy	Dialectical behavioral therapy
Motivational interviewing	Multi-systemic therapy

Whether therapists practice any of these or not, they would readily acknowledge that they view them as acceptable orientations to therapy that others offer. However, approximately 17,000 (Martin, in press) other orientations to therapy are ones that may be characterized as "theo-rectal." They include

After-death communications	Akashic record readings
Alchemy	Ancient wisdom
Anthroposophical therapy	Applied shamanism
Aura therapy	Christian Buddhism
Comedy therapy	Essential oil healing
Floratherapy	God-centered Christian therapy

God's Truth therapy	holographic scaling
Immanuel prayer process	Kabbalistic healing
Light laser therapy	Metronome therapy
Neuropsychiatry [not a psychiatrist]	Oriental medicine
Past life regression	Plant spirit medicine
Power animal retrieval	Punching bag therapy
Soul retrieval therapy	Splanka energy psychology
Time travel	Universal values therapy
Vedic astrology	Vibrator therapy

Along with a very large number of others, these so-called "approaches" or "orientations" to therapy are called "theo-rectal" because of where we believe they come from. They betray the needs and interests of clients who receive treatments from these approaches. Further, they betray the interests and welfare of the majority of therapists who work sincerely and persistently every day to provide the best clinical services that they can.

The relevance of this aside may be clear. It is a warning. It is an encouragement for clinical supervisors to be alert to the temptation of supervisees to select approaches that come from something other than the real clinical world. They should be alert to the possibility that supervisees may "just make up stuff" that has no relevance to the real clinical world. This is to suggest that, as a person of faith, I wish to affirm faith when I see it. However, such a readiness to affirm diversity cannot and should not allow supervisees who have no training and no apparent interest in receiving minimal training that would qualify them to offer or claim to offer an approach to therapy that flows from their faith. To say, "I'm a Christian, and, therefore, I provide Christian therapy," is not professional. It is comparable to saying, "I am a man, and, therefore, I provide masculine therapy," or "I am sexual, and, therefore, I provide sex therapy," or "I eat, and, therefore, I provide eating disorders therapy." To make these kinds of statements or numerous versions of them reveals ego-centrism – "Therapy is mostly about me, the therapist, and, therefore, I should provide therapy that expresses my interests, first and foremost."

Naturally, with its emphasis on how supervisees develop, a concern about how supervisors develop also emerged, especially when training supervisors became a broadly recognized necessity for all of the major mental health professional associations, such as the American Counseling Association (ACA) and the American Association of Marriage and Family Therapists (AAMFT). An expression of this may be seen in the fact that these associations established certifications for clinical supervisors. Also, the need for understanding supervisor development arose from the observation that experienced supervisors demonstrated more effective work than inexperienced supervisors (Russell & Petrie, 1994). As obviously reality-based as this observation may seem, though, it has not yet produced a model of clinical supervisor development about which clinical supervisor researchers and practitioners have consensus. Based on their review of research on theoretical models of supervisor development, Barker and

Hunsley (2013) conclude, "Perhaps the most striking finding from our review is the dearth of empirical studies focused on supervisor development." Despite the lack of studies that focus on supervisor development and a widely accepted and useful model of supervisor development, movement toward this has occurred. The importance of this movement is that it contributes to the burgeoning sketch of a picture of supervisor development.

The practice of psychotherapy has evolved toward specialization and tactical orientations, such as the treatment of eating disorders or sexual compulsivity or couples' therapy. Similarly, to accommodate this ongoing evolution, clinical supervision has become somewhat more specialized and tactical, too. Still, the search for a model of supervisor development proceeds, as if the need for it is the proverbial "itch that will not go away." To maintain this metaphor, scratching the itch has provided some extraordinarily useful concepts and insight. For example, Goodyear and others (Goodyear et al., 2015) identified "Ten Changes Psychotherapists Typically Make as They Mature into the Role of Supervisor." (p. 1044). The changes or, as they characterize them, "developmental themes," are as follows:

- Becoming able to perceive/act on complex response opportunities
- Learning to think like a supervisor
- Developing the ability to be oneself
- Learning to view oneself as a supervisor
- Developing the capacity to use reflection as a tool to monitor one's biases and one's impact on others
- Developing confidence in one's judgments about what constitutes effective counseling
- Developing confidence in one's competence as a supervisor
- Developing patience with the process of supervisee development
- Developing the courage to do the right thing in the gatekeeper role
- Learning to understand and manage power

The contribution of Goodyear and his associates holds the potential of elevating awareness of best practices in clinical supervision and growing a useful conceptualization of the development of competent clinical supervisors, with both of these being very much needed features of clinical supervision. As Gosselin and others (2015) note,

> *One of the major challenges in this area of research has been a lack of a clear conceptualization of what psychotherapy supervision development is and how it works. A definition is an important starting point for any assessment of the research literature by delineating the construct; that is, what constituted psychotherapy supervision development and what does not.*

Gosselin and others confirm an observation that all clinical supervisors may want to incorporate into their understanding of their work: "A second challenge in this area of research is that psychotherapy supervisor development models are largely untested and not grounded in the empirical literature."

While this book is not oriented primarily toward the research community, the considerably sophisticated observations and conclusions from the research community should be taken with high seriousness. Taken in this way, they invite the whole body of clinical supervisors to reflect on their work and to incorporate it into our practice of clinical supervision. The question, of course, is how this may be done.

At least, clinical supervisors and prospective clinical supervisors should believe that they begin their work at a stage of demonstrable incompetence and that their reasonable ambition and goal is to become demonstrably competent, knowing that demonstrable competence is not a fixed entity that once achieved never goes away. Instead, from the beginning of the practice of psychotherapy or the practice of clinical supervision, the need and obligation toward development endures until it is no longer practiced. So, regardless of the specific model that a clinical supervisor prefers, an essential understanding of supervisor development is that the supervisor continues to develop as a clinician and as a supervisor. "How may I be better than I am?" may be the indispensable question that clinical supervisors carry with them so long as they practice clinical supervision.

With or without a commonly accepted model of clinical supervisor development, there are common assumptions about important features of such a model. With no intention of presenting a complete set of assumptions about which mature clinical supervisors would agree, with reference to supervisor development, some of these assumptions include the following:

Clinical supervisors demonstrate good clinical skills throughout their work as clinical supervisors.

Beginning supervisors have anxiety about their work and low competence.

Beginning supervisors have uncertainty about their supervisory role.

Supervisors need supervision in the beginning of their work and from time to time during their careers in supervision.

Mature clinical supervisors study their supervision and consult with other supervisors, to ensure that their effectiveness is maintained.

Mature clinical supervisors demonstrate capability of honest and accurate assessments of their skills and effectiveness, along with a readiness to do this.

Mature clinical supervisors demonstrate grace/graciousness with their supervisees.

Surely, an emergent idea about supervisor development is that it should be evidence-based (e.g., Gosselin et al., 2015). However, at this time, approaches to supervision training and the models of supervision that have recently emerged are mostly not validated by research. As an incipient profession, clinical supervision preparation depends mostly on the history of practicing supervision and not on research. In addition, a lack of preponderant consensus about a model of supervisor development is itself a consensus. As Watkins observes, "Consensus seems to be that there is a critical need for empirical study of psychotherapy supervisor development (Watkins, 2012, p. 45). Nevertheless, some models appear to have become influential in promoting consensus. One of them was proposed by Stoltenberg, Delworth, and McNeill (1998).

Allowing for the lack of preponderant consensus about a model of supervisor development, some analysts of have offered ideas that enhance understanding of supervisor development. For example, Watkins (2012) writes about the common features of major models of supervisor development.

> *In surveying those models, the essential orienting points to bear in mind are: (1) all models are generally cast as either a three or four stage linear progression; (2) with Alonso's life-span model excepted, the models track supervisors from when they begin to supervise through the process of their becoming seasoned, master practitioners; and (3) as supervisors successfully progress through the stages, supervisory identity and skills are theorized to become increasingly enhanced, and supervisory self-doubt, insecurity, and negative affect about oneself as supervisor are theorized to become decreasingly in evidence.*
>
> (p. 48)

Watkins observes, "The models seemingly have their clearest, most identifiable distinctions at the beginning and end points; it is the middle parts that become a bit more fuzzy and difficult to track" (p. 70). In other words, most models advance the idea that beginning clinical supervisors exhibit uncertainty about their new role, express anxiety about their performance, and depend on experienced supervisors for guidance. In contrast, developed and skillful clinical supervisors generally present the following features.

> *Consolidation:* Solidified identity; theoretically grounded; able to effectively address parallel process and supervisee counter-transference phenomena
> *Integrated:* "Master supervisor"; highly skilled and integrated; able to effectively work with a wide variety of supervisees
> *Role Mastery:* "Master supervisor"; highest levels of awareness, skill, and identity achieved; consistency, stability, and consolidation predominate; highly committed to supervision as life-long learning experience; highly adept at working with supervisory transference, countertransference, and parallel process.
>
> (pp. 50–51)

Watkins confirms what experienced trainers of clinical supervisors believe to be true. Namely, there is no agreed-upon model of supervisor development or agreement about what such a model should include. However, he offers valuable insight about "four particular mechanisms that emerge as critical and pivotal for change and growth across models" (p. 71). He writes that these "elements seem to be both the prerequisites and lubricant for the initiation and maintenance of any sort of supervisor development process" (p. 71). The elements that characterize individuals who become skillful clinical supervisors are

> *(1) sufficient interest in being and desire to improve as a supervisor; (2) openness to one's supervisory self-experiencing; (3) capacity for and willing embrace of supervisory self-examination and self-reflection; and (4) action, practice, and experimentation (e.g., with regard to supervision skills, strategy deployment, and alliance formation).*
>
> (p. 71)

Possibly, those who wish to become skillful clinical supervisors and those who wish to train them successfully can utilize these elements in their pursuit of effectiveness.

Understandably, when clinical supervisors contemplate their role, they likely consider how their supervisees develop, much more than they consider how they themselves develop. No doubt, most of the literature on clinical supervision gives significantly more weight to developing supervisees than to developing supervisors. Among other goals, this book is intended to be a resource for helping supervisors to develop themselves. The focus of the book is how to develop an approach to clinical supervision. However, this somewhat narrow focus should not hide the importance of the growth and development of clinical supervisors, with specific emphasis on the knowledge, skills, and attitudes that they present to their supervisees and through which they assist in the professional development of their supervisees. Although its age is a factor in its relevance and utility, an excellent resource for supervisor development is Jane Campbell's book, *Becoming an Effective Supervisor: A Workbook for Counselors and Psychotherapists* (Campbell, 2000). Also, to accompany this book, we are currently preparing a workbook that we are tentatively titling, *Clinical Supervision: A Training Manual and Workbook.*

In chapter 21, "Practices Helpful to Developing a Philosophy of Clinical Supervision," several suggestions about practical ways to engage in developing a philosophy of clinical supervision can be found. They encompass a variety of practical activities that will assist supervisors and prospective supervisors toward becoming more effective. However, in the larger discussion of developing an approach to clinical supervision, a conceptualization of supervisor development may be needed, too. Clinical supervisors are encouraged to consider their personal, respective conceptualization of their development. This may be facilitated with the practices that are described elsewhere in this book. In addition, they may be facilitated through regular attempts to answer questions like these:

How may I be better at clinical supervision than I am?

What are my supervisees experiencing that I should understand better than I do?

What are the issues that inhere in my current growth as a clinical supervisor, and who may help me with these issues?

What, if any, are the unique vulnerabilities that I bring to my work as a clinical supervisor?
Is there a new and relevant research report about supervisor development about which I should know?

As this discussion transitions to a discussion of supervisee development, clinical supervisors will want to consider how their roles evolve in relation to supervisee development. Or, to frame this idea as a question, "How may the functioning of the clinical supervisor change as her or his supervisee develops?" What may be the differences in outlook, activities, and skills from a clinical supervisor who oversees the work of a new clinician and the supervisor who oversees the work of an experienced and appropriately effective clinician?

Conclusion

If a discussion of clinical supervisor development holds meaning for experienced or prospective supervisors, it is that they, in fact and almost inexorably, develop in multiple ways, including their knowledge of counseling and psychotherapy, their knowledge of clinical supervision, their skill in providing clinical supervision, and their growth as individuals in the role of clinical supervisor. Insofar as they develop, they may claim options for how to think about their development. Surely, one way of thinking about their development is to regard themselves as incomplete clinical supervisors whose abilities are compromised by their incompleteness. Alternately, they may regard themselves as incomplete and, therefore, choose to demonstrate their readiness to adapt to becoming a better version of themselves, even when such becoming involves high resolve and courage, just as they wish to see in their supervisees and their supervisees' clients.

12
SUPERVISEE DEVELOPMENT

Generally, clinical supervisors assume that, as a consequence of their oversight, their supervisees will develop toward becoming effective clinicians. Few, if any, clinical supervisors would want to believe that their supervision would not facilitate professional development in their supervisees or would make their supervisees less competent clinicians than they were when supervision began. The assumption that supervisees develop emerges from somewhat more specific assumptions, including the following:

> In the process of becoming competent, the counselor will progress though a number of stages that are qualitatively different from each other;
> Each stage requires a qualitatively different environment for optimum growth to occur.
>
> (Australian Institute of Professional Counsellors, 2011)

Experienced clinical supervisors would likely add another assumption to these. It is that the desired progress in the first assumption stands on the readiness of supervisees to expose themselves to the risks of trying to achieve effective professional functioning in their clinical work. Without such readiness or determination, the developmental stages would not likely occur.

For most supervisors, these assumptions or similar ones come somewhat easily. They may pose little challenge for supervisors. However, they necessarily pose a question that is very challenging: "If supervisees develop, what are the identifiable development stages through which they develop?" or "As supervisees develop, how may I recognize the developmental stages when my supervisees are going through them?" Understanding that the questions arise far more easily than their answers are found, the discussion here describes commonly found developmental stages of supervisees and offers a limited array of clues that may help supervisors to identify them as they occur.

To place the ideas here in a useable context, clinical supervisors, especially new ones, need to know that developmental models of clinical supervision have been advanced for approximately fifty years. Stoltenberg and McNeill (1997) offer this brief account of the emergence of developmental conceptualizations of clinical supervision:

> *In their 1987 book, Stoltenberg and Delworth review and critique seven developmental models of clinical supervision using Barlett's (1983) categorization framework. Hogan's (1964) four-stage model was presented as one of the earliest models (other than Fleming, 1953) relying on developmental constructs. Although the presentation of this model was quite brief and, therefore, lacked detail, it had an important impact on subsequent model building. Indeed, along with the cognitive developmental work of Harvey, Hunt, and Schroder (1961) and Hunt (1971), Hogan's model formed the basis for Stoltenberg's (1981) developmental model of supervision.* (p. 186)

While the history of developmental conceptualizations of clinical supervision continues to grow, these conceptualizations should be understood more as conceptual models than conclusive, evidence-supported approaches to clinical supervision. The current models of clinical supervision must continue to receive investigation so that supervisors who enact them can practice with appropriate professional confidence in them. At this time, collectively, their value may be similar to those of the theoretical models of psychotherapy from four or five decades ago. The theories of psychotherapy provided needed guidance for, among other things, conceptualizing clients' experience and shaping clinical decisions. However, the volume of evidence for many different treatments, such as treatments for disruptive behaviors in children or eating disorders in adults, has adequately and mostly neutralized the importance of these theories.

Allowing for the need to conceptualize the development of supervisees from broadly accepted research-based conclusions, a sampling of some of the current models is briefly presented here. A major category of supervision models that is not presented here is the theory-based models. The rationale for this is simple: Theory-based models, such as person-centered clinical supervision or psychoanalytic clinical supervision, express the ideological perspective of the supervisor, much more than a disciplined, evidence-based model of clinical supervision. Such approaches continue to decline in relevance and viability, being supplanted by research-based approaches to counseling and psychotherapy. The models briefly presented include

A stage development theory of counselor competence (Smith, 2006)
The Stoltenberg and Delworth model
The integration model
The discrimination model
The no-model model
Reflective practice model
Competence-oriented model of clinical supervision (COMCS) model

If a thorough discussion of models of clinical supervision were attempted, it would require considerably more space than this book should give to such a discussion. Instead of making this attempt, this discussion borrows from several commonly identified models of clinical supervision. For example, the concept embedded in the Littrell, Lee-Borden, and Lorenz model (Littrell, Lee-Borden, & Lorenz, 1976) is that supervision practices are closely correlated with supervisees' skills, similar to the calibration that clinicians make in their interaction with their clients. As a clinical supervisor or a clinician, this calibration shapes the practice of supervision or therapy in ways that make the prescriptive thinking of modeling more an artifact of the intellect than a wise supervisory or clinical intervention. Nevertheless, the correlation of supervisor practice with supervisee development in this model contributes substantially to an effective working model of clinical supervision.

A Stage Development Theory of Counselor Competence (Smith, 2006)

Similarly, Smith's developmental model briefly encapsulates clinical supervisors' experiential awareness of their supervisees' movement from incompetence to competence. Smith (2006) prepared a fairly simple model of counselor development. He referred to the model as "a stage development theory of counselor competence," clearly placing the emphasis on the development of clinical competence. It includes four stages. Each stage is assigned a descriptive title and a phrase that characterizes the individual supervisee – or "the individual" – in each of the four stages, as indicated in the following.

Number	Descriptive Title	The Individual
1	Unconscious incompetence	The "Unaware"
2	Conscious incompetence	The "Novice"
3	Conscious competence	The "Technician"
4	Unconscious competence	The "Artist"

In the earliest stage of this development, supervisees enact the social "scripts" that they have taken most of their lives to develop. Quite reasonably, because of their socialization to function in their individualistic ways, they should not be expected to know how to function as mental health care providers. As a manifestation of this lack of awareness, they conduct therapy in ways that replicate their so-far learned ways of relating with others. Usually, sooner or later, they become aware of how ineffective they are (i.e., "conscious incompetence"). With this recognition, they struggle, usually expressing uncertainty about what to do, as they attempt to conduct therapy. Their struggle, along with supervisory guidance, opens their experience of themselves and their potential capabilities as therapists to practice therapy based on clinical judgments, instead of thoughts and actions that come primarily from their socialization. Finally, as they continue to acquire clinical skills, confidence, and elevated prowess in conducting therapy, they acquire "unconscious competence."

The belief that, with the oversight of trained clinical supervisors, inexperienced mental health care providers can move from "unconscious incompetence" to "unconscious competence" compels attention. Very likely, experienced clinical supervisors have witnessed this movement and received gratification from the recognition that they have effectively assisted supervisees through this process.

The Stoltenberg and Delworth Model

With almost thirty years of analysis and critiques, the Stoltenberg and Delworth model (Stoltenberg & Delworth, 1987) continues to have positive resonance with many clinical supervisors. In short, they proposed three developmental levels of supervisees and eight developmental dimensions. The first level describes new counselors as lacking information, demonstrating insufficient skills, and being apprehensive about their clinical performance. The second level describes clinicians who are well into the process of development, showing comfort in their clinical roles, demonstrating competence in managing client information and interactions, finding positive meaning in their clinical work, carrying appropriate accountability for their interventions, and being at ease in exploring their personal issues. The third level is described as one in which supervisees exhibit self-reliance and relate with supervisors as colleagues and peers, in contrast with their dependence on supervisors in the first level. Significantly, Stoltenberg and Delworth affirm the importance of correlating supervisor functioning with supervisees' level of skill.

Stoltenberg and Delworth identify eight dimensions of supervisees' functioning, including these:

1 Intervention skills	2 Assessment techniques
3 Interpersonal differences	4 Client conceptualization
5 Individual differences	6 Theoretical orientation
7 Treatment goals and plans	8 Professional ethics

The Integration Model

Following Stoltenberg's "Complexity Model" (1981), the integrated model of clinical supervision came from Philip Rich (1993). The model expresses integration – or blending – because it draws from the supervision approaches that were extant at the time, including counseling, social work, and other types of professional orientations. The integration model addresses four functions of supervision, six stages of supervision, and six primary elements of supervision. Viewing the integration model of clinical supervision as "a basis for a uniform understanding of the supervisory process and its actual practice, supervisory training, and future research" (137), Rich identified the four functions of supervision as "facilitation, staff development, staff socialization, and service delivery" (138). To the functions, he added the six stages of clinical supervision, including "relationship building, planning, observation, analysis, conference or meeting, and follow up" (138) and completed his model with "six primary elements," including "facilitative environment, supervisory relationship, structural elements, supervisory skills, provision of learning experiences, and supervisory roles" (138).

The significance of this model is that it expresses the complexity of clinical supervision and attempts to account for this complexity in the delivery of supervisory services. As the model has evolved through the work of Stoltenberg, McNeill, and Delworth (1998), with contributions from others, it has become a commonly identified one in the literature on clinical supervision and a commonly sought one among clinical supervisors.

The Discrimination Model of Supervision

The discrimination model of supervision originated with Bernard, according to her and Goodyear's report in their book, *Fundamentals of Clinical Supervision, Third Edition* (2004). Their model posits three primary roles of the clinical supervisor: teacher, counselor, and consultant. In turn, each of these three roles carries three functions or "foci": intervention, conceptualization, and personalization.

Bernard and Goodyear (2004) characterize their model as a "social role model." In their non-theoretical model, they seek to account for the complexity of personal functioning, insofar as individuals have complex social roles that imbed beliefs and a large body of complex learning that comes with normative human development and its narrower professional development. They write, "The discrimination model is concerned specifically with interactions within the supervision session as these relate to immediate learning needs of the supervisee" (p. 97). The interactions that address the learning needs of supervisees presumably occur in such ways that the social roles of the supervisor and supervisee become clinically refined as their relationship develops. And, they add, the model "does not speak to the role of evaluator or monitor, which is important as a means to ensure quality of client care," although "its presence is assumed" (p. 97). While the meaning of this should be articulated by the authors, its apparent meaning is that the supervisee develops within social roles that emerge somewhat naturally from the development of the supervisory relationship, and the somewhat peripheral functions of evaluator or monitor do not normatively characterize most relationships.

The No-Model Model

The no-model model of clinical supervision acknowledges a common, if not typical, supervisory reality: supervisors provide supervision with little or no interest in, skill pertaining to, or preparation for supervising. According to Campbell (2006),

> *In this supervision model, clinical supervisors are selected or appointed because they are excellent therapists, clinicians, or counselors, not because they have training in supervision. Supervisors using this model say to themselves, "I am a competent clinician; therefore, I will be a competent supervisor. I will just do with my supervisees what my supervisors did with me." Usually, a no-model model represents a reactive, retrospective approach to supervision.*
>
> (pp. 35–36)

Campbell acknowledges that this common model is often a deficient one. She points out that supervisees are not clients and that, because of this, they require a different set of skills than therapy. She adds that supervisors who repeat the supervision that they received keep the past alive but likely provide marginal supervision. Adding to Campbell's thoughts about the no-model model of clinical supervision, another likelihood is that some supervisors provide supervision with little or no thought about their work. Maybe, a supervisor who described her supervision illustrates this. With enthusiasm and delight, she said, "I just love supervision. It's just so great to meet with beginners and enjoy them." Clearly, in response to inquiries from others, she could not elaborate on any aspect of her approach to clinical supervision.

Reflective Practice Model

A general acknowledgment is that the reflective practice model of clinical supervision has become increasingly common as a preferred understanding of clinical supervision. Hill, Crowe, and Gonsalvez (2016) observe that "The capacity for reflective practice is increasingly being incorporated into competency requirements for workers across healthcare domains (Falender et al., 2014; Mann, Gordon, & MacLeod, 2009)" (p. 265). This observation, though, should not obscure another observation. It is that agreement about what a reflective practice model is and how it works is not yet available. Allowing for a lack of agreement, the reflective model of clinical supervision holds certain beliefs about clinical supervision that define the core of what it is.

Within these beliefs, one emphasis is that "Reflective supervision is the regular collaborative reflection between a service provider (clinical or other) and supervisor that builds on the supervisee's use of her thoughts, feelings, and values within a service encounter" (Multiplying Connections, 2017). This emphasis focuses on dialogue that probes and refines the clinically relevant issues within the supervisee. Another emphasis is that reflective practice, including clinical supervision, is a process through which "practitioners gain skills to identify, name, and change various assumptions and biases in a systematic fashion to increase awareness, competency, and effectiveness" (Cooper & Wieckowski, 2017, p. 252). Further, Cooper and Wieckowski assert, "The process has a strong scientific base in the development of expertise through deliberate practice" (2017, p. 252).

This emphasis shifts the priority to supervised critical thinking and critical analysis of knowledge and experience. While there are other emphases in the very large discussion of the reflective practice of clinical supervision, at least two major assumptions occupy the attention of discussants. One is that reflection is inevitable. Reflective practice seeks to capitalize on this inevitability. The second is that reflective practice achieves its best results when it is intentional. So, the idea is that reflective practice captures the inevitability of reflection and refines it into effective clinical work through intentional, deliberative, relational, and integrative interaction and practice. This is a way of saying that reflective practice carefully examines the experiencing of self in the context of clinical work and integrates the findings from such examination into clinical work.

The reflective practice model of clinical supervision may encompass numerous specific supervision practices. It may be integrated with almost any major theoretical orientation to counseling and psychotherapy, including integrative therapy, solution-focused therapy, various psychodynamic therapies, and person-centered therapy. Typically, though, the reflective practice model of clinical supervision proverbially "takes on a life of its own." For example, this may be seen in the form, "Reflective Supervision: Some Guiding Questions," available from Clinical Supervision Resources (2017), an online service that offers free materials that are available for copying and using. Among many examples of reflective supervision interventions, the form includes direction for the supervisee to select "a clinical encounter" that evoked discomfort and uncertainty about how to proceed and then adds, "2. Encourage the supervisee to think about the situation. What were you trying to achieve? Why did you intervene that way? How did you feel about the experience? What do you think the client/other person was feeling/thinking/wanting?" While somewhat unsettled, the supportive evidence (e.g., Cooper & Wieckowski, 2017; Curtis, Duran, Elkins, & Venta, 2016; Calvert, Crowe, & Grenyer, 2016) for the practice of reflective clinical supervision confirms the belief that reflective practice leads to heightened self-awareness of clinical decision-making and clarity about specific ways to facilitate client change.

The reflective practice model of clinical supervision continues to receive broad-based attention within the discipline of clinical supervision. Despite this, some raise caution about its rise in visibility. Calvert, Crowe, and Grenyer (2016) conclude, "There is a dearth of research. regarding the purposeful engagement in the processes of the supervisory relationship to develop therapeutic relationship competencies, including reflective capabilities" (p. 1). This caution should be noted, although numerous examples of research efforts may be easily located.

For example, a recent and ongoing effort by Cliffe, Beinart, and Cooper (2016) aims to establish reflective practice as an evidence-based approach to clinical supervision, with particular emphasis on testing the validity of a short version of the Supervisory Relationship Questionnaire.

The Competence-Oriented Model of Clinical Supervision (COMCS)

Taking the concept of an integrated model, the following information represents an attempt to integrate some of the features of the supervision models presented earlier and others with observations from several years of providing clinical supervision and studying clinical supervision models. Appropriately, this attempt may be referred to as "comics" or, more accurately, the competence-oriented model of clinical supervision (COMCS). As an aside, providing a model of clinical supervision, especially knowing that many influences have helped to produce it, feels like we are mimicking others and, maybe, making a "comic" of our approach to clinical supervision. Nevertheless, we hope that the model presented here shows initiative, thoughtfulness, accountability, and risks that usually attend such an endeavor. The COMCS model stands on several assumptions. With ongoing growth in assumptions, it assumes that

- Prospective mental health clinicians evolve from demonstrable incompetence to demonstrable competence.
- Their evolution draws its energy or motivation from their readiness to change toward becoming effective clinicians.
- Their evolution may be described as proceeding through several indistinct and not-yet-refined developmental stages.
- The content of their development includes knowledge, skill, outlook, and tasks.
- Their evolution depends on the guidance, teaching, nurturing, direction, and collegiality of supervisors.
- Their clinical functions can be understood as professionally accountable or not, insofar as they exhibit the qualities of high-functioning therapists, such as a strong proclivity for complex thinking, strong relational skills, personal self-care, emotional attunement, and a high tolerance for ambiguity, among others.
- Research-based conclusions about highly effective therapists substantially contribute to understanding clinical supervision, with particular emphasis on helping supervisees to conceptualize their appropriate professional ambitions and setting goals for clinical supervision. Sharing and discussing the article by Skovholt and Jennings (2004) may be a feature of enacting this assumption.
- Competent professional functioning may be defined. In fact, numerous definitions are readily available. More than definitions, though, the

accurate measurement of competence is necessary. As a reference that provides important insights in this regard, the recent article by Spengler and Pilipis, "A comprehensive meta-reanalysis of the robustness of the experience-accuracy effect in clinical judgment," gathers evidence from numerous research efforts that address competence in counseling and psychotherapy (Spengler & Pilipis, 2015).

Clinical supervisors should articulate a conceptual clinical framework for their supervisees, to ensure that they fulfill their obligations to supervisees. This is to say that each clinical supervisor should have clear ideas about what supervisees should know, how supervisees should function as clinicians, the level of self-awareness that supervisees should demonstrate, and the appropriate level of professional attitudes that supervisees should exhibit. However, the primary emphasis in supervision should be helping supervisees to develop their conceptualization of their clinical work and not teaching supervisees about conceptualizing clinical supervision.

With these assumptions in view, clinical supervisors should possess and expect their supervisees to possess solid basic, general knowledge of clinically relevant assessments, diagnosing, human development, substance abuse, clinical theories, intervention techniques, sex addiction, multicultural issues, neuroscience, professional ethics, and much, much more. However, each of these categories of knowledge is indefinitely large. Each one – and many others – could occupy the entire career of a clinician. Neither supervisors nor supervisees should know everything about all of these clinically relevant categories. By analogy, an excellent physician may need to know almost everything about bones, if she or he is an orthopedic physician, but should not be expected to know as much about pancreatic cancer as bones. Likewise, a psychotherapist may need to know almost everything about play therapy and childhood development, if she or he specializes in treating children, but should not be expected to know as much about sex addiction as play therapy.

For any model of clinical supervision, but with clear emphasis in COMCS, the criterion for much of clinical judgment and supervision centers on clinical relevance. If supervisees work with self-harming adolescents in an inpatient facility, they should show initiative toward gathering clinically relevant information, developing competencies that relate specifically to this population, reflecting on their personal experience of adolescence, and more. The criterion that inheres in these expectations is clinical relevance. Mostly, clinical relevance refers to the essential importance of the needs of the client. If supervisees are treating self-harming adolescents, they may not want to invest much energy in pursuing clinically relevant information about terminally ill seniors or developing clinical competencies that relate to this population, for example.

However, because supervisees are virtually always involved in what is being supervised, they should engage in ongoing reflection on gathering, clarifying, and discovering ways to utilize information about themselves. If the clients are a couple that includes a chief of staff at a hospital and a bank president, how comfortable or uncomfortable is the supervisee with them? Or, if the client is an over-anxious four-year-old boy, what is the supervisee's reaction to trying to translate her clinical understanding of four-year-olds into skillful clinical work with a young child? Or, yes, if supervisees' needs for affection and/or acceptance are easily translated into sensitive "mating antennae," how may they react to a client who appears to be nicely suited to provide affection and acceptance? The emphasis here is on the clinical relevance of supervisees' self-awareness to the specific needs of their clients.

The evolution of change from incompetence to competence, then, must be measured by the primary criterion of clinical relevance. Clinical supervisees who are new to clinical work may be expected to deliver marginal performances, with regard to competence, insofar as they are not expected to have mastered much of anything. In other words, they may not know much about what is clinically relevant, or, if they know about clinically relevant things, they may not know how to deliver what they know in a way that is truly effective. Generally, the earlier in the supervisee's experience that a supervisor is involved, the more the clinical supervisor seeks to evoke self-guidance from the supervisee but also offers mentoring and teaching.

In most academic training programs for mental health care professionals, clinical work begins late in such programs and continues after the trainee has completed and, presumably, mastered several bodies of basic content. As noted previously, these include such content areas as assessment, diagnosis, intervention techniques, documentation, human development, psychopharmacology, and others. The importance of this in this discussion is that the knowledge base of most supervisees is reasonably well established by the time they have completed their academic training. Because of this, supervision justifiably places a much greater emphasis on how knowledge is utilized and expressed than on whether a supervisee has it. The COMCS emphasizes this knowledge base, too, and presumes that it is adequately and solidly in place for most beginning supervisees.

With the discussion, so far, as a précis, what does COMCS look like? As a partial answer to the question, the information in Chart 12–1, "Competence Model of Professional Development," illustrates the COMCS.

In anticipation of others' need to understand this integrated model of clinical supervision, the following observations are offered as guidance:

The model characterizes movement from incompetence to competence.

The model identifies categories of movement. They are knowledge, skill, outlook, and tasks.

"Knowledge" accounts for the considerable body of professional information that may be relevant, with regard to many clinical experiences that are being supervised. A supervisee who treats individuals and groups in a substance abuse program would enter this work with a foundational knowledge of substance abuse but would also demonstrate readiness to gain increased sophistication in this area of clinical work as she or he is being supervised.

"Skill" refers to the demonstration/performance/expression of clinical judgment. Generally, it refers to the question of how supervisees utilize the considerable body of knowledge that they brings into clinical work and supervision. While a broad range of skills are necessary for good clinical work, COMCS places high priority on strong analytic skills and strong relational skills. "Analytic" refers to the skills that include information gathering, raising questions that take the clinician and client beyond the obvious, and processing information and making good clinical sense of it. "Relational" refers to the skills that include a capacity to adapt to many different kinds of client presentations, empathic alertness, speaking with compassion or confrontation when it or other responses may be needed, and much more.

"Outlook" refers to a somewhat complex array of personal features that may broadly be summed up in the word *attitude*. However, outlook is much larger than attitude. It includes supervisees' attitude toward clinical work and clients, to be sure, but it also includes the degree of optimism or pessimism about themselves and clinical work, the range of thoughts about their personal engagement with others as a way of influencing others to meet their needs, the degree of fear-based thoughts and feelings when dealing with personal or clients' crises, feelings that may be sought-avoided-accepted, tolerance of similarities and differences with clients, personal motivation, and much more.

"Task" refers to the many tasks that must be completed when an individual does clinical work. The completion of tasks may or may not involve the development of skill. Instead of developing professional skills, tasks more likely than not involve personal discipline in getting them finished in a timely and correct manner. The tasks may include the timely completion of forms of documentation, scheduling appointments, following up on referrals, keeping agreed-upon schedules with meeting clients and others, ensuring that all necessary forms (e.g., informed consent, release of information) are included in client files, bringing needed materials to supervision meetings, and so on.

These four categories of movement from incompetence to competence appear in Chart 12–1.

If a clinical supervisor hopes to complete a model of supervision that is useful and effective toward developing supervisees, the one outlined here may be helpful. However, because it is an outline, it may cause more questions to be asked than it answers. As it is, though, clinical supervisors may want to consider raising their individual questions about each of the four categories (i.e., knowledge, skill, outlook, and tasks) so that the COMCS becomes individualized and useful.

Chart 12–1 Competence Model of Professional Development

INCOMPETENCE > > >	**> > > COMPETENCE**
Held/Expressed With Uncertainty	**Held/Expressed With Autonomy**
Low Professional Accountability/Efficacy	**High Professional Accountability/Efficacy**

Knowledge
- Development of recognition and validation
- Development of growth and enrichment
- Development of expanded knowledge
- Growth of meta-knowledge (e.g., complex thinking, clinical reasoning, curiosity)

Clinical Skills and Transcendent Skills
- Clinical skills
- Relational skills
- Self-management skills
- Clinical leadership skills
- Engagement skills
- Activity-oriented skills
- Assessment skills

Transcendent Skills
- Emotional attunement to self and/or client
- Adaptability
- Clinical judgment
- Critical thinking
- Conceptualization skills

Outlook/Attitude
- Proclivity for relationships
- Appropriately valuing self
- Attitudes toward self and others
- Facility with feelings
- Adaptability/reactivity
- Meta-emotions
- Relevant personal values
- Tolerance of ambiguity
- Motivation

Task Completion Competencies
- [This may be almost anything that needs to be done in relation to clinical work.]
- Keeping accurate and current documentation
- Timely attendance of meetings
- Nurturing referral network / managing referrals and contacts
- Preparing for sessions with clients
- Following normative organizational policies and procedures
- Consultation with numerous others (e.g., probation officers, physicians, attorneys)
- Testifying in court/depositions
- Preparing letters for schools, employers, and others
- Billing and related matters
- Attending to licensing and certification requirements

Issues of Knowledge in the COMCS

Clinical supervisors generally assume that their supervisees know enough to be functioning in their identified clinical roles. For example, supervisees should be expected to know the code of ethics (e.g., ACA's, APA's, or others) that guide their professional ethical behavior and that provide the ethical boundaries within which they operate. Clinical supervisors would not likely assume, though, that their supervisees know – this is to say, have sufficient experience with – how to implement clinical decision-making because they have not done this if they are beginning clinicians. Similarly, beginning and relatively inexperienced clinicians may know the diagnostic categories in the DSM-5 but demonstrate low effectiveness in utilizing what they know, revealing both the knowledge of practice and their level of skill in practicing. The issue in clinical supervision is one of expanding awareness/knowledge of "real life" in the conduct of mental health care but also one of developing clinical skills.

Another issue related to knowledge involves the supervisee's demonstrated expansion of knowledge. This is to say that, inevitably, supervisees – along with long experienced clinicians – learn from their clients and acquire a great deal of knowledge about their clients and client experiencing. For example, beginning clinicians may have little or no vocabulary that enables them to converse with their clients, say, with regard to a thirty-one-year-old male who displays hallucinations or a sixteen-year-old girl who engages in compulsive sexual expressions with multiple, serial partners. When the hallucinating client speaks of his fear about being betrayed by his senses, he is giving the therapist a way to have a meaningful dialogue with him. "So, you really can't trust yourself right now. It's confusing to hear things and not know whether you are really hearing them?" Likewise, assuming that beginning clinicians/supervisees have little or no experience with a sixteen-year-old girl who presents the behaviors identified, they will discover new "language" and other manners of communicating that, in clinically appropriate ways, will be integrated into dialogue with this client.

This discussion of the issues of knowledge assumes that the supervisee comes into supervision with a comprehensive but not necessarily useful and surely not encyclopedic knowledge of clinical work. The supervisee's body of knowledge comes mostly from graduate courses, although important categories of knowledge may have come from life experiences and undergraduate studies. This body of knowledge changes, though, when the supervisee begins clinical work. It changes in, at least, three ways, as described in the following.

The first kind of change in knowledge involves *the development of recognition and validation*. This development is not so much the development of clinical skill but the skill of attaching information to clinical reality. For example, a new clinician may be working with a father who escaped from his home when it burned but lives with the horror of knowing that three of his four children died in the fire. Among many struggles that the father presents is that he says,

> *I feel like I'm going crazy. Really, I do. I know something bad happened to my kids. But, sometimes, I can't even remember their names. It's like they didn't exist. And, when we go the house, my wife tells me that I don't even recognize the place. She's really nice about it, but she's right. I just feel like my brain goes dark and I can't see what I see. It's weird. I mean, it's just weird.*

New clinicians begin to recognize that they know something that is immediately relevant to their clinical work. In the situation with the grieving father, the recognition is that naïve clinicians see what they already know as dissociation. And, in recognizing that they know dissociation and that this knowledge may be usefully related to their understanding of clients, the supervisee's knowledge is validated.

The second kind change in knowledge involves *the development of growth and enrichment*. Growth and enrichment complement the first kind of developing knowledge, recognition and validation. Quite beyond recognizing that something like dissociation may be seen in clients, the experience of encountering dissociation – or any of an interminably long list of clinical situations – demands that supervisees grow their knowledge of dissociation so that it is enriched by the experience of being with a client who presents dissociation. Virtually all experienced clinicians understand that the best of information about clients' experiences is not complete when it is primarily intellectual or academic information. However, when, within the perspective of the developing clinician, information about clients' experiences fuses into a living awareness of the clients' experiencing, the supervisee grows and enriches knowledge.

The third kind of change in knowledge involves *the development of expanded knowledge*. Again, as a complement to the other expressions of developing knowledge, supervisees inevitably expand their knowledge as a consequence of functioning as a clinician. Expanded knowledge is the addition of knowledge that clinical experience demands. While the addition of knowledge is not unique to each individual, it likely appears to be. Generally, though, the addition of knowledge comes from encounters with client circumstances and the demands that arise from these encounters. For example, no doubt, many experienced clinicians remember when they first heard a reference to "T-F-C-B-T" and knew that they did not know what it was. Or the reference may have been one that reported, say, in an article, "cognitive bias modification" or "CBM" and, again, left the reader wondering what "CBM" was. Such encounters with new knowledge and the demand of professionalism that the clinician encounters further evoke the pursuit of new knowledge constitute the features of expanded knowledge. As another illustration of expanded knowledge, the publication of a new DSM poses the demand that clinicians study it and adapt to using it effectively.

Similarly, when many of us began to practice counseling/psychotherapy, neuroscience and its importance to our practice were, at best, extremely remote. Now, the relevance and importance of neuroscience presses us to expand our knowledge of mental and emotional functioning well beyond historic understandings of psychological processes. Among many good and recent books that facilitate this understanding is David Presti's *Foundational Concepts in Neuroscience* (Presti, 2016). As a researcher whose training includes a doctoral degree in molecular biology and biophysics and another doctoral degree in clinical psychology, he is especially well informed for helping to inform the rest of us. And as the rest of us seek information about neuroscience, we expand our knowledge.

Issues of Skill in the COMCS Model

Therapy is a whole. It cannot and should not be fragmented into arbitrary subcategories of therapeutic skills. Further, no matter how strongly and effectively it may be exercised and no matter how persuasively it may be articulated, attention to a specific clinical skill is not sufficient for a reasonably professional conceptualization of clinical skills. For example, a therapist may be quite strong in building a good alliance with clients – a skill – but simultaneously be quite weak in offering appropriate self-disclosure – a clinical skill. Another way to say this is that one clinical skill is not discrete and complete by itself, such as the two already mentioned: building therapeutic alliances and the therapist's self-disclosure.

A therapist executes clinical skills. A therapist cannot be subdivided into parts of a therapist, although her or his specific skills may be conceptualized, examined, and developed separately by the therapist or others. In addition, clinical supervisors and others can facilitate the development of specific skills. The importance of skill development as an outcome of clinical supervision cannot be emphasized too much. After all, it is the implementation of therapeutic skill that defines therapy more than anything else. This is the doing of therapy.

Another prefatory issue in thinking about clinical skills in the COMCS model of clinical supervision is that clinical skill should be distinguished from clinical and personal assets. Clinical and personal assets encompass many features of being a person who provides clinical services. Such assets may include certain personal characteristics, such as high intelligence or religious faith or optimism or honesty. None of these assets are necessarily therapeutically significant. The lack of these assets, though, would almost surely be associated with clinical ineffectiveness. They become significant when they are expressed through specific clinical skills.

Generally, clinical skills are what therapists do. Every clinician who meets with a client does something to engage with a client, take actions toward a client, or in some way express clinical judgment. "Something" may be listening or taking notes or teaching about normal childhood development or offering supportive comments to a client or sharing an important and clinically relevant self-disclosure or assigning a task to a client or any of a very large number of other specific actions. Indeed, it is this very large number of specific actions that challenges clinical supervisors who wish to conceptualize them and assess how well a supervisee may deliver them that usually proves to be a daunting and even confusing reality for clinical supervisors. To assist clinical supervisors with their interest in conceptualizing clinical skills, COMCS offers a typology of these skills. With definitions and illustrations of the following types, the typology includes these major categories:

Clinical Skills

Relational skills
Self-management skills
Therapeutic leadership skills
Engagement skills
Activity-oriented skills
Assessment skills

Transcendent Skills

Emotional attunement to self and/or client
Adaptability
Clinical thinking and judgment
Critical thinking
Conceptualization skills

Relational skills. These skills encompass the ways a mental health clinician interacts with clients. Such interactions may be illustrated in multiple ways. For example, when clinicians model focus and reflective thinking for clients, they are exhibiting relational skills. Or when clinicians initiate conversations with clients about the quality of the relationship between themselves and their clients, especially in such ways that display openness to improving their relationship, they are exhibiting relational skills. Similarly, clinicians exhibit relational skills, when they choose to self-disclose or when they provide self-care for their clients or when they confront difficult client issues in ways that welcome troubling and often painful disclosures from their clients.

Self-management skills. Self-management skills may overlap with relational skills or other types of clinical skills, as should be expected of most of the skills that are discussed here. After all, as noted earlier, a clinician cannot be subdivided into discrete skills, simply because all of these skills inhere in a therapist who displays them. Each skill, though, may be separately studied, including self-management skills. These types of skills answer the question: How do I manage myself during my interactions with my clients?

In short, self-management skills exhibit the degree to which a therapist reacts to clients' presentations. Or, stated another way, how well does the therapist improvise in response to surprises or contain the temptation to react to a client in ways that may not be clinically appropriate? The need to improvise or contain responses may be seen in numerous examples, such as the following:

> *The client(s) is a couple. He is twenty-five years of age, and she is twenty-six years of age. The couple has been together for almost four years, including living together for three years. Both of them report that the relationship has been a pretty good one, with no betrayals or violence or other major complaints. With this lack of major "explosions" in their relationship, he says, "She is often hard to live with. I have to be very careful to say just the right thing or she will sulk and withdraw until I apologize, although I haven't done anything wrong. She's just too needy. And, she says this, too, sometimes." She describes a situation that emerged at a cocktail party that the couple hosted at their home. She reports that she saw him talking with one of their female guests, a married friend whom they have known for several years. Then, with no obvious provocation, she says, "Men are dogs. You can't trust them. I will never trust a man. I don't care how good he looks. Men are dogs. He's a dog. You're a dog. I hate dogs. Men are dogs." Escalating well beyond the circumstances that brought them to counseling, she continues to rant.*

In this case, the client refers to the therapist as "a dog." In response to this client, how may a therapist manage himself? Maybe, another example that calls for self-management skills could be helpful.

> *The client is a thirteen-year-old female. The therapist has met with her for eight sessions. During these sessions, the client has said almost nothing. She says that she wants therapy. However, as therapy proceeds, the client displays considerable vulnerability, seeming to fear almost everything, including the therapist. Sometimes, she merely shrugs in response to any question or statement from the therapist. Sometimes, she cries, as if internal stimuli overcome her. Sometimes, she looks at the therapist, seeming to plead for help and lacking words to ask for anything. Sometimes, almost becoming someone else for short periods of time within sessions, she shows signs of dissociation. The number of sessions grows, increasing to twelve and then seventeen. Then, with her hollow, sad expression, looking at nothing in particular, she says, "They did bad things to me." She cries uncontrollably. The therapist feels the client's pain – trauma, betrayal, confusion, physical injury, rage, humiliation, fear, sadness, disgust, isolation, and more. The therapist knows that "this precious and lovely little girl was gang raped."*

In this case, the client presents a compelling and desperate need for help. Albeit slowly coming, the client is receptive to help. In response to this client, how may a therapist manage herself or himself?

These two client situations may cause little or no reaction from those who read them. Their situations are, after all, merely words on a page. However, for therapists who sit with these clients, little or no reaction lacks plausibility. Instead of little or no reaction, almost all therapists, with emphasis on those who may treat these clients early in their clinical experience, will react. Their reactions are quite understandable. To be angrily and irrationally referred to as "a dog" is not likely to be a matter of simple indifference. Likewise, recognizing that her life is forever changed, having a reaction to a devastated, gang-raped teenage girl is understandable. These reactions require self-management. Managing reactions illustrates the necessity of self-management skills.

Self-management skills encompass much more than managing reactions to clients. They involve other clinically useful practices. Some of these include self-disclosure, various expressions of preferences, focusing, and attention giving. Almost any expression from a therapist may be clinically useful and potentially helpful. For example, the feature of self-disclosure that makes it clinically useful and potentially helpful is that it comes from a clear clinical rationale.

Clinical leadership skills: Numerous clinical interventions require clinical leadership skills. Based on clear clinical reasoning, a therapist may encourage, if not direct, a client to read material that relates to the client's clinically relevant needs. This calls for clinical leadership. Similarly, when receiving a new medication, the patient is commonly directed by a pharmacist to raise questions and read about the medication. When pharmacists discern that a patient may not understand how to follow directions for taking a medication or may misunderstand how a medication may affect the patient, the pharmacist will engage the patient in a "pharmacy-education" conversation.

Among therapists, one of the familiar practices that easily illustrates the need for clinical leadership skills is psycho-education. In short, psycho-education refers to didactic – or teaching – sessions with clients. Commonly, psycho-education may be needed because a client or family has encountered a confusing problem with which good information may help. Or a client or family may lack experience that enables them to make necessary changes. An illustration may help to clarify the need for clinical leadership skills. This one comes from recent clinical experience.

The client is a twelve-year-old girl. She is the adopted daughter of a couple who has two biological children, a son aged seven and a daughter aged nine. The client came into her adopted family around age three because her biological mother and father were severely addicted to drugs. She was grossly neglected. When her parents were arrested, the client, then almost three years of age, was found in a rodent-infested apartment. She showed signs of malnutrition. For a short time, she required hospitalization so that her medical condition could be stabilized. Now, at twelve years of age, she comes to therapy because, according to her adoptive parents, "she just refuses to be a part of the family." Asked for details, they report that their daughter "doesn't like to be with us. She gets angry when we try to talk to her about how much we love her. She just doesn't appreciate all we have done for her. We would do anything for her. We do all we can to make her secure and to let her know that she is loved, but she just doesn't respond." The therapist concludes that the client suffers from serious attachment problems and that her adoptive parents mistakenly equate the sincerity of their feelings and attitudes toward the client with their belief that the client is capable of responding to them proportionate to the depth of their sincerity. The therapist concludes that the adoptive parents will likely gain from instructions about reactive attachment problems.

Clinical leadership should be understood as a feature of clinical practice. It is a way to provide clinical services. As such, it surely may be expressed in several ways other than didactic interventions. These other ways may include gathering clinically relevant materials for clients, such as reading materials from the National Institute on Aging (NIA), when a client may be trying to find ways to care for her spouse whose dementia has become hurtful and confusing. The NIA has free materials that are prepared for individuals such as this client. Or the need for leadership skills may be seen in the therapist's interest in connecting a client, such as the spouse who is caring for her partner with dementia, with a network of caregivers or other professional resources. While networking of various kinds cannot supplant direct clinician-therapist interactions, clinicians can show helpful and purposeful leadership on behalf of their clients by developing networks of professional caregivers or partnerships among clients or connections that promote information sharing among families with common problems, such as reactive attachment, substance abuse, or dementia.

Client engagement skills: These skills demonstrate a therapist's response to the question, "How do I engage my clients in the process of change?" Typically, these are the skills that may be most commonly associated with counseling and psychotherapy. Collectively and separately, they reveal the action that occurs when therapy happens. Maybe, the briefest characterization of client engagement skills is to say that the therapist asks probing questions, and the client responds with reflective, searching answers. And from this simply characterized process, client change occurs. [Most clinicians understand that all questions are not the same. They know about and utilize open questions, closed questions, experiential-focused questions, conceptual-oriented questions, leading questions, confrontation questions, information-gathering questions, and so on.] However, the term, *client engagement skills* surely refers to more than asking questions. It may also refer to offering an affirming statement to a client, such as "I know it hurts to think about how you were victimized. I want you to know, though, that I really admire your courage in talking with me about what happened." Or it may refer to supportive statements, such as "You've made some really hard decisions. And you have worked hard to get to the point where you can make decisions. I have to tell you I really look forward to seeing how things unfold for you as you act on these new things. This is exciting and new for you. I can hardly wait to see what happens. Go for it."

For approximately twenty years, several authors have contributed depth and range to understanding client engagement skills. Surely, Allen Ivey, along with his colleagues, is one of these authors. His and their book (2014) *Intentional Interviewing and Counseling: Facilitating Client Development in Multicultural Society* is one of these books. From it and other sources, a long list of client engagement skills may be listed, including the following.

Summarizing	Attending	Probing
Interpreting	Eye contact	Vocal tone
Confronting	Sequencing	Pacing
Questioning	Reflecting/mirroring	Paraphrasing
Observing	Influencing	

Activity-oriented skills: These skills emphasize the therapist's ability to engage clients in specific, clinically relevant activities. Typically, these kinds of skills demonstrate the therapist's sophisticated awareness of activities and the specific clinical rationale for engaging a client(s) in these activities. The list of potential activities is virtually an unlimited one. For examples, we sought to identify activities that mental health care providers use in their therapy. In reviewing their websites, we located references to the following activities, along with hundreds of others:

Hiking	Piano	Sailing
Mazes	Photography	Flower arranging
Yoga	Prayer	Meditation
Boxing	Running	Riding llamas
Painting	Play	Circus arts
Dancing	Drama	Guided imagination
Cooking	Writing poetry	Sand tray
Chess	Lifting	Punching bag
Clowning	Sculpture	Swimming

An individual clinician is highly unlikely to use most or all of these activities. However, almost inevitably, individual clinicians will involve their clients in activities. Commonly, for example, they will make assignments, such as assigning a couple the task of having structured conversations or planning a romantic outing. Or following the invaluable research from Pennebaker (2016) and others, such as Borkin (2014), Martin (2004), and Wright and Bolton (2012), a clinician may assign a client the activity of writing, because the evidence indicates that client gains from writing are substantial. A clinician may create a plan for practicing a new interpersonal skill, such as asserting one's needs. Such a plan calls for a client to engage in specific activities. A clinician may engage a client in roleplaying or in eating differently. For example, recently, an obese couple came with the specific request for help in acquiring self- and couple-discipline toward eating differently.

Together and separately, these activities and many others may be effectively utilized in therapy, when therapists know and understand the clinical relevance of the activity and demonstrate skill in making them clinically appropriate ways of helping their clients. Importantly, a therapist's interest in an activity is not a sufficient rationale for utilizing an activity in therapy. Recently, a new supervisee said, "I'm really into martial arts. I can hardly wait to use them in therapy." Through these comments, the supervisee reveals that he wishes to make therapy about himself and not so much about his clients. More broadly than martial arts, many clinicians wish to offer "Christian therapy" or other ideologically driven therapies and, because of this wish, even when they lack any form of relevant preparation, engage their clients in "prayer" or other expressions of the clinician's ideology.

Assessment skills: After years of clinical practice, these skills often become "second nature." They seem to become a feature of the individual therapist's way of engaging with and thinking about clients. Evaluating supervisees' assessment skills gives priority to the skill of the therapist and only secondarily to the types of assessments that may be attempted. Importance is placed on how well assessments are attempted and not so much which assessments are attempted. With this emphasis in view, several categories of assessment skills may be considered, including the following:

Information gathering skills: With virtually all clients, information gathering is an assessment skill because facts often determine the direction of counseling, regardless of a client's description of her or his problem. The importance of information gathering may be seen in the common refrain, "What you don't know CAN hurt you." For example, a thirty-eight-year-old male comes for therapy, with the complaint that he suffers with "sexual dysfunction." Specifically, he says that he needs help because he cannot get, let alone sustain, an erection. On hearing of this man's complaint, the therapist's assessment skills require her or him to gather clinically relevant information. Considering the possibility that beginning therapists may not know what is clinically relevant, their supervisors may facilitate their supervisees' attention to needed information. This may involve gathering information about medications that may interfere with sexual functioning. Or it may be obesity or depression or diabetes or distress or anxiety or significant discord with one's partner or substance abuse or fatigue or heart disease or any of several additional factors. Without careful information gathering, a therapist may fail to accurately assess her or his client's needs.

Case conceptualization skills: With virtually all clients, much of the treatment is determined by a therapist's understanding of what the client's problems are. Case conceptualization answers the question, "What good clinical understanding does the clinician have of this client's problems?" From the earliest days of the mental health movement, Sigmund Freud and others recognized that psychotherapists lacked mechanisms for precisely measuring their patients'/clients' problems. With this recognition, they invented conceptual-psychological approximations of their clients, knowing that psychoanalysis or, later, person-centered therapy or cognitive therapy depended for its success on the clinicians' skill in developing a clear understanding of the client's problems from their respective theoretical points of view. Today, while the classical theories continue to decline in importance – and will, no doubt, disappear – practicing clinicians must depend on refined conceptualizations of their client's problems so as to elevate the likelihood of success. Elsewhere in this book, a model and example for conceptualizing clients' problems are presented.

Clinical evaluation skills: Clinical evaluation skills involve several types of iterations. One is utilizing *assessment instruments*, such as the Beck Depression Inventory, the Minnesota Multiphasic Personality Inventory, or any number of others. With all instruments of this kind, supervised development of assessment skills is necessary. Another iteration of evaluation skill is *diagnosing*. Whether diagnosing is a desired activity or not, it is a necessary one, in the context of current mental health delivery systems. Another evaluation skill is *risk assessment*. With many clients, risk assessment skills play a small role. However, with many others, these skills rise to life-and-death importance. Because of this, supervisees will need to develop skill toward reaching clinically useful determinations about a client's risk factors and protective factors, weighing each one's importance to the foreseeable well-being of the client. Another evaluation skill is *treatment planning*. As an evaluation skill, treatment planning will establish sophisticated and practical goals, possibly following the acronym, S.M.A.R.T. or goals that are specific, measurable, achievable, realistic, and timely. In other words, supervisees' skill in treatment planning demonstrates their skill in effectively assessing the client's problems and needs.

Issues of Outlook and Attitude in the COMCS

Typically, in the beginning of their clinical work, supervisees demonstrate heightened uncertainty about who they are as clinicians and what to do in their new role. Also, typically, the fog of uncertainty lifts relatively quickly, allowing them to see their clients, instead of distracting preoccupation with themselves. Beyond this quite understandable and easily recognized uncertainty, supervisees display themselves in their somewhat unique, individual ways. For one, it may be that he has succeeded in many of his relationships by being a "charmer." So, instead of treating his clients in clinically appropriate ways, he seeks to charm them into making important changes. For another, it may be that she has "always performed well" and defines herself as a performer. So, instead of treating in her clients, she hard-headedly persists in seeing her work as a test of her abilities. For another, it may be that he avoids conflict, largely because he cannot tolerate the threat of his anger. So, instead of treating his clients in clinically appropriate ways, he becomes hyper-vigilant to the threat of his clients becoming angry, including becoming angry at him. These expressions of individuality that may interfere with supervisees' potential for delivering effective therapy are relatively common but not necessarily typical of supervisees. Nevertheless, the attitude and outlook that supervisees, along with every other clinician, take to their clients matters a great deal. The truism seems indeed to be true: "You can make almost any stupid mistake and clients are quick to forgive you, so long as they know you care, but you can't make a stupid mistake, if clients believe that you don't give a damn about them." This is a matter of attitude and outlook.

In unusual but easily recognized cases, the critical importance of the attitude of the therapist is simply that many clients have only the expectations of their therapist to believe that their lives may be better than they are or even that they may be able to survive. Goodwill matters. Optimism matters. Enjoyment of therapeutic work matters. Welcoming change matters. Inviting challenge matters. Wholesome values matter. Without these outlooks and attitudes, along with others, effective therapy may not be possible.

Issues of Task Completion Competencies in the COMCS

Clinical work holds great appeal for clinicians. At least, after many years of preparation for their multiple and complex roles, they enter clinical work with the refined ambition of making lives better for their clients and finding personal fulfillment through their work. However, usually, far from their naively anticipated ecstatic fulfillment that often fueled their interest as they entered their graduate programs, they encounter tasks that usually cause them to wish for relief from the tedious depersonalization that they seem to require. Nevertheless, as supervisees mature into their professional roles and rightly claim the demanding accountability that attends to these roles, they accept these tasks as necessary activities through which they often provide needed assistance for their clients. For example, usually clinicians come to see positive value in conversations with medical directors of insurance companies because these conversations sometimes lead to payment for services that clients would not otherwise receive. Or they come to see that keeping accurate and current documentation of their clinical services, such as assessments, treatment plans, progress notes, and more, enhances their clinical work but also protects both their clients and themselves. They come to see that consultation with others, including probation officers, family planning services, attorneys, psychiatrists, and other physicians; testifying during court proceedings; and preparing letters for human resources professionals at clients' places of employment and specialized agencies, such as substance abuse clinics or eating disorder clinics, enhances the services that they provide for their clients. The competencies associated with clinical work may include billing and related matters, managing taxes, arranging for client-related meetings, establishing policies and procedures for managing a clinical practice, attending to licensing and certification requirements, nurturing a referral network, and much more.

This model may not be welcome by some clinical supervisors. This is quite okay. The aim of presenting it is to provide an illustration of a model of supervisee development, with the implication of its importance, and not so much to prescribe a model. Along with others who have offered models of clinical supervision, we readily acknowledge that all of us who provide clinical supervision have a long way to go before we hold a consensus view of supervisee development. The distance between here and there may be long enough that a single model will never receive a majority of support among clinical supervisors, let alone unanimity. However, a conclusion to which almost all clinical supervisors would and should agree is that each one of them/us should have given serious consideration to their/our views about what counseling/psychotherapy is and what clinical supervision is. Or, stated differently, all clinical supervisors express their model of clinical supervision, whether they do this tacitly and probably inadequately or with thoughtful professional deliberation and intentionality.

Conclusion

This chapter presents a brief overview of several major models of clinical supervision and a detailed discussion of the model that Martin and Turner developed, the COMCS. If readers draw conclusions from this presentation, the most important one may be that models of clinical supervision continue to evolve, just as clinical supervision generally continues to evolve. Along with other books, this book provides a picture of the ongoing evolution of clinical supervision as a specialization within the larger profession of counseling and psychotherapy. The evolution of clinical supervision will continue indefinitely. It will become increasingly effective and professionally accountable. These are the underlying assumptions and beliefs of this chapter.

13

A PHILOSOPHY OF CLINICAL SUPERVISION

This chapter serves two purposes. One, it aims to provide a description of the primary philosophies of clinical supervision, with the expectation that this will enable readers to possess an orientation to philosophies of clinical supervision and such an orientation will equip them with a frame of reference for interpreting the philosophy of supervision that appears in this chapter. Two, it aims to present an example of a philosophy of clinical supervision. It is a philosophy that one of the authors composed.

Philosophies of Clinical Supervision

This discussion is intended to offer descriptions of primary orientations to clinical supervision. These orientations are variously referred to as "models," "philosophies," "approaches," and "orientations," among others. No matter what the preferred term may be, each one is intended to indicate that the one who offers clinical supervision has an approach that reflects training, understanding, and accountability. Therefore, this discussion is designed to assist those who wish to compose a philosophy of clinical supervision.

Adapted from Bernard and Goodyear (2004) and Powell and Brodsky (2004), the characteristics of a good model of clinical supervision include the ones listed here. A good model of clinical supervision

Emerges from the individual who provides clinical supervision, beginning with the supervisor's self, personal and clinical style, and, more generally, approach to leadership.

Exhibits precision, clarity, and consistency.

Shows comprehensiveness, using current scientific evidence-based practices.

Converts into operational and practical clinical supervision, providing specific concepts and practices in clear, useful, and measurable terms.

Becomes outcome-oriented to improve counselor competence; make work manageable; create a sense of mastery and growth for the counselor; and address the needs of the organization, the supervisor, the supervisee, and the client.

According to a publication from the Substance Abuse and Mental Health Services Administration (Center for Substance Abuse Treatment, 2009),

> *It is imperative to recognize that, whatever model you adopt, it needs to be rooted in the learning and developmental needs of the supervisee, the specific needs of the clients they serve, the goals of the agency in which you work, and in the ethical and legal boundaries of practice. These four variables define the context in which effective supervision can take place.*
>
> (p. 9)

The emphasis here is that effective clinical supervision serves the needs of clients and the professional developmental needs of the supervisee. This emphasis elevates the significance of developing a philosophy of clinical supervision, in that a philosophy of clinical supervision enables the supervisor to chart a course for effectiveness.

These ideas, though, necessitate the question, "What would a philosophy of clinical supervision look like?" In response to this question, a good place to begin is to describe the basic types of clinical supervision philosophies – or models.

Historically, there have been five primary types of philosophy of clinical supervision. They are 1) competency-based models, 2) treatment-based models, 3) developmental models, 4) blended or integrative models, and 5) reflective models. Surely, with thought and practice, clinical supervisors may be able to identify more than five models of clinical supervision. Nevertheless, as a way to orient individuals to basic models or philosophies of clinical supervision, these five are briefly described here.

Competency based models (e.g., micro-training, the discrimination model [Bernard & Goodyear, 2004], and the task-oriented model [Mead, 1990]) focus primarily on the skills and learning needs of the supervisee and on setting goals that are **s**pecific, **m**easurable, **a**ttainable, **r**ealistic, and **t**imely (SMART). They construct and implement strategies to accomplish these goals. The key strategies of competency-based models include applying social learning principles (e.g., modeling role reversal, role playing, and practice), using demonstrations, and using various supervisory functions (teaching, consulting, and counseling) (Center for Substance Abuse Treatment, 2009).

Treatment-based supervision models train to a particular theoretical approach to counseling, incorporating EBPs into supervision and seeking fidelity and adaptation to the theoretical model. Motivational interviewing, cognitive–behavioral therapy, and psychodynamic psychotherapy are three examples. These models emphasize the counselor's strengths, seek the supervisee's understanding of the theory and model taught, and incorporate the approaches and techniques of the model. The majority of these models begin with articulating their treatment approach and describing their supervision model based upon that approach (Center for Substance Abuse Treatment, 2009).

Developmental models, such as Stoltenberg and Delworth (1987), understand that each counselor goes through different stages of development and recognize that movement through these stages is not always linear and can be affected by changes in assignment, setting, and population served. (The developmental stages of counselors and supervisors are described in detail in the following.) (Center for Substance Abuse Treatment, 2009).

Integrated models, including the blended model, begin with the style of leadership and articulate a model of treatment, incorporate descriptive dimensions of supervision (see the following), and address contextual and developmental dimensions in supervision. They address both skill and competency development and affective issues, based on the unique needs of the supervisee and supervisor. Finally, integrated models seek to incorporate EBPs into counseling and supervision (Center for Substance Abuse Treatment, 2009).

The reflective practice model stands on the belief that the ability to reflect on one's experiencing of and behavior in a particular situation leads to productive change in one's experiencing and behavior. It involves giving attention "to the practical values and theories which inform everyday actions by examining practice reflectively and reflexively. This leads to developmental insight" (Bolton, 2010, p. xix).

The reflective practice model is a "purposeful way of learning from experience, challenging assumptions and biases, and questioning personal behavior" (Bolton, 2010, p. xx). Like other models of clinical supervision, the aim of the reflective practice model is to advance the clinical competence of supervisees (Curtis et al., 2016). The theme of advancing competence comprises three broad sub-themes including clinical supervisors engaging in reflective practice, promoting reflective practice in supervisees, and committing to life-long learning. Elements of this theme were evidenced within other themes, such as supervisory alliance and diversity, calling attention to the interwoven nature of competencies and some of the difficulties in attempting to establish distinctly separate competency domains. The majority of extracts featured within this theme were broad, generic statements, such as "Demonstrated skills in reflective practice," "Ability to facilitate reflection," and "Commitment to lifelong learning and professional growth" (Olds & Hawkins, 2013).

Prospective clinical supervisors are encouraged to study these primary models and to gather a body of knowledge and understanding that will help to enable them to develop their individual philosophies of clinical supervision. In addition, they may be able to create a somewhat fully developed model through various practices. Some of these practices are described later in this book.

An Example of a Philosophy of Clinical Supervision

Note: One of the authors of this book, Francis A. Martin, has utilized his written philosophy of clinical supervision to communicate with prospective supervisees, students, peers, and trainees in professional development events. He understands that his philosophy of clinical supervision may or may not have resonance with others' philosophies of clinical supervision. In the context of this book, it is intended to be an example of a philosophy of clinical supervision, mainly in terms of encouraging others to compose their philosophies of clinical supervision and not so much in terms of being a model of what a philosophy should be.

Much of what is written in this book comes from a very simple goal: To offer help for supervisors' efforts to develop their own approach to clinical supervision. To extend this simple goal, this chapter offers an example of a philosophy of clinical supervision. The example is by design brief, flowing from the belief that extremely more than is said could be said. The goal is to be helpful to the extent that help is needed and not to display details and information that is not needed. Also, if a statement of a philosophy of clinical supervision were to incorporate as much as possible here, much of the rest of the book would be duplicated in this chapter.

In advance of a reader's observation that the statement of my philosophy of clinical supervision includes personal references and "I" statements, the fact of these references and statements is readily acknowledged. My belief is that a statement of a philosophy of clinical supervision should be crafted by each clinical supervisor so that supervisors relate with their supervisees in a coherent and deliberative manner. The following information is my attempt to explain my reasoning for relating with my supervisees as their clinical supervisor.

To advance understanding of my philosophy of clinical supervision, I offer a conceptual context in which these beliefs are utilized. This is to say that, just as I hold ideas about what characterizes a good therapist, I should have ideas about what characterizes a mentally-emotionally healthy individual. After all, facilitating the emergence of the mentally-emotionally healthy individual defines many therapeutic interventions. Similarly, I should have ideas about how to conceptualize mental-emotional problems, because this is what clinicians should be able to do. These two ways of conceptualizing human experience form much of the context in which a philosophy of clinical supervision may be expressed.

The Conceptual Context of My Philosophy of Clinical Supervision

My strong belief is that mental health care is *health care*. With this emphasis, I conclude that, contrary to many who practice counseling/psychotherapy, the normative standards of health care should be standards of care with which we aspire to comply, knowing that much of what we attempt to do is considerably more complex and ambiguous than most of what other health care providers do. Moreover, this is a way of saying that equipping supervisees to practice mental health care invites supervisors to clarify for themselves and their supervisees what they believe they are trying to do and to accomplish.

Within the boundaries of competence and broadly accepted standards of health care, I believe that I am trying to engage clients in a process of change. Usually, the "change" that the client and I are trying to achieve involves re-thinking, re-feeling, and re-acting self-negating patterns of thinking, feeling, and acting. If I do this well, I will draw from the best evidence from practice-oriented research that I may find and from the best of consultations of which I may avail myself.

And, naturally, I rely on my clinical experience to contribute to my understanding of how I may conduct psychotherapy. Ultimately, because I am the one in the room with a client(s), I am accountable for what happens there, not the researchers or consultants whose wisdom helps to inform me about my clinical work. I must understand that their wisdom does not necessarily or inevitably translate into effective treatment.

Also, as I facilitate change for my clients, this requires me to identify the best evidence that supports my view of what mental health looks like, with the emphasis on "health." The evidence should shape my view of mental health and, therefore, equip me to see movement toward mental health in my clients and mental health in them when they gain it through psychotherapy. In other words, if I seek to identify mental health in my clients, what may I see when I find it? With no need to persuade anyone else that the signs of mental health are ones that they should accept, here are mine. However, earlier in this book, we present a somewhat objective report about the qualities of mental health. (Readers may refer to Chapter 3, "What Do I Believe about Conducting Mental Health Care?")

Recognizing that my obligation is to facilitate health for my clients, I believe that the first characteristic is that *the mentally healthy persons carry an ever-present awareness of their freedom to choose*. Surely, many of our clients give us pictures of themselves as individuals who have relinquished their freedom to choose. They are the ones who

See their small mistakes as catastrophic errors;
Believe that no one could ever love them because they are so bad and undeserving of love;
Cling to irrational fears of speaking to all strangers, including friendly ones;
Succumb to narcissistic self-indulgence to cover their self-loathing; and
Compulsively demand perfection of themselves and suffer their inevitable failure to achieve it.

The examples of individuals who are "locked in rooms with open doors" and who have relinquished their freedom to choose are virtually innumerable. Moreover, all of us, including mental health professionals, are acquainted with this vulnerability. Despite this vulnerability, sometimes, we sustain our freedom to choose. Except for self-consciously choosing to take a side – for my team or my religion or my country or my values or other sides – the mentally healthy person prefers freedom instead of sides. Mentally healthy persons avoid the traps of social convention that require sides to be taken and that sometimes mandate sacrificing mental health. Instead, they place value

As much on cooperation as on competition,
As much on having a clear point of view as on accepting points of view that are different,
As much on unity with others as on a readiness to create disunity on behalf of a moral position,

As much on affirming life as on a readiness to sacrifice to defend life, and
As much on gathering resources that make her or him secure as on generosity with resources.

In maintaining this freedom, mentally healthy individuals show balance in their lives. They often take a long view of difficult circumstances and work toward long-term solutions to difficult problems, instead of giving in to immediate, short-term responses that often exacerbate problems more than solving them. Their management of problems usually leads to outcomes that are somewhat more positive and durable than the outcomes of others.

Extending this idea, mentally healthy persons act with generosity, placing emphasis on ensuring that others have needed resources, particularly those resources that they cannot provide for themselves. Typically, healthy persons maintain awareness of the pressure to take sides, to align with those who can bring benefits to them, but choose life-affirming actions instead of self-aggrandizing ones. Drawing both admiration and enmity, they often stand in contrast with an American culture that is too often self-indulgent, self-promoting, and even greedy, a culture in which the "have-nots" have persistently increased as a proportion of the population for almost four decades.

Mentally healthy persons have a heightened and effective sense of proportionality. This simply means that the mentally healthy person keeps things relatively clear and free of distortions. This characteristic of the healthy person may be expressed in numerous ways. Here are some of them.

Generally, they feel good about themselves but not defensively or naively great.
They take justifiable pride in good or excellent relationships or in work or other activities but know that pride is much more about the future and the potential that the future holds than a record of self-satisfying accomplishments. They operate as if pride is good – based on real accomplishments – but that hope is better than pride.
They are searching, curious persons who know that there are answers to many of life's pressing questions and that the answers are almost always tentative. They understand that life holds more adventure and change than fixed and certain things.
They understand that adversity comes with living and that this fact only partially describes human experiencing, insofar as companionship, good food, good sleep, and other "feel good" realities come with life, too. So, more likely than not, they understand that adversity or its opposite are momentary and that something significant happens after either one. It is this cognizance of "something" that permits the healthy person to maintain openness to possibilities.

The mentally healthy person demonstrates cognitive complexity. In other words, the mentally healthy person accepts the fact that life is complex and adapts to this fact. For example, the human body is extraordinarily complex. This leads to the acceptance of believing in the expertise of physicians. More than this, though, the mentally healthy person is not a concrete, either-or thinker. This feature of the healthy person may be confusing. In application, this kind of thinking means that the mentally healthy person shows high tolerance for uncertainty, likes puzzles in many forms, and invites new experiences, including discovering new acquaintances. In practical terms, this means that parents can both show devotion to their child and recognize the child's imperfections. Similarly, in marital relationships, spouses can demonstrate their devotion to each other and accept their relational vulnerabilities.

The mentally healthy individual demonstrates cognitive complexity, but this is not to suggest that they reside only in communities of intellectuals. Instead, healthy persons may be found in many kinds of groups, including among mechanics, professional athletes, artists, and various other occupations; in universities, quilting clubs, and religious groups; at all income levels; and more. They fill many different kinds of occupations and live in a wide array of communities. Moreover, even when they are passionate about following their special interests, they usually show interest in many different kinds of activities. For example, one may be a skilled quilter but also take on the adventure of running marathons. Or, for example, one may be a devoted hunter but also develop his talent as an artist.

Whether they are more or less expressive with their feelings than others, *mentally healthy persons are considerably more attuned to their feelings*, commonly demonstrating a capacity for expressing a wider range of feelings than others. In their relations with others, they show a readiness to be receptive to a wide variety of expressions of emotions, too. Generally, this equips them to be attuned to their own feelings and, therefore, to effective self-care and other-care.

Mentally healthy persons possess strong and positive relational skills. The idea of strong relational skills is often associated with leading political figures. While the difference between healthy persons and political figures cannot be narrowed or statically set, it is one of health, more than obvious effectiveness. The healthy person relates in a manner that affirms and endorses health in others, while politicians commonly seek benefits for themselves, sometimes denying benefits for those whom they seek to influence. Typically, healthy persons emerge from a history of relationships in which they have been positively valued. In addition, they almost universally believe that strong, mutually affirming relationships form the basis for effective living. Sometimes as a stated philosophy of life and sometimes with simple intuition, they know that their significance, their mattering, comes from relationships and not so much in promotions at work, academic degrees, awards won, money earned, the number of high-profile names that may be "dropped" so as to gain vicarious value, or other familiar markers of success. Instead of finding their value through "knowing important people" or through having praise from others, they find their importance in enduring and positive relationships.

Adding to this list, here are some other features of a mentally healthy person:

Practices self-acceptance but not self-indulgence.
Expresses an attitude of gratitude and avoids being judgmental.
Maintains a clear conscience.
Accepts responsibility and solves problems.
Treats others well – fairly and respectfully.
Laughs and enjoys humor but not hostile humor.
Finds genuine meaning, if not happiness, in living.
Avoids sacrificing people to advance self-interests.
Monitors and regulates emotional expressions, in contrast with emotional impulsiveness.
Enjoys time alone.
Accepts evaluations from others, indicating security in oneself.
Readily acknowledges the contribution from others to her or his well-being.

Caution: Life gives us problems. Anyone who reads this faces problems. The recognition of this fact of life may cause many individuals to mislead themselves. They may conclude that their problems define them as lacking mental health or the potential for mental health. Instead, the importance of this recognition is that it affirms life as it is but also that no one has all of the qualities that may characterize mentally healthy individuals or that these qualities may be indefinitely sustained without interruption. In other words, mental health is fluid and ever changing. Indeed, the ever-changing nature of mental health compels mental health care providers to provide mental health care, mindful of helping their clients to discover what they are capable of and of creating health for them. After all, it is their hope and belief that their professional services will engage their clients in a process of change that moves their clients toward increased mental health.

Mental health care professionals and the clients whom they serve can benefit from knowing about some of the characteristics of mentally healthy individuals. The characteristics may appear to be ideal and unreachable. Viewing them this way is quite understandable. After all, it is unlikely that one individual will possess all of these characteristics. Even with this limitation, knowing about these characteristics gives counselors and psychotherapists something that they seek to become and maintain for themselves. Instead of being used as negative comparisons, these characteristics are best used as sources of hope and encouragement.

Significantly, just as mental health should be conceptualized by clinical supervisors, mental-emotional-relational problems should be conceptualized, too. The importance of this is that it provides necessary clarity and reassurance for supervisees, when they know that their supervisor has attempted to understand and articulate their view of clients' mental-emotional-relational issues. Without this, supervisors may appear merely to make up stuff and, therefore, confuse supervisees and, possibly, expose incompetence. With this in mind and as a feature of my philosophy of therapy and clinical supervision, I have sought to be clear about how I conceptualize clients' issues, without being dogmatic about it or prejudicial because of it. Instead of dogma and prejudice, I demand of myself that I welcome alternate conceptualizations from supervisees. Further, I welcome opportunities to challenge their conceptualizations of their work, just as I hope that they will challenge mine. At this time, some of the features of my way of conceptualizing client's issues are condensed into Chart 13–1, "Conceptualizing the Client's Experience/Presentation."

The beginning of conceptualizing clients' issues is "need." While this topic alone could occupy a large book, much less than this should be written here. In short, the idea of beginning with need is that therapy is a response to clients' needs. At least, the need is to lower the intensity of or eliminate clients' pain. Beyond this, the need may be one of searching for ways to redeem a failing marriage or to rid the client of the compulsion to masturbate or to equip a five-year-old to sleep in her own bed instead of being overly anxious and in bed with her parents or to help a new widower to adjust to the biting loneliness of being alone. While these possibilities give the appearance of singular needs that may be addressed with focused attention on them, the human reality is that needs are far more complex than this list of possible needs may indicate. Nevertheless, needs energize us to act. For example, most of us seldom become pre-occupied with food when we have plenty to eat and eat as frequently and as much as we wish. Without food, though, the need for it may occupy us in an all-consuming manner, channeling nearly all of our actions toward getting something to eat. Instead of hunger for food, though, counselors and therapists are much more likely to treat clients whose need for relational connection – belonging, caring, affection, companionship, and more – is far more pressing, even when clients actively undermine their potential for relational connection. Likewise, instead of hunger for food, counselors and therapists are much more likely to treat clients who "hunger" for relief from nagging loneliness, panic attacks, irrational compulsions, and many other "hungers." The emphasis here is that the source of concern and the energizing force that bring clients to mental health care are needs. While clients may engage in their relationships in ways that defy the possibility of meeting their relational needs, the needs do not disappear but continue to motive them toward relationships. For example, a long married couple may have maintained an angry and adversarial relationship for many years. Why have they done this? Too simply stated, they likely learned that authentic intimacy was much too risky and frightening. So, instead of authentic intimacy, they activate their respective needs for intimacy through angry and adversarial actions. This is not satisfying for them, but it enables them to stay together, with the illusory expectation that somehow they will meet their needs with each other.

The expression of need appears in a client's behavior or actions. While the behavior may tell clinicians relatively little about the client's needs, it usually gives them reasons to begin treatment. For example, the twelve-year-old boy sneaks out of the house at night to visit his girlfriend. Once they discover this, his parents bring him to therapy. Clinicians may not know why he sneaks out of his house to visit his girlfriend, but they know from his parents' report that he

Chart 13–1 Conceptualizing the Client's Experience/Presentation

Need	Intervening Variables				Behaviors/Actions
Needs Are Multi-Variable	**Environmental Factors**	**Physiological Factors**	**Social-Relational Factors**	**Personal Characteristics**	**Presentation of Person**
Type Intensity Frequency Duration Non-discrete Motivation	Climate Geography War/combat Social context	Multi-variable Genetic Disability Sex	Family Other relation Cultural values Social norms Expectations	Cognitions Assumptions Beliefs Relational Style Mental/emotional needs Behavioral habits Perceptions of resources Affective habits MORE	Observable Reported Troubling behaviors Actions Expressions of personal pain
	ILLUSTRATIONS-----------		**ILLUSTRATIONS**------------		**ILLUSTRATIONS**
Needs are complex A need may be to relieve pain, seek food, rest/sleep, seek pleasure, be sheltered, breathe, belong, receive, love, have social place, and much more	War Economic depression Economic boom Freezing weather Noise	Blow to head Pancreatic cancer High temperature Addictions Nutrition Anemic	Language Attitudes Values Relational shaping War/combat Gender roles Religion Employment Single parenting	Introverted Pessimistic Expressive Passive Curious Adventuresome Athletic Courteous Rigid	Almost anything crying running away contemplating raging writing worshipping whistling hitting others eating reading cursing

does this. Or we may not know why a forty-eight-year-old female involuntarily moves from one job to another, but we know that she does this. So, needs may be the beginning of conceptualizing client behaviors, but it is usually the behaviors that we see first.

Then, at the risk of oversimplifying this approach to conceptualizing a client's issues, the challenge of making sense of a client's behavior comes from filtering into the clinician's body of knowledge about the client several kinds of information that enable the clinician to make sense of – or conceptualize – the client's behavior. The clinician gathers information about clients' characteristic ways of thinking about their situations, their ways of relating with others, their characteristic ways of managing clinically relevant experiences (e.g., conflicts, mistakes, intimacy, problem-solving, achievement, and many others), and more.

For example, a male plumber may seek therapy because his wife has grown weary of his avoidance of conversation and intimacy with her and has "mandated" that he "get help." While his avoidant behavior is the identified cause of his coming for therapy, the clinical conversations lead to the therapist's conclusion that the plumber's perfectionistic driven-ness pushes him to get everything perfectly right and to punish himself mercilessly when he fails to get everything perfectly right. And, paradoxically, instead of achieving the perfectionism that he believes is a "must" for him, he maintains his belief that he lacks talent, motivation, worth, and value for anyone else. This triggers the false idea that if he pushes even harder, he can get closer to the perfectionism that he expects of himself, and this, in turn, further secures his inability to achieve the standards that he expects of himself. The unfortunate consequence of his mismanagement of his need for intimacy with his wife results in alienation from his wife.

In this case, something like cognitive-behavioral therapy (CBT) may be needed, insofar as the client gives the clinician a picture of his distorted beliefs. The client's distorted beliefs have contaminated his relationship with his wife. And, if the couple came for therapy, the clinician may judge that the client's perfectionism is a problem but that equipping members of the couple with effective relational skills may help to mute the plumber's internal voice of perfectionism. So, CBT may be supplanted with something like emotion-focused therapy (EFT).

The underlying assumption of this way of conceptualizing the client's issues is that usually the first set of facts from the client involves observable behaviors or actions and that these actions come from needs. A necessary and auxiliary assumption is that needs are quite healthy features of being human and that healthy needs are often skewed and expressed in ways that ensure that they cannot be met. For example, the thirty-seven-year-old male who aggressively pursues sex partners – the sex addict – may be desperately hungry for affection and intimacy but fears affection and intimacy or feels rage toward those who have denied him these things. He ensures that he will not meet his needs for affection and intimacy by aggressively pursuing multiple sex partners. After all, as he frequently finds and discards sex partners, he acquires added evidence with each new partner that no one truly wants him or could love him. Maybe, an easier example is the committed alcoholic who medicates his loneliness by drinking. Predictably, his need for loving and durable relationships, will not be met because of his drinking.

Caution: This brief overview of a way of conceptualizing clients' issues is necessarily limited. Because of this, it may raise more questions than it answers. It is not intended to be complete. Instead of an attempt at completeness, and more than a comprehensive way of understanding clients' issues, it is a way of expressing by example the obligation for clinical supervisors to claim their individual way of conceptualizing clients' issues.

My Philosophy of Clinical Supervision

The following information extends and amplifies several parts of this book. It is composed in a way that expresses my beliefs about my approach to clinical supervision. It is somewhat circumscribed because of my interest in not replicating huge parts of the rest of this book in this chapter. For example, elsewhere in this book, a definition of clinical supervision is given. It need not be duplicated here. Similarly, the administrative tasks in clinical supervision are discussed elsewhere in this book. Along with many other features of an approach to clinical supervision, they, too, need not be duplicated here. As expressions of my philosophy of clinical supervision, these beliefs are intended to reveal the fine-grain of beliefs about clinical supervision that are complements to several other features of clinical supervision that the rest of the book discusses. Because I frame these beliefs in this way, they come as statements that express my understanding of clinical supervision in ways that are intended to complement the numerous contributions that I have gained from others.

The highest priority is to ensure that clients are okay, meaning that, at least, they are not harmed and, better, that they receive the best help of which the supervisee is capable. As a practical matter, in the supervisory meeting, I want to know whether a client may be in jeopardy, crisis, or another circumstance – suicide, abuse, impulse toward dangerous behavior, or other risks – that may hold potential harm for the client. While this is unusual, I want client welfare to be an essential priority during supervision meetings. To do otherwise places the supervisee at risk, too, insofar as the supervisee may be treating, for example, a suicidal client who may die. If possible, I will do all that I can to protect a supervisee from such a dreadful outcome.

I should provide a supervisory environment that is welcoming and safe for supervisees. Without welcome and safety, supervisees are not likely to engage in the appropriate risk-taking that necessarily attends their professional growth. Extending this idea, the process of supervision involves mutual confidence and trust. While my influence in the supervisor-supervisee relationship is usually higher than the supervisee's, especially early in the supervisory relationship, I have an obligation to build mutual confidence so that my need to protect my professional interests does not become a problematic issue between us. More than protection, though, I conclude that a supervisee is not likely to develop well toward competence when the environment of supervision is unduly threatening.

My commitment to a welcoming and safe supervisory environment holds potential for failure, especially when it prohibits needed engagement with supervisees around their poor clinical judgment and performance. Offering a welcoming and safe supervisory environment is necessary. It is necessary, too, to maintain client welfare as the highest priority and, because of this, confront a supervisee's inadequacies openly, honestly, and in a professionally accountable manner. Thus, in conducting clinical supervision, confrontation is a necessary skill and intervention but so are support, encouragement, and empathic guidance.

I should give attention to what a supervisee needs. Supervisees' ability to articulate their needs, insofar as professional growth and development come from a need to grow and develop, indicates the potential for identifying and responding to clients' needs. For example, supervisees who opt for pleasantness and conflict avoidance because they feel high discomfort with their anger are not likely to relate well with angry clients. In such cases, their mismanagement of anger becomes a need that they ought to acknowledge and from which they ought to gain.

I want to engage supervises in assessing their performance. Such an assessment should involve weakness, failure, miscues, and related concerns, but it should also reveal strengths, assets, effectiveness, satisfaction, and related positives. From this perspective, several possible priorities emerge. One is that supervisees will be encouraged to gather information, especially with regard to what they should know but do not. Another is that supervisees are encouraged to risk delivering new interventions with clients, so as to expand their repertoire of interventions and, presumably, their effectiveness. Another is that supervisees are encouraged to sharpen their awareness of themselves so that they are relatively freer to engage clients in gaining their own, increasing self-awareness. An underlying assumption is that supervisees' self-assessment is likely to be more important over the long-term than the supervisor's assessment of their performance.

I should help supervisees to construct their view of therapy. This includes their understanding of how clients change and how to engage clients in the process of change, their understanding of themselves as therapists, and ways to assess progress throughout the therapeutic process. This implies a constructionist view of therapy, without in any way limiting therapy to such a view. More than an orientation to therapy – either theoretical or narrowly clinical – this is an acknowledgment of the need of all therapists to become socialized or professionalized into the work of therapy and to claim a positive professional identity. However, a benefit of this is that it readily converts and directs a supervisory conversation into ways that supervisees may conceptualize and, therefore, operationalize their work, in a clinically and theoretically broad-based way. This assumes that the conduct of counseling and psychotherapy is much more intentional than reactive and more disciplined than spontaneous, but reactive and spontaneous, nevertheless.

When I have relevant information that supervisees lack, I should find ways to share the information and to help supervisees to find ways to expand their knowledge. This takes multiple forms. On one occasion, this may take the form of sharing information from research about adolescents who self-harm. On another occasion, it may take the form of sharing information about male identity development during the childhood or adolescent years. In other words, at times, I am a teacher.

I should understand that influence between the supervisee and clients matters a great deal and that, similarly, influence between supervisors and supervisees matters a great deal, too. And, analogously, I should assist supervisees in exploring the range of their influence with clients, as somewhat simultaneously, supervisees explore their rightful and needed influence with me and other mental health professionals. This may involve discussions of power and how it is used in therapy. It may facilitate conclusions about ways for supervisees to experiment with their power with clients and with me. Also, this may facilitate dialogue between us that helps supervisees to clarify for themselves the bases of power that may be operative in treating specific clients.

More than understanding power, though, influence is centered in growth and professional development. To illustrate this, if a developing clinician treats substance abusers in an inpatient program, these are the clients who shape and to a large degree determine the clinician's professional biography. Alternately, if a developing clinician treats couples in a private practice, these are the clients who "write" the clinician's professional biography. The idea of a biography clearly has limits. It is merely a way to say that clinicians learn from the clinical experiences that they have and not from the ones they do not have. Clinical supervisors must take this into account, especially when their professional experience is significantly different from their supervisees' experience.

I should recognize and confirm for supervisees their movement toward increasing competence. This, too, takes many different forms. It may simply be an acknowledgment of normative stress from working hard to improve clinical skills. It may be empathic support in response to a supervisee's productive struggle to manage a difficult client. It may be an affirmation of the gains that the supervisee has made toward mastering certain skills.

I want both of us to enjoy the supervisee's burgeoning competence, confidence, and effectiveness. On occasion, a supervisor may wish to pose the question, "What do you have to offer clients now that you did not have when you began to work with them?" The question may be expressed in many different forms. It may refer to the supervisee's development of specific skills with which the supervisee has struggled. It may refer to specific clients with whom a supervisee has demonstrated clinical effectiveness. Just as counselors want to help their clients to establish a clear picture of their gains in counseling, supervisors want to help their supervisees to establish their gains in developing counseling competence.

I should help supervisees to gather and utilize the best evidentiary information that supports their clinical judgment. This helps both of us to avoid ideological traps. This is to say that supervisors and supervisees should avoid the multiple ideologically oriented therapies that lack the best evidentiary support. The ideology may be one of the traditional theories of therapy, such as psychoanalysis or various expressions of humanism, or others that are non-clinical, such as Bible-based Christian therapy or past life regression or any of thousands of others. More than avoiding ideological traps, though, the discipline of utilizing clinical approaches that express research-based support should be integrated into therapy and into clinical supervision, insofar as possible and practicable. This assumes that therapy continues to require therapists to render sophisticated "guesses" about many clinical things.

I should place a positive value on the clinical experience of supervisees, with emphasis on the necessity of maintaining openness to a supervisee's possibly superior way of conducting therapy. This means that the supervisee's judgment about what to do in conducting therapy may be very different from what I may do, and, no doubt, at times, it may be better. I should be ready to affirm this. Surpassing the supervisory relationship in importance, the relevance of placing a positive value on the supervisees' clinical experience is that their experience becomes an ever-increasing body of clinically relevant evidence and, therefore, criteria for selecting treatment interventions. This is a major reason for requiring clinical supervision. Supervisors want their supervisees to gain from their clinical experience. And unless their experience is marginally competent or harmful to clients, I should affirm the experience and encourage its ongoing improvement.

In the context of conducting clinical supervision, I should provide a model of a therapist and therapy, while inviting supervisees to explore their ways of conducting therapy. This means that I should be able to conduct therapy as an example for supervisees. This may involve demonstration sessions among supervisees or recordings of sessions with clients. At least, it would involve reports about and reflections on recent clinical experiences. The emphasis here is that clinical supervisors must maintain their skills through providing mental health care for clients, through real practice. Without this, their clinical acuity declines.

I should facilitate supervisees' self-awareness, with emphasis on how the process of conducting therapy changes them. This means that I should try to increase supervisees' attunement to themselves. It means that supervisees will gain skill in utilizing their reactions to clients as a source of information about the client and insights about how to deliver appropriate clinical interventions.

I should demonstrate a readiness to conceptualize client behavior. This means that, as I indicated earlier, I have clear ideas about what mentally healthy individuals may look like. However, insofar as most of what clinicians do is to treat individuals who bring mental-emotional-relational problems, if not mental illnesses, I should have refined skill in conceptualizing client behavior and a skill in communicating this to supervisees. This is much more a matter of modeling clinical judgment than it is soliciting imitation.

To the best of my ability, I should personify the assets that research identifies as qualities of effective therapists. Clearly, clinical supervision is not therapy for supervisees. However, insofar as possible, it should express the values that inhere in therapy. Two categories of assets are contained in these ideas. One contains the assets of effective therapists. Among others, this category includes a proclivity for complex thinking, tolerance for ambiguity, strong relational skills, and others. The other category contains the values of therapy, including the autonomy of clients and supervisees, respect for differences (i.e., diversity) between clients and therapists in one clinical situation and between supervisors and supervisees in the supervisory situation, and others. All clinical supervisors should have reasonably clear understandings of what characterizes effective therapists.

I should practice supervisory interventions that, except for unusual circumstances, endorse and affirm the judgment of the supervisee. As an aside, the exceptions to this would come as expected ones, including potential harm to a client or supervisee, urgent need for re-direction of the supervisee's clinical actions, ethical or legal violations, or others. These exceptions are rare. The interventions, though, are common. They include didactic, confrontational, supportive, experiential, relational, and other interventions. The discussion of supervisory interventions elsewhere in this book is intended to report interventions that I often consider when I meet with supervisees but also possibly to invite other clinical supervisors to expand their repertoire of supervisory interventions.

I should be alert to the reality of process and change in my experience of supervision, supervisees, therapy, and other features of living as a professional mental health care provider. If there ever were "glory days" in my professional history or the collective history of psychotherapists, I cannot go back to them. Likewise, I should not perpetuate beliefs that there may have been glory days or that, if we are good enough, we can create or re-create them. This is a way to say that as a clinical supervisor, I should be alert to my supervisees' potential for change, along with being alert to my potential, too, and to the recognition that their change or mine may not make us better at what we do. Our collective hope and honest expectation is that we will truly get better. Risking getting better, though, is as important as getting better. One necessarily precedes the other.

To remove any unintended ambiguity about this idea, an illustration may be helpful. Around the time when I began my work as a counselor, I heard numerous quips about being human, such as "No brain, no personality." The truth of such a quip seemed to be self-evident. However, it assumed that I may have known what this truth meant, particularly with reference to the implications of brain functioning for mental health care. Back then, I could not have imagined how critically important brain scientists would become to our understanding of our attempts to help clients. Now, I understand that, contrary to what I may have presumed to understand back then, I should attempt to expand my professional development well beyond what I may have presumed. Now, I believe that I should read emerging and relevant sources, such as David Presti's book (2016), *The Foundational Concepts of Neuroscience: A Brain-Mind Odyssey*, or listen to Thad Polk's twelve lectures (2015), *The Addictive Brain*, and read the accompanying book.

I should coach supervisees to practice within the boundaries of their competencies, while also coaching them to experiment with new competencies. Insofar as I coach supervisees to do either of these things – containing a supervisees' practice within their boundaries of competencies or urging them to try new competencies – I am accountable for the results of such coaching. This is what professional ethics require. This is what law requires. This is what normative standards of clinical supervision require. And this is what I require of myself.

While I must guard the integrity of mental health care, I should also welcome new providers of mental health care services, my supervisees, and, later, my colleagues. I am a "gatekeeper." I take this to mean that I should sometimes close and lock the gate but that with most supervisees, I should keep it open. This is an important and usually non-challenging feature of my work as a clinical supervisor. However, as unusual as it may be, screening a supervisee out of professional mental health care poses major challenges to my professional judgment. I seriously want supervisees to succeed but must at times recognize their failures and inappropriateness for service as counselors and psychotherapists.

Assuming each of us becomes a good therapist at a pace that is nearly unique, I want to assist supervisees with a pace of change that works for each one of them. This means that, just as many of us do, supervisees sometimes get trapped in skewed, comparative thinking in which their comparisons of themselves with others may not help them. Most therapists lean toward introversion. Notoriously, introverts often compare themselves unfavorably with extroverts. Instead of this, I wish to coach all supervisees to set growth goals for themselves and to seek markers of change that enhance their individual development. Whatever the pace of growth of a supervisee, I encourage growth at a pace that a supervisee claims for herself or himself.

I will work hard to try to ensure that talented therapists-in-the-making find meaningful fulfillment in their service as clinicians. This involves their need to see themselves as effective therapists. More than this, though, it involves delivering the best possible services, including services that lead to positive outcomes or not-so-positive outcomes for their clients. This is to say, that, just as an oncologist may deliver superior services, say, to individuals who suffer with lung cancer, knowing that some of these patients will die, good therapists deliver superior services, too, knowing that client outcomes do not necessarily define good therapy or good therapists. This recognizes that all categories of clientele are not the same and that, because of this, the rate of positive outcomes among various categories of clients cannot be the same.

As a long-serving clinician and clinical supervisor, my ideas and beliefs about therapy and supervision continue to grow and to be influenced by the livingness of therapy and supervision. This is the professional life I live. Surely, in retrospect, this life has involved changes that I could never have imagined in advance of making them. And, for me, the stirring and permanent lesson in this is that, in prospect, this will be true again and again into the future so long as I continue to practice therapy and supervision. A single response to this recognition is not feasible. Surely, at times, it is dread. At another time, it is much too familiar a thought to be useful or motivating. At other times, it is a little more weight than I wish to carry. Mostly, though, it evokes within me the feeling and conclusion that this is truly a great life. *All of this – dread, familiarity, weightiness, a great way to go, and much more – are features of my experience that I wish to share with supervisees.*

Conclusion

Clinical supervisors, with emphasis on beginning supervisors, often struggle to define for themselves a way to understand their work as supervisors. Experienced clinical supervisors recognize this struggle and challenge. Both of them, beginning and experienced clinical supervisors, are encouraged to study the material in this chapter, with the aim of defining and claiming their individual approach to clinical supervision, only because it is one clinical supervisor's attempt to share his philosophy of clinical supervision and surely not because it is an ideal one. Further, they are encouraged to reconcile themselves with an all-too-familiar reality of clinical work. Namely, no matter how experienced and skilled they may be, experienced clinicians and clinical supervisors continually reflect on and anticipate specific areas of growth.

14

THE EXPERIENCE OF CLINICAL SUPERVISION

The aim of this chapter is to bring readers more directly than other chapters into the experience of clinical supervision, with the emphasis on helping to actualize and express a philosophy of clinical supervision. To accomplish this, the chapter invites readers to reflect on what happens during supervision meetings, to provide examples of supervision dilemmas, and to consider possible responses to these dilemmas. It is these responses that express a philosophy of clinical supervision.

What Happens in a Supervision Session?

Sessions with supervisees require that their clinical supervisors attend to multiple levels of accountability, knowing that a supervisor cannot attend to all of them at the same time. And, just as much of life comes without advanced notice, the items that get attention are those that command it. This is a truism of conducting clinical supervision and therapy. A client's suicidal ideation may command an entire session with a supervisee. Or a supervisee's avoidance of her attraction to "a really cute guy" may command attention. Or the supervisee's need for support, following the coincidental and premature departure of five of his clients, may command attention. Or success in helping a client to reach clinically important goals and the clear and maybe first-time success with a client command attention and celebration. Obviously, the idea is that what happens in a supervisory session involves supervisors and supervisees in predictably improvisational moments. For both, improvisational skills are essential to their effectiveness.

However, quite apart from improvisational moments, supervisors and supervisees should establish agreed-upon plans and priorities for their sessions. The following plans and priorities may be helpful for those supervisors and supervisees who wish to negotiate an agreed-upon plan for their meetings. The information about plans and priorities comes in two parts. One part describes priorities to which many supervisory sessions give attention. The other part describes interventions that supervisors may need to initiate with supervisees.

Supervisory Priorities

Very likely, supervisors who wish to clarify priorities for their sessions with supervisees have already discussed their philosophy of clinical supervision, their supervision style, and other features of their approach to clinical supervision. Also, they have likely provided a great deal of information for supervisees, as a matter of ensuring informed consent, usually because they wish to do this but also because supervisory standards of care require it. And, quite apart from setting priorities for their meetings, both supervisors and supervisees have clarified other contextual issues, such as the frequency, the duration, the general content of their sessions, and many of the role expectations of each of them.

Extending the definitions of meetings and the expectations for both the supervisor and the supervisee(s), in the order of their importance, the priorities of meetings may look like the following:

Among the clients who are being treated by the supervisee, do any of them present critical and/or emergent issues? As many clinicians and supervisors know, this usually refers to clients who may be at risk of suicide, overdosing from drug usage, or harming themselves in other ways. It refers to extreme disturbances, such as crippling depression or disabling dissociation or prodromal or active psychotic symptoms. It refers to past or impending harm to another person, with particular regard for children and elderly persons, and other extraordinarily aggressive thoughts toward others, such as intentions to harm "an unfair boss." The list of emergent issues could easily include many more than these. Also, the environment in which these things arise conditions the degree of criticality that may be associated with each. For example, if the context is an outpatient, private practice, many of these things would be alarming to the extent of requiring immediate action, whereas if the setting were an inpatient, hospital setting, little immediate action may be needed.

What does the supervisee need? Frequently, beginning clinicians ask, "What would you do with . . .?" or "How would you handle this situation?" For beginners, these kinds of questions make sense. They reveal that beginners really have very limited ideas about what to do with many client situations and that they lack confidence in trying to do something with what they know.

"Lost" beginners, though, generally disappear somewhat quickly, once they gain recognition of being able to practice what they have prepared to practice. For an extended period of time, then, once the newness of a clinical role has worn away, supervisees persist in exploring the dimensions of their roles. Instead of obsession with their uncertain or confusing performance as clinicians, they usually rapidly gain awareness of their potential impact on clients. Toward gaining this awareness, supervisees present ever increasing and complex needs. Instead of trying merely to be comfortable with clients, they demonstrate openness to experiencing the clinical process and growing from it. So, from this, their needs may involve learning how to make clinical use of their clients' refusal to change, daring to test clinical understanding of their clients in ways that their clinical supervisor may not usually share, or any number of an enormous variety of needs. And the more clearly they can present their needs, the more a clinical supervisor has to work with and the more likely she or he is to be effective in supervising others.

Supervisees' needs may evoke many different kinds of responses from their clinical supervisors. Some of these responses, or interventions, are discussed here as "supervisor interventions."

What is the supervisee doing with clients? The answer to this question likely involves most of what happens in a clinical supervisory session. The session is used to share clinical information about clients. Explicit or not, the talk about clients answers questions, such as the following: Is anything new happening with this client? What concerns the supervisee about her or his work with this client? Is there anything with which the supervisee needs help? In addition, the session is used to discuss client issues and how the supervisee may be responding to them. And, with regard to what the supervisee is doing with clients, the remaining topic is what the supervisee may be planning in her or his work with clients.

What does the clinical supervisor need to know? This question suggests that the clinical supervisor should have questions that ensure good client care and that facilitate the supervisee's development. The number of questions is almost limitless. Nevertheless, some of the common ones are

What is your experience of this client?
How do you make sense of – or conceptualize – this client/client's presentation?
Is there anything that gets in the way of working well with this client?
Have you considered interventions that you have not tried yet?
What, if anything, causes you concern about this client?
Would you discuss your decision to intervene in this way, try this particular technique, or respond to the client in this way or another?
What is there about this client that you need help with?
What do you need from me during this supervision session? More broadly, what do you need to gain from supervision and/or how do you need to develop professionally?

What happens next? In some way, the supervisory session needs to address the matter of how the supervisee proceeds with clinical services with each client. This is a matter of clarifying the initiatives that the supervisee expects to take with each client, while understanding that no one can precisely predict what a client may bring to the next clinical session.

After all that we have discussed about this client, what is your next, best question about this client?

> What do you anticipate from this client, given your understanding of this client?
> Describe your plan for the next session.

Beyond what happens during a session and in anticipation of supervisory sessions, Bernard and Goodyear (2004) encourage the use of a structure for planning a session. As a means of preparing for supervision sessions, they recommend a set of questions that may be useful for supervisees and, therefore, supervisors. They refer to their questions as "Leads to Assist the Supervisee in Preparing for the Supervision Case Conference" (p. 214). Their leads prompt the clinical supervisor to interact with supervisees with probes that are "relevant to (A) the initial counseling sessions and (B) subsequent counseling sessions." Their probes appear here.

1 A Briefly describe the client's presenting problem.
  B What were your objectives for this session?
2 Describe the dynamics of the session (your own reactions to the client and the interactions between you and the client).
3 A Describe other important information that was learned during the session, including contextual information.
  B Summarize key issues discussed during the session.
4 Describe relevant cultural or developmental information as it relates to the presenting problem(s).
5 A What is your initial conceptualization of the client's issue(s)? (Be sure that your comments are theoretically sound.)
  B Explain changes (or expansions) of your conceptualization of the presenting problem(s).
6 List relevant diagnostic impressions, including DSM code . . .
7 A To the extent possible, describe an initial treatment plan for this client.
  B Explain changes (or expansions) of your treatment plan for this client.
8 Based on your treatment plan, what are your objectives for the next session?
9 To what extent were your objectives for this session met?
10 Does any aspect of this case raise ethical concerns for you?
11 Share any personal reflections on this session.
12 What specific questions do you have for your supervisor?

These themes of supervisory sessions offer only a loose structure. As a necessary adjunct to this structure and, probably more important, is the matter of what the supervisor does during supervisory sessions. Or what are some of the common supervisory interventions and how may they be understood? These questions are addressed in the next session.

Supervisor Interventions

Experienced clinicians who are also clinical supervisors very likely understand that serious limitations should buffer their readiness to inform the rest of the world about how extremely well they have mastered their roles and practices. Just as they recognize their limitations, they are usually inclined to deal graciously with the limitations that they see in their supervisees. So, if nothing else may be taken from the discussion of supervisor interventions, it is that they should be delivered graciously, with exceptions, of course.

Generally, experienced clinicians who are also clinical supervisors recognize that they have a repertoire of interventions at their disposal and that, just as clinicians must exercise good clinical judgment, supervisors must exercise good supervisory judgment. This means that the following interventions are offered here as recommendations for beginning supervisors who sometimes lack these "tools" and for experienced clinical supervisors who may wish to add tools to their practice, based on the belief that good supervisor judgment is called for when any one of them or combinations of them are utilized. Maybe, the criteria for good supervisory judgment are supervisors' conclusions that their interventions rest on a confident belief that the client(s) and the supervisee are beneficiaries of the intervention.

Each kind of supervisory intervention may be utilized singularly or in various combinations. And, depending on the urgency of the clinical situation and/or the needs of the supervisee, each one may be delivered with high intensity or low intensity. Most interventions are delivered with low intensity. However, when the risks are high, the intensity often rises to match the demands of the risks.

In Chapter 6, "What Are the Roles of the Clinical Supervisor and Supervisee?," several supervisory interventions are defined and discussed. They include the following types of interventions:

Didactic	Conceptual
Informational	Confrontational
Directive	Supportive
Experiential	Relational
Questioning	Supervisor disclosure
Supervisor modeling	

Managing Supervisory Dilemmas

The title of this chapter, "The Experience of Clinical Supervision," anticipates that it will help readers immerse in the experience of clinical supervision, albeit in necessarily limited ways. To invite readers to experience clinical supervision, the chapter includes three vignettes for consideration. Each of the vignettes presents a different kind of situation that calls for supervisory interventions. They are intended to be illustrations of possible interventions and not as prescriptive ones. The implied expectation is that the vignettes will illustrate common challenges for supervisors and ways to respond to these challenges. Almost by definition, the discussions of these vignettes are incomplete. The clients, the supervisees, and the supervisory interventions pose far more complex realities than these brief illustrations can thoroughly capture.

Vignette One: Alicia and Octavius. As a recent graduate from her master's program and a new, not-yet-licensed counselor, Alicia is employed as a counselor in an agency that serves a broad, representative clientele from her mid-sized industrial city. Recently, she has been treating Octavius, a twenty-six-year-old male. Alicia appears to have completed a successful intake with Octavius and has begun treatment in ways that complied with normative clinical, ethical, and legal standards.

Alicia presents her work with Octavius to her supervisor. As she discusses Octavius, she appears to be directive in her approach. She tells Octavius what to do. She brings forms for him to complete, such as applying for a new job. She plans events and activities for Octavius, apparently assuming that he should be engaged in these activities, such as applying for acceptance as a student at a local college and arranging for him to meet a mentor.

Alicia's supervisor, Dr. Roger Duron, has begun to feel concerned about her clinical work with Octavius. From her recorded sessions with Octavius, "Dr. Roger" notes that Octavius expresses high ambivalence about how to accommodate Alicia's initiatives, as if he may not comprehend what she is doing. He decides to address his concerns about Alicia's clinical performance with Octavius.

Duron's supervisory approach to Alicia utilizes questions, including these.

As we review your therapy and presentation of Octavius, what do you need? What may I help with?
Can you describe your clinical approach to Octavius? Or, what needs does Octavius present, and how does your approach try to meet these needs?
Your actions with Octavius are pretty directive ones. How did you select these particular actions? Can you describe your decision-making process?
What is your impression of Octavius's response to your initiatives?
When you review the treatment goals for Octavius and your interest in helping him to achieve these goals, how do your actions fit with these goals?
What is it like for you to be with Octavius? Can you describe your experience of being with him?
What would you like to do differently with Octavius?

To place Alicia's actions in a context, new therapists/counselors often demonstrate their trained and, maybe, ingrained habits of performing and achieving in their earliest clinical experiences. In Alicia's situation, she may well be viewing Octavius as presenting challenges of "assignments" that she should complete. In doing this, she is likely acting from positive regard for Octavius and with positive intentions toward helping him, although she delivers her positive intentions in transparently non-clinical and probably unhelpful but not harmful ways.

In anticipation of addressing his concerns with Alicia, what may Dr. Duron consider to be important? Or, to frame the question in another way, which of Duron's assumptions or beliefs about clinical work, clinical supervision, and new counselors may be operative in this situation, and which interventions may be most useful? The answer to these questions may easily devolve into numerous complicated speculations about Duron's assumptions and beliefs. This devolution will be avoided here.

As suggested in the preceding paragraphs, a supervisor is likely to observe that Alicia's interest in Octavius is a positive and appropriate one. This observation diminishes the likelihood of utilizing some supervisory interventions, such as confrontational, directive, relational, and informational ones. Maybe, a useful approach to Alicia could be a didactic one through which the supervisor provides lessons about common feelings and actions among beginning therapists. Similarly, maybe, supervisor's disclosure may be useful, if he shares his early struggles with Alicia's out-of-control impulses toward achievement- and performance-oriented therapy.

In response to Alicia, our preferred response involves supportive, questioning, and experiential interventions. The preceding questions express this preference. With regard to an experiential intervention, Alicia needs to experience herself as an achievement-oriented new therapist and decide how and whether to utilize the assets that come with this way of viewing herself. At least, she should recognize her impulse to achieve for her client and expecting her client to change as a result of her achievements. No doubt, Alicia has adapted to the success of achieving. In the context of delivering therapy, though, this is sometimes counterproductive. With regard to a supportive intervention, Alicia needs to receive encouragement to take risks toward relating with her client in ways that are uncharacteristic of her way of relating with others. As an outcome of these interventions, the desired expectations are that Alicia will experience her good intentions, identify her overly performance-conscious approach, experiment with utilizing her assets differently, define her success in satisfying but in real clinically appropriate ways, and help her client to discover his power to make changes.

As a necessary understanding to facilitating change for Alicia, her supervisor should do more than assume that a supervisory alliance is solidly in place. This means that her supervisor should give explicit attention to their relationship and act in such ways that confirm that it is a safe one in which Alicia may take needed risks toward making needed changes. This may be expressed in many ways, such as this one: "Alicia, I want to make sure that you are okay with what happens here – that you are safe in supervision, while you adapt to your new role as a therapist. An important part of my job is to ensure that you are safe. If you feel unsafe, please tell me. If you aren't safe here, this may be a statement about my failure to help you in this way. So, I really want to hear from you. Can you comment about this?"

Vignette Two: Kaitlyn and Rachel. [This is one of the vignettes that appeared at the beginning of this book, in the "Introduction." It is discussed very differently here from the way it was discussed earlier.]

Kaitlyn, a fourteen-year-old female, sat stoically, emitting no signal that she may be emotionally or cognitively present. Her sullen, avoidant manner indicates that she does not want to be in therapy. In short, she is "shut down."

Kaitlyn currently resides in a group home where she has been for almost a year. She was taken into state custody around the age of two years, when child protective service workers discovered that she was severely neglected. She was immediately adopted but was soon returned to state custody. Kaitlyn's current placement follows a turbulent history of eighteen foster care placements. In the group home, Kaitlyn has required several critical interventions. These have come from loud and belligerent behavior, fighting with other girls in the group home, initiating unwanted sexual interest toward other girls, arguing/cursing support staff and clinical staff, and others.

Initially, Kaitlyn was removed from her parents' home and placed with a foster family at the age of two, following substantiated allegations of neglect and abuse. Today, Kaitlyn carries physical scars from abuse from birth to four years of age, from physical abuse by her biological parents and, soon thereafter, her adoptive parents. Her physical victimization includes beatings, cuts, sexual assault, burns with cigarettes, and more. In addition, she carries significant emotional "scars" from these experiences. During her stay in her first foster home, she became known as "the demon child," confirming the conclusion by her foster parents that Kaitlyn was aggressive, explosive, oppositional, and more. After six months in her first foster placement, the foster parents expressed their exhaustion and requested that Kaitlyn be removed from their home. In successive placements, Kaitlyn similarly exhausted her foster parents. When she was ten years of age and living in her eleventh foster home, she received abuse, again, from an older foster brother and sister. They repeatedly raped Kaitlyn. These experiences seemed to "fuel the fire" of Kaitlyn's anger and oppositional behaviors.

Now, Kaitlyn receives therapy from one of your supervisees, Rachel. As Rachel began to treat Kaitlyn, she described Kaitlyn with appropriate clinical terms, allowing for conversational and somewhat colloquial descriptions during supervision meetings. After three sessions with Kaitlyn, Rachel indicated that she was no longer struggling with uncertainty about how to treat Kaitlyn. In reporting about her work with Kaitlyn, your supervisee says, "I knew what to do. I got tired of hearing 'fuck you' from this kid. It's just not appropriate for a child to speak to an adult the way she speaks to me. I told her not to speak to me that way. And, I told her, 'God won't put more on you than you can handle.'" Gesturing with her hands pointing from her eyes, as if to suggest that Kaitlyn should forget her past and move into a nice future, she continued, "And, I told her, 'Your eyes are for looking forward, not backward. You can't change anything in the past. You've got to look forward. You've got to have hope. This is what God wants for you.'" Rachel added, "Her attitude sucks. She will never make it this way. And, I told her, 'You're a lovely girl. God wants good things for you. And I will never give up on you. You are precious.'"

Rachel has presented Kaitlyn to you. You are Rachel's supervisor. So, what may you do next? The answers to this question depend on contextual factors, such as Rachel's status as a therapist. To provide this context, the following information may be helpful.

Rachel has functioned as a therapist for approximately three years. She is nearing the time when she may apply for her license as a psychologist. Due to family exigencies, she needed to move from her first internship to her second, current internship. In her two placements, she first served in an inpatient program that treated disturbed youth. In her second internship, she has served a wide range of clients, including children, adolescents, adults, individuals, families, and groups, with each encounter stretching her clinical repertoire.

Rachel is noted for her casual manner and speech. Also, she is known for her conscientious attention to detail, thoughtful clinical analyses, ease of gathering and retaining information, and openness to feedback from her peers and supervisors. However, somewhat paradoxically, she is known to be excessively rigid in expressing her views about her clients and in her approach to them, sometimes with hints of her strongly held religious views. Prior to her report about Kaitlyn, though, Rachel's religious views had been only hinted about and almost entirely unknown to those in her professional environment.

Many clinical supervisors would likely have a strong emotional response to Rachel's illogical, anti-clinical, and shaming statements to Kaitlyn. Although they may not be typical, strong responses to supervisees – not to mention clients – are not uncommon. For example, when supervisors and clinicians hear that a child has been brutalized, a neutral response is unlikely, even when they know that their clinical judgment rises in importance and subdues their visceral responses – disgust, indignation, sadness, and more. Nothing in supervisory work requires supervisors to be neutral, but good supervisory/clinical judgment should almost always overcome their visceral responses. This may be the initial challenge of responding to Rachel. Allowing for this initial challenge, the question about what responses may be offered to Rachel must be considered.

One preference would be to initiate questions, a questioning intervention.

> When you say to Kaitlyn, "God won't put more on you than you can handle," what do you want to communicate to Kaitlyn? Or, more succinctly, "You had a lot to say to Kaitlyn. What did you want her to get from what you said?"
>
> Can you describe your decision-making in saying these things to Kaitlyn? What is your clinical rationale for saying these things to Kaitlyn?
>
> As you reflect on what you said to Kaitlyn, what would you change?

Obviously, many more questions than these may be raised. The preceding questions imply that the supervisor may be confronting Rachel with her serious misstatements and poor clinical judgment. This could easily be more explicit than the questions imply and entirely appropriate.

Rachel, as you spoke to Kaitlyn, I felt myself responding to what you said. I felt shamed by what you said. And I believe that Kaitlyn probably felt this, too.

Rachel, I'm concerned about your comments to Kaitlyn. Your comments were shaming, much too religious, and entirely inappropriate.

Rachel, your comments to Kaitlyn probably hurt her. They may have permanently impaired your relationship with her.

Other supervisory responses to Rachel may be conceptual, directive, experiential, or didactic ones. A *conceptual intervention* may emphasize Rachel's need to give serious thought to her thinking about Kaitlyn and the expectation that Rachel will develop a clear and clinically relevant conceptualization of Kaitlyn. With deliberation and insistence, this should be done in a supervisory session. A *directive intervention* may emphasize Rachel's obligation to take corrective, reparative action toward Kaitlyn or, possibly, to refer Kaitlyn to another therapist. An *experiential intervention* would bring Rachel into active reflection on and feeling about her experience with Kaitlyn. A reasonably appropriate speculation about Rachel's experiencing of Kaitlyn is that Kaitlyn triggered Rachel's negative self-assessments and that, from this intolerable negative self-assessment, Rachel cognitively positioned herself as superior through her affiliation with God's instructions for Kaitlyn. Shaming Kaitlyn may have been a way to say, "Shut up" or "You can't be sullen and quiet with me and cause me to feel ineffective, you stupid twit; I don't want to hear from you, anyway." Another useful supervisory intervention may be a didactic one. In response to Kaitlyn more than Rachel, but with Rachel's need to understand Kaitlyn, discussions about reactive attachment may be needed. A *didactic intervention* may involve discussions but likely should include serious reading and reporting, too. Because this may send Rachel into a convenient avoidance of her faulty decision making, a didactic intervention may not be the best one with which to begin.

Vignette Three: Katie and the Flasher. The supervisee is Katie and the supervisor is Dr. Martin. "Dr. Martin, I know you're going to think I'm crazy, but I have a client and I don't want to work with him." This statement comes from a young female therapist who has applied for her license but has not yet received it. She continues to offer treatment, under supervision. This is her explanation of not wanting to work with her client.

"I've been treating this man – a forty-four-year-old man – for about six months. A couple of sessions ago, he disclosed that he likes to expose himself to girls. He says that he has not done this for a long time, long before I began to work with him. He talks about how frustrated he is because he wants to expose himself to girls. He says that he used to do this quite a lot. I tried to get him to tell me how much he did this, but I couldn't get a clear picture. I get the idea, though, that he may have gone through a long period of time when he flashed girls, maybe, every month or so. Anyway, here I am with this man. And it feels so creepy. I'm afraid that he will expose himself to me. And, then, what do I do? Anyway, I just don't want to work with him anymore."

Katie's experience with her flasher client poses an interesting challenge. The challenge contains inherent conflicts. On the one hand, from the point of view of normative male-female relationships in most and multi-varied interactions, no one would want Katie to place herself in a position where she will be flashed with views of a man's penis. Neither a man nor a woman should tolerate random, unwanted exposures of nudity, say, at a grocery, a public park, church, or a sporting event. On the other hand, mental health care brings men and women into relationships that are not normative. In these non-normative relationships, clients often disclose secrets about which no one else in the world knows. Experienced clinicians have heard disturbed and disturbing secrets about illicit sexual affairs, illegal political donations, embarrassing rages against strangers, anxious confessions about Trichotillomania (hair-pulling disorder), irresistible compulsions to clean and re-arrange closets, and, yes, agitated worry about a history of flashing children. This is to ask whether this supervisee's worry about treating this client is a product of her socialization – normative male-female relationships – or a statement about her view of clinical work with this client – a man whose disturbance involves a history of flashing? In other words, is this a conventional social issue, or is it a clinical issue?

Katie's supervisor may want to engage her in a process of reflecting on her experience with this client. This is a questioning intervention.

What are your impressions of this client? (e.g., Is this client seeking your approval of his flashing? Is this client trying to seduce you? Is he engaged in trying to re-think and change his behavior? Is the client trying to prepare you for being flashed?)

When you hear about this client's concern about his history of flashing children, what is your personal, subjective response to him? (e.g., Is Katie's response one of disgust, arousal, intrigue, fear, sympathy, or others?)

What is the clinical significance of your responses to this client?

When you indicate that you prefer not to work with this client, what are you saying about you? What are you saying about your role in relating with this client?

Blended with a conceptual intervention, a supervisor self-disclosure may be useful for Katie.

A conceptual and self-disclosing intervention: One of the real struggles for all of us, as we transition from non-clinician to clinician, is how to claim a useful and honest professional identity or role. In the beginning, we do not know how to do this. Usually, as we work with clients, we gain awareness of how mental health professionals function and almost inexorably align ourselves with this kind of function. This is a way of saying that we slowly claim a professional identity and our professional roles.

For example, when I was just beginning, I remember when I met a new client, a young woman who was morbidly obese. My initial reaction on seeing her was disgust. My reaction triggered mixed thoughts. One was that I should be much more open to supporting and accepting this woman than I was. Another was that she really was disgusting. I felt the tension. As I worked with her, I heard about the disgust that she felt about herself. In the end, the work went very well. And this client helped me to discover some important insights about being a professional health care provider. For one thing, she helped me a great deal to confirm that my reactions to a client may be honest and real but that they may not matter much. Whether I felt disgust or not may not matter. Whether I felt sympathy or not may not matter. Or whether I felt attracted to her or not may not matter much either. What really mattered was whether I could be a professionally accountable person with her, including my personal and professional obligation to show respect for her. So, regardless of my reaction – sort of like being a physician in an emergency room and seeing a gunshot wound – no matter how easy or difficult it was to see her, my job, my professional identity, and my sincere commitment to helping her required me to subdue my reactions and provide the best possible service for her. To my surprise, this particular client also helped me to recognize that my reactions to a client may be a good guide to helping a client. So, as crude and even as disappointing as it may sound, my initial reaction of disgust matched her reaction to herself. For both of us, the question was not whether we should have felt disgust or any other feeling but how we made sense of the reaction and what we chose to do with it.

Another conceptual intervention may be to engage Katie in thinking about how she conceptualizes this client.

Katie, what do you know about flashers? Are you okay with having a discussion about this?

What do you conclude about what may drive/push this client to flash others, including children?

Considering your reaction to this client, I wonder whether you may want to look for material, including some good research, that may help you to understand flashers.

Common Challenges in Clinical Supervision

This discussion seeks to bring into focus several of the common challenges that supervisors encounter. The challenges involve ones that supervisees present to their supervisors but also ones that supervisors bring to the supervisory relationship and ones that both supervisors and supervisees face. In advance of this brief discussion, a comment is needed. It is that this is a conscientious sampling of common challenges and not an encyclopedic presentation of them.

Tracking supervisee development: Experienced clinicians and clinical supervisors recognize that their best awareness of the growth of clients and/or supervisees is limited. This means that tracking and professionally interacting with supervisees requires ongoing supervisory adjustments. To illustrate this challenge, the significance of tracking supervisee development may be seen in the fact that supervisees generally change their thinking about counseling/

psychotherapy from being task oriented to being relationally oriented. And, in the beginning of their clinical work, supervisees may need their supervisors to be somewhat more task oriented than relationally oriented, even when the two of them give serious attention to conceptual and relational issues (Lochner, 1996; Kitzrow, 2001; Schanz, 2016).

Gathering/having sufficient information: A truism of conducting clinical supervision is that supervision is supervision; it is not directly providing clinical service. Maybe, supervision may be considered to be "vicarious therapy," insofar as supervisors "think clinically" when they supervise other clinicians. Indeed, this may be regarded as a necessity of clinical supervision. However, in most supervisory situations, the supervisee has direct experience with a client and the supervisor does not. At least, this means that supervisors should give careful attention to what they may not know. And, usually, in seeking to know – or to gather and have sufficient and relevant information about the process of therapy and the client – the supervisor may wish both to follow a protocol for gathering relevant clinical information and persist in asking herself or himself, "Are there questions about this client and/or supervisee that I have not yet answered?" or "What may I need to know that may be more important than what I now know?" Many resources for such a protocol may be used, but we have found Sturmey's book, *Clinical Case Formulation* (Sturmey, 2009), to be very useful with regard to an outline of information that may need to be gathered.

Supervisee's refusal to be clinical: Probably, practicing clinicians recognize that they have evolved into their roles as clinicians and out of their socialized way of relating with others. From their personal experience of evolving in this way, they likely remember the awkwardness and, maybe, clumsiness they felt when they tried to be "clinical" instead of their familiar and comfortable selves. They understand and see the challenge of intentional evolving into a clinical role and identity in their supervisees. However, they see some of their supervisees refuse to evolve into a professional role and identity and persist in expressing their socialized identity. Obviously, this may take many forms, but clinical supervisors likely recognize their supervisees who are entrenched in a pleasing mode of relating, overly committed to directing others usually as a way to demonstrate that they are "right," or easily enmeshed with the pain of their clients so that they exude their clients' pain (i.e., parallel process) are inclined to save their clients from themselves. Each of these becomes another common challenge for clinical supervisors. In response to a supervisee's refusal to be clinical, supervisors may invite or direct their supervisees to be clinically accountable through conscientious and persistent interventions.

Supervisee's excessive deferral to their supervisors: Typically, supervisees are dependent on their clinical supervisor because, at least when they begin to treat clients, supervisees have no clinical experience upon which independence may be based. However, as supervisees develop or should develop, excessive dependence may be maintained. The explanations for supervisees' excessive and deferential interactions with their clinical supervisor may not be readily available to either the supervisee or the supervisor. However, regardless of the explanation for it, such interactions pose a challenge for clinical supervisors. It suggests that supervisees are overly dependent and likely avoidant of appropriate autonomy in relating with their clients.

Supervisee's conflation of their good intentions and valuable insights with clinical judgment: No doubt, the positive attitude and good intentions that clinicians take to their clients are important professional assets. For effective clinical work, though, they are not in themselves sufficient. "I meant to do it" or "I didn't mean to do it" is not an expression of appropriate clinical judgment. Attitude and intentions inhere in clinical work but become effective to the extent that they demonstrate clinical skill and a commitment to their refinement of clinical skill.

Cognitive style differences between supervisors and supervisees: Experienced clinicians and experienced clinical supervisors have little doubt about the reality of multiple cognitive styles. Translating this understanding into clinical supervision, though, can be challenging, particularly when the supervisor and the supervisee bring different cognitive styles to the supervisory relationship. One floats freely into abstractions and patterns of thought, while the other one steps with deliberation and caution into an orderly gathering of details and conclusion-reaching. One listens to her or his own sensing of the experience and utilizes this to help with clinical judgment, and the other one thinks analytically about the client's and his or her own experience of the clinical encounter. For much longer discussions of cognitive differences in supervisory relationships, see Wolfsfelda and Haj-Yahiaa, 2010; Lochner, 1996; Kitzrow, 2001; Schanz, 2016.

Relational style differences between supervisors and supervisees: Along with cognitive style differences in the supervisory relationship, relational style differences may pose challenges, too. And, like cognitive style differences, experienced clinicians and clinical supervisors recognize relational style differences. In the supervisory relationship, one may attach to others readily and comfortably, while the other one warms to others slowly (Riggs & Bretz, 2006). Or one may hold beliefs about the way men relate with women, while the other one holds beliefs that seriously depart from the beliefs of the other one (Hindes & Andrews, 2011). Or one may be inclined toward introversion, while the other one is inclined toward extroversion. Or one may express confidence in her or his own internal informational awareness, while the other one expresses confidence in pursuing questions. Or one may be socially refined and inclined to deal with conflict in a highly finessed way, while the other one may be inclined to be outspoken and blunt in her or his communications. Well, the options here are virtually endless, too. The almost too obvious emphasis and point here is that clinical supervisors should give attention to possible relational differences between themselves and their supervisees.

Lack of relevant clinical experience with both the supervisor and supervisee: Almost inevitably, clinical supervisors encounter supervisory-client situations with which they have little or no experience. Only to illustrate this, I – Francis A. Martin – remember all too well a supervisee's presentation of a four-year-old male whose profile appeared to be a psychotic one. While I have extensive experience in treating children and adolescents, I had not treated a four-year-old who seemed to be psychotic. Many experienced clinicians who are supervisors lack relevant clinical experience with some categories of clients' needs. This lack may be clinical work with terminally ill individuals or eating disordered clients or elderly victims of sexual assault or others. Whatever the lack may be, astute clinical supervisors will be alert to this deficiency and actively seek ways to address it.

Numerous ethical and/or legal dilemmas: Ethical and legal challenges come with the work of providing clinical supervision. Clinical supervisors should prepare for them, not so much from fear, but from a clear understanding of ethical and legal obligations to clients and supervisees and a readily useable set of procedures for managing these obligations. Major ethical dilemmas are quite familiar but also rare. The rare ones are the ones that are dreaded most by clinical supervisors, including supervisees' stunningly poor and harmful clinical work, inappropriate accommodations of clients' disturbed behaviors (e.g., drug usage), client abandonment, inappropriate intimacy with clients, or others. These lapses in ethical and legal behaviors by supervisees may require actions against a supervisee outside of the supervisory relationship. The not-so-consequential ethical and legal challenges involve numerous possibilities. Such challenges occur when supervisees' decide to utilize an intervention with which they have no appropriate preparation. Or they may give advice that fails to address a client's already self-defeating behaviors. Or they may offer presumed insights from their own life experiences, not recognizing that their insights have little or no relevance to their work with clients.

Conclusion

No doubt, clinical supervisors face challenges. Some of the challenges will be disturbing. However, the larger picture of clinical supervision is that it improves needed services to clients and facilitates the needed development of supervisees toward becoming effective clinicians. Quite simply, clinical supervision can be and usually is immensely fulfilling.

The experience of clinical supervision encompasses numerous variables. Among them, several may be readily identified, including the age of the supervisor, the age of the supervisee, the gender of each of these individuals, the physical setting in which they meet, the clientele whom they serve, the level of competence that each of them brings to their respective roles, their respective clinical histories, their unique personal issues, and much, much more. Allowing for the extraordinary complexity of clinical supervision, this chapter has described the experience of clinical supervision with the aim of creating understanding of some of the commonly recognized processes of clinical supervision. Acknowledging that this chapter is limited, at least, by the variables for which it does not account, readers are encouraged to adapt the material in this chapter to their individual situations so that they may enhance their clinical supervision.

15

ADMINISTRATIVE TASKS IN CLINICAL SUPERVISION

This chapter orients prospective and practicing clinical supervisors to several of their administrative tasks. The rationale for this chapter comes as a familiar one to most experienced and competent clinical supervisors. It is that the effective management of administrative tasks elevates the likelihood that client welfare will be assured as the priority for clinical supervisors and supervisees. In addition, the effective management of administrative tasks helps to protect the professional interests of supervisors and supervisees. This to say clinical supervisors can manage their risks by effectively managing the business of clinical supervision.

Commonly, clinical supervisors do not see these tasks as the more desirable features of their work. Nevertheless, they usually recognize that the likelihood of their effectiveness rises measurably if they attend to these tasks. This presentation of these tasks has emerged from the clinical experience of the authors, their supervised clinical work, their training in clinical supervision, their teaching of clinical supervision, and, most important, their practice of clinical supervision. Careful preparation for providing clinical supervision, with clear and broadly supported thinking about what clinical supervision is, significantly helps to protect everyone involved in clinical supervision (i.e., clients, supervisees, and supervisors) and maintains appropriate supervisor accountability for compliance with normative standards of competence for clinical supervisors.

Prospective clinical supervisors understandably step into the role of clinical supervisor with confidence, based on their enjoyment of and effectiveness in providing clinical services to clients. Before prospective clinical supervisors meet with their first supervisee, several kinds of preparation are necessary. Surely, consulting with experienced supervisors and receiving oversight of their early efforts toward providing clinical supervision are valuable features of beginning to supervise other clinicians. However, consulting with experienced supervisors is hardly a sufficient basis upon which to begin to supervise other clinicians. Therefore, toward becoming an effective clinical supervisor, this chapter offers guidance about how to manage administrative tasks that inhere in providing clinical supervision. Here is a list of the major tasks that receive attention in this chapter:

Preparing for clinical supervision
Initiating clinical supervision
Creating agreements between supervisees and supervisors
Establishing objectives for clinical supervision
Maintaining documentation
The supervisory relationship
Monitoring critical situations
Tracking ethical and legal issues and managing risk
Assessing supervisees (refer to Chapter 13)
Conducting supervisory sessions (refer to Chapter 14)

Preparing for Clinical Supervision

Supervisor preparation varies extremely. The variances come from differences among the types of major licenses (e.g., professional counselors, psychologists, and social workers), clinical training programs, agencies and organizations that conduct clinical supervision, and regulations in states. The numerous variances that emerge from these sources are more than this chapter can report. Instead of trying to account for all or most of the differences, it discusses the minimally appropriate kinds of preparation that are necessary for those who begin to provide clinical supervision.

The operative assumption here is that clinical supervision is a practice. Among other things, this means that academic preparation without practice, including supervised supervision, is not sufficient as a basis upon which to begin independent clinical supervision. Academic preparation, though, shows itself in the preparatory trajectory of most clinical supervisors. This stands as the recommendation here. Academic preparation – the study of clinical supervision – is important, but it is not sufficient. Further, the recommended categories of information in which prospective supervisors receive training include the following:

Legal Requirements and Regulations of Clinical Supervision

While clinical supervisors understandably have little interest in functioning as attorneys, they must know about and understand many specifically legal definitions and constraints on their practice of clinical supervision. Their knowledge and understanding should be broadly based so that it includes

Case law [e.g., Andrews v. U. S. 1984 (LEAGLE.com, 2018) and Simmons v. U. S. 1986 (Justia US Law, 2019)]
Common legal constructs (e.g., contract, scope of practice, normative standards of care, direct liability, vicarious liability, informed consent, and others)
State-specific laws and regulation, if any, that define clinical supervision

Normative Ethical Standards for Clinical Supervisors

While this is a body of knowledge that supervisors should know, the importance of knowing ethical standards is that clients, supervisees, and supervisors can more likely than not be protected from harm when supervisors comply with professional ethics. The emphasis on compliance with professional ethics is to ensure a high quality of care for clients.

Knowing and understanding professional ethics for clinical supervision is an obvious imperative. Knowing and understanding the professional ethics with which supervisees must comply is necessary, too. This is particularly important when a supervisee pursues a license that is different from the license of the supervisor. For example, when a supervisee pursues a license as a social worker and receives clinical supervision from a professional counselor, the professional counselor should understand the professional ethics for social workers.

Roles of Supervisees and Supervisors

As supervisors enter into their role as supervisors, they should understand and demonstrate the features of good clinical supervision. Among other things, this means that, even when they draw from their clinical skills during supervision, they are not functioning as clinicians. Their new role encompasses rightful expectations of oversight of another professional's clinical work, evaluation, and feedback; modeling of professional demeanor and behavior; knowledge of specific clinical populations; competency in clinical work; support of supervisees; and much more.

Competent Counseling and Therapy

The accruing evidence is that competence among counselors and psychotherapists continues to decline (e.g., Goldberg et al., 2016; Spengler & Pilipis, 2015). With or without this evidence, a necessary question for prospective and practicing clinical supervisors is "What characterizes a good therapist?" The importance of the question is that, when it is answered well, it gives clinical supervisors goals toward which to work and standards by which to measure the progress or lack of progress of their supervisees. Numerous assessment instruments that supervisors will find to be helpful may be easily located. These include the one that we developed for this book. However, there are others, such as the Counselor Competencies Scale (Lambie, 2017).

Philosophies and Theories of Clinical Supervision

The importance of studying, reflecting, and integrating into practice the various approaches to clinical supervision is that they may be intentionally utilized. Without such intentionality, clinical supervisors will more likely practice their favored approach to counseling and psychotherapy than a philosophy and theory of clinical supervision. Further, the added importance of this intentionality is that it enables clinical supervisors to develop their individual models of clinical supervision. This category of preparation may be labeled as "models of supervision," "approaches to clinical supervision," "philosophies of clinical supervision," and "theories of clinical supervision."

Supervision Techniques and Interventions

For the discussion of this topic in this book, refer to Chapter 6 and Chapter 14.

Evaluating Clinical Supervisees

Attention is given to this topic elsewhere in this book. In the current discussion, suffice it to say that a critically important function of clinical supervisors is evaluating their supervisees. The underlying commitment of evaluating clinical supervisees is that they develop their competence as clinicians so that they establish themselves as professionally competent mental health care providers.

Common Problems in Clinical Supervision

For the discussion of this topic in this book, refer to Chapter 14.

Supervisor Development

For the discussion of this topic in this book, refer to Chapter 11.

Supervised Supervision

Preparing to provide clinical supervision must involve supervised supervision, just as preparing to deliver clinical services as a counselor or psychotherapist requires supervision. No one becomes a highly skilled counselor or psychotherapist without supervision. Likewise, seldom does a clinical supervisor become a highly skilled supervisor without having her or his early development as a supervisor supervised.

Formats of Supervision

Generally, discussions of formats for clinical supervision refer to individual, triadic, and group supervision. Surely, these formats should be understood, with reference to their advantages and disadvantages.

Current Research on Relevant Aspects of Clinical Supervision

Like all professions, clinical supervision continues to evolve. Some of its evolution comes from research that provides fresh insights, challenging conclusions, innovative practices, refinement of evaluations of supervisees, directions for the future, and much more. Skilled clinical supervisors who maintain their effectiveness also maintain an awareness of research about supervisor effectiveness and related matters.

Supervisory Relational Issues and Dynamics

Just like clinical service for a client, the supervisory relationship is fundamentally important in clinical supervision. And, just like the counseling relationship, the relationship between a supervisee and a supervisor involves many layers of significance and activity. During a supervisory session, the energy of both the supervisee and the supervisor may be invested in assisting the supervisee with heightened anxiety about a new and demanding client, while the next session may be invested in mutually sharing ideas about legislation that will re-shape aspects of their work. All things considered, though, a new supervisor should have prepared to enter the supervisory relationship with useful understandings of the issues and dynamics that inhere in the relationship. Some of these are discussed elsewhere in this book. For now, with regard to relational issues and dynamics within the context of good supervisory judgment, the clinical supervisor should make the supervisory relationship as safe and secure as possible, demonstrate candor and honesty in the relationship, provide modeling for effective personal and professional functioning, and continually try to be clear about relational priorities.

Administration of Clinical Supervision

Most matters of significance happen within the supervisory sessions. However, several administrative obligations of the clinical supervisor can "make or break" the success of supervision. Discussed at length in this chapter, these obligations encompass more than these brief comments. Suffice it to say that they include quite an array of activities, such as scheduling sessions, preparing for sessions, documenting sessions, preparing written evaluations, and so on.

Within the ongoing development of clinical supervision as a specific kind of distinct professional practice, certifying adequate preparation for it has become somewhat common. Moreover, among state governments, it is becoming a common mandate for those who seek to become clinical supervisors. Two of the most sought certifications are those offered by the American Association of Marriage and Family Therapists (AAMFT, 2019) and the National Board for Certified Counselors (NBCC) / Center for Credentialing and Education, an agency of the American Counseling Association. Information about the AAMFT supervisor certification may be located at www.aamft.org/supervision/supervision.aspx. Information about the supervisor certification by NBCC/ACA may be located at Center for Credentialing and Education (2019). Retrieved from www.cce-global.org/Credentialing/ACS.

Initiating Clinical Supervision

Several checklists for beginning clinical supervision with a new supervisee are readily available (e.g., Center for Substance Abuse Treatment, 2009, and Prest, Schindler-Zimmerman, & Sporakowski, 1992). All of them need to be adapted to fit the context in which clinical supervision is provided. For example, a checklist for a clinical supervisor in a university counseling center will likely be very different from a checklist for a clinical supervisor in an agency that requires its clinicians to comply with a specific treatment model, such as multi-systemic therapy or behavioral therapy. Allowing for the need to adapt a checklist to the context in which clinical supervision occurs, one of the commonly available checklists appears in *Clinical Supervision and Professional Development of the Substance Abuse Counselor* (Center for Substance Abuse Treatment, 2009). The checklist appears in Chart 15–1: Initial Supervision Session(s) Checklist.

Chart 15–1 Initial Supervision Session(s) Checklist

Education, Training, and Clinical Experience

_____ Educational background
_____ Training experience
_____ Setting(s), number of years
_____ Theoretical orientation
_____ Clinical competence with various issues, models, techniques, populations, presenting problems, treatment modalities
_____ Sense of mission and purpose in the field
_____ Educational plans and professional goals of the supervisee
_____ Training and awareness of cultural and contextual issues in counseling
_____ Training and awareness of community networking in counseling

Philosophy of Supervision

_____ Philosophy of therapy and change
_____ Purpose of supervision

Previous Supervision Experiences

_____ Previous supervision experiences (e.g., format, setting)
_____ Strengths and weaknesses as counselor and as supervisee
_____ Supervisee's competence with stages of counseling process
_____ Supervisee's level of development in terms of case planning, notes, collateral support, and networking
_____ Supervisory competence with various issues, models, techniques, populations, therapy groups, and modalities
_____ Methods for managing supervisor-supervisee differences

Supervision Goals

_____ Goals (personal and professional)
_____ Process of goal evaluation and timeframe
_____ Requirements for which supervisee is seeking supervision (e.g., licensure, professional certification)
_____ Requirements to be met by supervision (e.g., total hours, individual or group supervision)

Supervision Style and Techniques

_____ Specific expectations the supervisee or supervisor has of the parties involved (e.g., roles, hierarchy)

_____ Type of supervision that would facilitate clinical growth of the supervisee

_____ Preferred supervision style (didactic, experiential, collegial)

_____ Parallels between therapy and supervision models

_____ Supervision focus (e.g., counselor's development, cases)

_____ Manner of case review (e.g., crisis management, in-depth focus)

_____ Method (e.g., audio- or videotaping, direct observation)

Theoretical Orientation

_____ Models and specific theories in which supervisee and supervisor have been trained, practice, and/or conduct supervision

_____ Extent to which these models have been used clinically

_____ Populations, presenting problems, and/or family forms with which the models have been most effective

_____ Interest in learning new approaches

Legal and Ethical Considerations

_____ Ultimate responsibility for clients discussed in supervision in different contexts (e.g., licensed vs. unlicensed counselor, private practice vs. public agency)

_____ Number of cases for which the supervisor will be responsible

_____ Emergency and back-up procedures

_____ Awareness of professional ethical codes

_____ Confidentiality regarding the information discussed in supervision

_____ Confidentiality issues when more than one supervisee is involved

_____ Specific issues in situations where dual relationships exist (e.g., former client)

_____ Process for addressing supervisee issues (e.g., burnout, countertransference)

Other

What do we need to know about each other that we have not already discussed?

Adding to this checklist, a supervisor may need to ensure that it includes a discussion of the methods and timing of evaluating the supervisee's clinical performance. The larger additions, though, are likely to be ones that accommodate the clinical setting in which supervision occurs. Generally, the principle that guides the initiation of clinical supervision is that the supervisor engages in good faith, professionally accountable practices for clinical supervisors. For example, just as service for clients requires the informed consent, the practice of good clinical supervision requires informed consent from supervisees. Obviously, initiating clinical supervision involves more than informed consent. The next two tasks add to the obligations that inhere in initiating clinical supervision.

Creating Agreements Between Supervisees and Supervisors

Agreements between supervisees and supervisors should include all necessary items that relate to effective treatment of clients and protect the professional interests of supervisees and supervisors. Typically, the most common forms of agreements are contracts and informed consent documents.

Contracting for Clinical Supervision

The specific details of a contract between a supervisee and a supervisor depend simply on the features to a contract to which both of them agree. However, beyond the preferences of these two individuals, the common and necessary features of contracts for clinical supervision include the following:

Frequency of meetings
Dates for beginning the contract
Terms for ending the contract
Incorporation of professional ethics
Incorporation of laws and regulations
Fees
Availability for crises
Important exclusions
Rights of supervisee
Rights of supervisor
Purposes of clinical supervision
Confidentiality and limitations placed on confidentiality
Compliance with agency policies, if applicable

A search of the Internet will easily yield several clinical supervision templates. Here are sites where such templates may be located:

http://c.ymcdn.com/sites/www.naswoh.org/resource/resmgr/imported/Supervision%20Contract%20Template.pdf
Substance Abuse and Mental Health Services Administration. (2008). *Competencies for Substance Abuse Treatment Clinical Supervisors.* Rockville, Maryland: Author.
http://drsharman.com/wp-content/uploads/2010/07/ClinicalSupervision.pdf
http://cfalender.com/Supervision%20Contract.pdf
www.cgcounseling.org/upload/Supervision%20Contract%20new.pdf
www.robinfriedmantherapy.com/uploads/1/5/4/9/1549976/_supervision_agreement.pdf

Each of the templates at these sites is very different from the others. The differences may be confusing. However, the advantage of having a variety of templates is that it collectively answers almost any question that a clinical supervisor or prospective clinical supervisor may have about contracting with supervisees. Also, the variety emphasizes that a "standard" contract may not exist and that, because of this, supervisors should aim to create contracts that uniquely accommodate the needs of the supervisor and supervised, the agency in which they may serve, and the legal jurisdiction in which they provide services. As noted earlier, a dictum that we follow is "Whatever may be a concern, such as fees or procedures for handling clients' crises, can be included in a supervisory contract."

Thomas (2007) provides an excellent discussion of contracting through informed consent, although her discussion needs to be updated. Despite the limitation of datedness, Thomas's discussion provides careful analysis and insights into contracting and informed consent. In addition, it includes supervisor/supervisee cases that bring the reader into the landscape of these activities, along with several specific recommendations for fulfilling the obligations that come with clinical supervision.

Informed Consent in Clinical Supervision

Often, clinical supervisors integrate informed consent into their supervision contracts. More commonly, though, informed consent is a separate document and activity. Typically, informed consent in clinical supervision refers to the obligation of the clinical supervisor to inform prospective supervisees about their training, clinical experience, preparation for providing clinical supervision, common demands of clinical supervision, the supervisor's beliefs about mental health care and clinical supervision, the means of evaluating supervisees, and other relevant matters. The primary aim of providing professionally accountable informed consent is that supervisees can know and understand the opportunities and constraints of the supervision process and receive appropriate assurance about expecting effective clinical supervision. As a matter of professionally accountable practice, informed consent can and should be kept in the context of a wider array of agreements between supervisors and supervisees. For example, this discussion has made reference to the obligation of supervisors to establish a contract with supervisees. Further, the discussions that follow contribute to a context in which contracting and informed consent become parts.

Whether a formal agreement is reached or not, clinical supervisors carry the burden for the performance of supervisees. Because of this, supervisors should initiate discussions, if not formal agreements, about virtually all aspects of clinical functioning and professional accountability. A set of standards that are promulgated by the Association of Counselor Educators and Supervisors (Association for Counselor Education and Supervision, 2011) nicely illustrates the broad range of considerations, when the supervisory relationship begins, under the heading, "The supervisor explicitly states clear parameters for conducting supervision."

The supervisor and supervisee agree on time, place, and duration of supervision sessions.

The supervisor and supervisee discuss how the supervisee will prepare for each supervision session relevant to the supervision format (e.g., individual, triadic, group).

The supervisor clearly delineates supervisor and supervisee responsibilities regarding the preparation for and conduct of supervision.

The supervisor and supervisee agree on cancellation and rescheduling procedures for supervision sessions.

The supervisor and supervisee agree on payment for supervision (as appropriate and permitted by state law).
The supervisor provides the supervisee with his or her emergency contact information, parameters for contacting the supervisor in emergency situations, and specific instructions for emergency protocols.
The supervisor provides necessary forms and other documents to be completed by the supervisor, supervisees, and others as appropriate to the particular supervisee, setting, and/or credentialing body.
(p. 3)

Numerous procedural expectations may be added to this list. For example, the supervisor may wish to establish a schedule though which supervisees report about their accrued clinical hours, their conclusions/insights about their growth as clinicians, or other clinically relevant schedules. Or, for example, the supervisor and supervisee will likely need to establish the time and method of payment for services, if this fits the situation.

Establishing Objectives/Goals for Clinical Supervision

Insofar as one of the reasonably anticipated outcomes of clinical supervision is that the supervisee makes progress toward becoming an appropriately autonomous clinician and an increasingly effective one, the clarified goals from the supervisee are likely more important than the goals of the supervisor. The highest priority in setting goals for supervisees is to ensure that both the supervisee and the supervisor discuss clear conclusions from research about some of the important characteristics of effective psychotherapists. They should know what they are trying to achieve.

With regard to goals for supervisees, a good next step is to assess the supervisee's current level of functioning and, on the basis of this assessment, clarify clinically relevant goals for the supervisee. In this text, we have advocated for the competence-oriented model of clinical supervision (COMCS). The specific indicators of competence in this model provide a solid basis upon which to build goals for supervisees. For example, the following list of skills provides categories of thinking about specific clinical and transcendent skills that mental health care providers need to develop. If nothing more than a self-assessment from the supervisee and discussions about this with a clinical supervisor are translated into clinically relevant goals for the supervisee, clinically relevant goals may be set.

Clinical Skills

Relational skills
Self-management skills
Clinical leadership skills
Engagement skills
Activity-oriented skills
Assessment skills

Transcendent Skills

Emotional attunement to self and/or client
Adaptability
Clinical judgment
Critical thinking
Conceptualization skills

The COMCS approach to clinical supervision provides several helpful features, with regard to setting goals for supervisees. However, the qualities of highly effective psychotherapists provide another set of aspirations that supervisees and supervisors may wish to consider as ones that can assist them in their goal setting. For a discussion of these qualities, refer to Chapter 12, "Supervisee Development."

Just as treatment goals for clients are usually fluid and dynamic, the goals for supervisees should be regarded as fluid and dynamic, while simultaneously being specific, realistic, measurable, and achievable. This means that during the course of clinical supervision, the goals should be re-visited and possibly re-negotiated. For example, both the supervisee and the supervisor should understand that one of their highest priorities is to meet the clinically relevant needs of clients. The goals for the supervisee should serve this priority and, because of this, may need to be re-negotiated.

Toward clarifying goals for supervisees, a supervisee may say something like this:

> *I feel like if I seriously confront a client, I'm going to break something. My nature is to be supportive, not confrontational. So, confrontation is hard for me. I just don't do it. For me, therapy is about being as supportive and welcoming as I can be. I don't like being confronted, either. When it happens, I feel like I'm being attacked. So, I avoid doing it to other people.*

A discussion of supervisees' difficulty in confronting clients may reveal that they hesitate or refuse to confront clients in clinically appropriate ways because they fear the possibility of being rejected by clients. They follow the belief that if they are "nice and empathic," clients will reciprocate with niceness and empathy. While niceness and empathy are virtuous behaviors in many circumstances, they hardly establish a sufficient basis upon which to conduct effective psychotherapy. Therefore, a possible goal for such supervisees could easily center around the idea that they should develop clinically relevant assertiveness skills. Once such a goal is established, it should receive attention during clinical supervision meetings.

Generally, clinical supervisors bring knowledge and skills that are significantly more advanced than the knowledge and skill of their supervisees, while this is obviously not universally applicable to all clinical situations. For example, a supervisee may have extensive experience with service to clients in a shelter for victims of domestic violence, while the clinical supervisor has no experience with this clientele. Similarly, both the supervisee and the supervisor may need to acquire new skills in the delivery of an approach to psychotherapy that is new to both of them, such as radically open dialectical behavior therapy (RODBT). These situations and other similar ones that may arise place the burden of discovering new competencies on clinical supervisors, insofar as they should work within the boundaries of their competence.

Early in the supervisory relationship, goal setting requires attention. Beyond making a good beginning, though, as clinical supervision proceeds, the supervisor should give attention to the goals to which the supervisee and supervisor have agreed. Giving attention to agreed-upon goals serves important functions. One, it helps supervisees and supervisors to be clear about necessary priorities. Two, if supervision is done well, it invites supervisees to display their progress toward reaching their goals. Three, it provides a basis on which supervisees and supervisors can review the supervisees' work with clients and the specific clinical judgments that illustrate the supervisee's progress toward reaching goals or the lack of progress. Finally, it establishes a foundation for evaluating the clinical work of supervisees.

Maintaining Documentation

Just as client care requires documentation, clinical supervision requires documentation, too. The relative status of these two kinds of documentation may be understood but is seldom discussed. Most states define for mental health care providers what the client's clinical record should include. Usually. this is not the situation for clinical supervision. No doubt, such definitions and regulatory requirements for documenting clinical supervision will come. At this time, the trend toward such regulations is clear. For now, though, the questions about documentation are simple and clear. One, what should be included in a supervision record? Two, what should be included in a clinical supervision session and recorded from a session?

What should be included in a supervision record? Aasheim (2012) cites Falvey as recommending that the following items be included in a supervision file (p. 256):

Supervisee information/contact information form
The supervision contract
Additional contacts relating to the supervision relationship (e.g., contacts with agency, with another third party payer, with the university or training program
A copy of the supervisee's job description or, if a student trainee, the program requirements
A copy of the supervisee's malpractice insurance
The supervisee's résumé
The supervisor's professional disclosure form

The supervisor's informed consent document
Copy of the supervisor's license/pre-licensure information
Copy of all relevant codes of ethics
All evaluations or assessments of the supervisee's work
Attendance and payment log to track actual time spent in supervision and related payment or invoice information
Supervision notes from session

When relevant, the following items should be considered for inclusion in a supervisee's file:

Date of termination
Status of termination (e.g., met requirements of program or for licensing or terminated for failure to make progress)
Letters of recommendation
Policies and/or manuals of agency or university, if relevant
A record of sessions missed

What should be recorded from and included in a clinical supervision session? We propose that the following items be included in a supervision session note.

Name of clinician who was supervised
Date of session
Length of session
Type of session (e.g., face-to-face, telephone, group or individual)
Method of case(s) presentation (e.g., oral only, paper document, DVD)
High-risk concerns, if any, about clients (e.g., suicide potential, duty to warn, ethics-related and/or legal concerns) and conclusions reached and/or actions taken
Identifiers for clients whose care was supervised
Description of any specific directive or advice given to the supervisee
Feedback given to supervisee, with regard to major categories of supervisee development [Refer to assessment form in Appendix and to the chapter on supervisee development]
Date and time of the next scheduled session
Signature of supervisor

Depending on the context in which supervision occurs, supervisors may want to encourage and/or require supervisees to maintain their own record of supervision sessions. Such a record should be aimed toward helping supervisees to develop as clinicians. The supervisee's record may include much of the information that the supervisor maintains. However, toward helping supervisees to develop as clinicians, additional kinds of information may be useful primarily for supervisees but also for supervisors. Here are some examples of the kinds of information that supervisees may want to include in their documentation:

A record of meetings with their clinical supervisor
Self-evaluations of their progress toward achieving their goals in supervision
A reflective journal that gives attention to ethical and/or legal issues
A record of resources needed and secured, such as, say, an article on attachment issues in adults or information about radically open dialectical behavioral therapy (RODBT) – or whatever specific resources may be needed
A reflective journal that gives attention to their professional growth
A detailed analysis of cases, such as one with a client who has achieved clinical goals quite successfully or a client who has failed miserably

Obviously, documentation is important. At least, its importance in clinical supervision is that it confirms that supervision occurred. More than mere confirmation, though, the record of clinical supervision increases the likelihood that mental health care has been delivered according to high standards of client care. Unfortunately, when client care has not been delivered according to minimally appropriate standards or when a supervisee has failed to develop, a supervisor's record is needed so that the difficult decision to terminate supervision, refuse to endorse a supervisee for licensing, or to terminate a supervisee's employment may be effectively protected and justified. And, increasingly, several external entities are reviewing clinical supervision documentation. These include licensing boards, agencies that employ supervisees or supervisors, insurance companies, professional associations, and various agencies that certify specific clinical expertise.

The Supervisory Relationship

The effective management of the supervisory relationship would seem to be an obvious task for clinical supervisors. It is. While the supervisory relationship necessarily engages both supervisees and supervisors in a qualitative, personal, professional, and shared activity, supervisors bear a much heavier burden for ensuring that their relationship works well. And, insofar as the relationship must work well so that clinical supervision is effective, the management of the relationship becomes a necessary task for clinical supervisors.

Because clinical supervisors usually regard their supervisees as "junior colleagues," they almost always seek to regard them with respect, showing appreciation for the normative, sometimes painful, struggles and exhilarating achievements. The uniquely personal dimensions of their relationship are likely to be an existentially real feature of clinical supervision. Surely, the service of clinical supervision as it is expressed through these personal dimensions necessarily includes several features for which the clinical supervisor is largely accountable. Adapted from Gallon, Hausotter, and Bryan (2005), these features include the following:

Emotional, professional, and relational safety
Mutual trust
Mutual respect
Open and flexible style of relating, as opposed to a defensive style
Appropriate, mutual autonomy
Capacity to learn from mistakes and failure – or even to enjoy such events
Readiness to model effective self-management
Timely and prompt attention to supervisory meetings
Sensitivity to ordinary issues of life (e.g., family illness and financial stresses)
Sensitivity to supervisee's professional and personal developmental needs
Careful and caring attention to power differentials
Clarity about the roles of supervisees and supervisors, including the rights and responsibilities of both

As administrative tasks in clinical supervision, the importance of these features of a good supervisory relationship is that effective clinical supervision is much more likely with them than without them. Given this, it serves as a directive for clinical supervisors to ensure that they place a rightful and professionally accountable emphasis on the needs of their supervisees and not on their own needs. With no exaggeration of the significance of the centrality of a good relationship in effective clinical supervision, the Council of Representatives of the American Psychological Association (2018) advanced the following position in its *Guidelines for Clinical Supervision in Health Service Psychology*:

> *The quality of the supervisory relationship is essential to effective clinical supervision (e.g., Bernard & Goodyear, 2014; Falender & Shafranske, 2004; Holloway, 1995; O'Donovan, Halford, & Walters, 2011). Quality of the supervision relationship is associated with more effective evaluation (Lehrman-Waterman & Ladany, 2001), satisfaction with supervision (Ladany, Ellis, & Friedlander, 1999), and supervisee self-disclosure of personal and professional reactions including reactivity and countertransference (Falender & Shafranske, 2004; Ladany et al., 1999). The power differential is a central factor in the supervisory relationship and the supervisor bears responsibility for managing, collaborating, and discussing power within the relationship.*
>
> (Porter & Vasquez, 1997; p. 17)

The Association for Counselor Education and Supervision (ACES), a division of the American Counseling Association, prepared a guide for clinical supervisors, "*Best Practices in Clinical Supervision*" (2011). In the guide, ACES asserts that "The supervisor operates with an awareness that the supervisory relationship is key to the effectiveness of supervision as well as the growth and development of the supervisee" (p. 7). Apparently, both APA and ACA are clear about the importance of the supervisory relationship in effective clinical supervision. Extending the emphasis on the importance of the supervisory relationship, the added importance of supervisor self-care should be emphasized, too. The method of self-care surely emerges from the intention to maintain self-care. And intentionality emerges from the recognition of its importance. The method, then, may be almost anything that facilitates and maintains self-care. It may be viewing funny videos, engaging in relaxation techniques (e.g., walking, massage, exercise, deep breathing, meditation), reading, multiple forms of socializing, attending concerts, eating well, and, of course, sleeping and resting, along with many other possibilities.

In their study of self-care among supervisors, Blount et al. (2016, p. 367) emphasize that "*Self-care* was defined as the necessity of taking care of one's *self* in order to be a better asset to supervisees and clients. The self-care theme supports the idea that 'you cannot give away that which you do not possess' (Bratton et al., 2006, p. 15)." Expanding the breadth of their view, they add that supervisor self-care "is consistent in the counseling and other helping professional literature (Lawson, 2007)" (p. 367). Correctly, they assert, "[We] we must take care of ourselves before we are able to care for others" (p. 367). Finally, among their conclusions, they state, "Through the supervisors' process of reflection and recognition, they were able to respond with care and compassion to their supervisees" (p. 367). Noting that healthy supervisors can mitigate against un-health in their supervisees, Blount and her colleagues add that

> *Similar to other wellness research in the helping professions (Lawson, 2007; Myers & Sweeney, 2005b; Skovholt, 2001), self-care is paramount to supporting personal wellness, as well as having the capacity to promote wellness in others – supervisors with supervisees and in parallel, supervisees with clients.*
>
> (p. 368)

Clearly, a healthy supervisory relationship and a supervisor's self-care have significance, but are they administrative tasks? Our answer is "Yes." Our reasoning for this answer is simple: Clinical supervisors should give their supervisees a model of solidly personal and professional executive decision making, effective self-care, and self-management. To assert this view in one more way, supervisors should manage themselves in such ways that they give supervisees a model of healthy relating, even when their relationship with supervisees involves conflict or other potentially unpleasant dynamics. When supervisors claim their professional role – analogous to actors claiming their roles – constraints and opportunities come with the role. With regard to the supervisory relationship, supervisors express, fill, or "play" their role in such ways that their personal, relational needs take a relatively low priority and, commensurately, the needs of supervisees and their clients take a very high priority.

"Executive decision making" by clinical supervisors refers to several actions that affect the supervisory relationship. These include establishing a schedule for meeting and ensuring, thereby, that clients and supervisees receive the services and oversight that they need. They involve compliance with professional ethics, laws, and regulations and agency policies and procedures, when such policies and procedures are relevant. They involve many more decisions and responsibilities than these. In addition, they involve decision making that relates specifically to the conduct of clinical supervision, such as deciding about the content of a supervision contract. Depending on the circumstances and needs of supervisees and their clients, a clinical supervisor may need to direct the supervisee to prepare in quite specific ways for supervisory meetings, including which clients will be presented, which client issues should be discussed, or possibly what kind of in-between sessions consultations a supervisee will need to pursue.

Monitoring Critical Situations

The obligation to monitor critical situations comes somewhat naturally, because supervisors are concerned about the welfare of clients who may be at imminent risk. Among many possibilities, clinical supervisors should monitor the status of clients who exhibit or who have relevant histories with any of the following behaviors:

Suicidal ideation	A history of suicide attempts
Homicidal ideation	Attempts to harm others
A history of harming others	

Boundary threat (e.g., extravagant gifts, attempts toward sexual seduction)

With regard to the status of these clients, clinical supervisors will likely want to give priority attention to the status of these clients during supervisory meetings. Also, depending on the supervisor's judgment, the supervisor may wish to maintain contact with the supervisee between supervisory meetings. Whether such monitoring occurs within or between supervisory meetings, supervisors should keep careful records of such monitoring so that the documentation supports the needed conclusion that clinical care for these clients met normative professional standards of care.

Tracking Ethical and Legal Issues and Managing Risk

No one can provide risk-free clinical supervision. Just as risk inheres in virtually all human activity, whether the activity is driving an automobile or visiting a friend's home or whatever the activity may be, risk also inheres in clinical supervision and in mental health care, generally. Clinical supervisors should know about risks in providing clinical supervision, but they should also know about managing risk so that they reduce the potential for adverse consequences. While some of the following recommendations for managing risk may seem to be self-evident, each one should be taken seriously.

Above all, monitor the welfare and well-being of clients.
Consult with other mental health care supervisors.
Consult with attorneys, with regard to risk management.
Consult with your insurance carrier.
Monitor the welfare of supervisees.
Comply with all relevant laws.
Comply with regulations.
Search for relevant case law.
Maintain liability insurance.
Ensure that supervisees maintain liability insurance.
Practice within the scope of competence.
Ensure that supervisees practice within the scope of their competence.
Monitor supervisees' clinical performance.
Give attention to supervisees' clinical judgment and decision making.
Review updates of changes in clinical supervision (e.g., attend professional meetings or review licensing laws).
Read research about clinical supervision, including – but much more than – best practices in clinical supervision, risk management strategies, and effective management of common supervision problems.
Identify potential problems with supervisees and document actions taken in response to these problems.
Comply with agreements with supervisees.
Follow normative practices in clinical supervision (e.g., informed consent, keeping agreed-upon schedules, providing competent and relevant feedback to supervisees).
Meet regularly with supervisees, ensuring that client welfare can be monitored.
Demonstrate commitment to professional boundaries in supervisory relationships.
Review ethical standards, with clear emphasis on ethical standards that relate to clinical supervision.
And, of course, keep good records!

Risk management should be taken seriously by clinical supervisors. However, they will not likely ever be the object of a legal complaint. Such complaints are rare. Furthermore, the most important work of clinical supervisors is not risk management. It is developing competent mental health care clinicians. It is this worthy aspiration that motivates clinical supervisors and that keeps them safe, particularly when they provide a model of professionalism that demonstrates commitment to the highest professional and personal ethical standards and when they seek to ensure that their supervisees do the same.

Assessing Supervisees

Inevitably and necessarily, supervisors evaluate their supervisees. The emphasis on this as an administrative task comes as another reminder of its importance. Because large parts of this book give attention to evaluating supervisees, only the reminder is offered here, along with encouragement to review the parts of the book that give attention to assessing supervisees, particularly the discussion of the competence-oriented model of clinical supervision (COMCS). Appendix A includes a supervisee evaluation form that clinical supervisors may utilize in their work. It is based on COMCS.

Conducting Supervisory Sessions

Earlier in the book, the chapter, "The Experience of Clinical Supervision," discusses much of what happens in clinical supervision meetings. The discussion here adds to the earlier discussion. The material here is intended to answer the question, "What do clinical supervisors do during supervision sessions?"

During a conversation with two experienced clinical supervisors who at the time were providing clinical supervision for two individuals who were prospective licensees, the supervisors asserted that their supervisees did not need to have contact with or conduct counseling/psychotherapy for the sessions to count as supervision. Puzzled by this, we inquired about what happened during their meetings with supervisees. They indicated that they discussed cases. So, we wanted to know about whose cases were discussed, if no one in the room actually provided services to clients. They explained that their supervisees were also administrators at their agency, and as administrators, they oversaw the work of their administrative subordinates and that this counted for clinical work that they could supervise. Obviously, their explanation of their supervision fell extremely below minimal professional standards, not to mention failing to pass the proverbial "smell test."

This is to say that supervision sessions require that clinical supervisors provide supervision for clinical work. While miscellaneous, other topics of discussion, such as weather or traffic or illness, inevitably arise, clinical work must be the primary focus of clinical supervision meetings. Apart from this obvious requirement, several additional requisite activities for supervision meetings may be listed. They include the following:

Because documentation of what happens in clinical supervision sessions increases the effectiveness of both supervisors and supervisees, supervisors should take notes during and after clinical supervision sessions. Maintaining good records of supervision contributes to effective client care and good supervisee development. Of course, though, another reason for taking notes is that it potentially adds a layer of protection against ethics or legal complaints. Also, implicit in keeping a record of what happens during clinical supervision sessions is that it communicates professional accountability to supervisees.

Clinical supervision sessions should be held when they are scheduled. This involves having a schedule and ensuring that, within the normative range of human limitation, supervisors and supervisees keep their commitments to meet. Our experience is that this simple expectation of supervisors and supervisees can be easily abrogated. For example, what need for sensitive decision(s) may arise, when a supervisee misses a session or two and requests of a clinical supervisor that the supervisor allow the truant supervisee to be allowed to "make up" some sessions by attending meetings with one of the supervisor's other supervisees? Or, for example, if a supervisee's clinical work falls below minimal professional expectations and if this supervisee's clinical supervisor fails to keep scheduled meetings, the supervisor may not be able to justify difficult but necessary corrective actions toward the supervisee.

Clinical supervision meetings invest primarily in "covering" clinical cases. Typically, this involves discussions of the clinical work of supervisees. This may seem to be self-evident. However, the importance of discussing the clinical work of supervisees is that, while client welfare is the higher priority, the professional development of supervisees stands as a close second priority. In other words, giving attention exclusively or almost exclusively to clients' needs may not help supervisees to develop. For example, when the supervision meeting gives almost exclusive attention to diagnosing clients, collaborating toward understanding and strategizing about clients' problems, and identifying specific clinical techniques that may be utilized, the professional needs, including potentially large deficiencies, of supervisees may be missed. In such a case as this, clinical supervision will have failed the supervisee.

Insofar as many supervisees need endorsement of their candidacy for licensing or certification, supervision sessions should give attention to the supervisee's progress toward meeting the requirements for licensing or certification. Almost universally, the mutual expectation of clinical supervision is that the supervisor will endorse or refuse to endorse the supervisee's candidacy for licensing or certification. Because of this, the importance of mutual understanding of the requirements for licensing or certification necessitates that discussions about these things become topics to be covered during supervision meetings.

Clinical supervisors protect the integrity of supervision sessions. Among many other standards, such as confidentiality, supervisors ensure that the setting, such as an office, conference room, or coffee bar, offers appropriate security for sensitive information and supervisor or supervisee disclosures. In other words, supervision meetings should be conducted in such places that clients, supervisees, and supervisors are protected from inadvertent disclosures. While clinical supervisors bear primary accountability for protecting the integrity of supervisory sessions, most supervisees willingly and readily share this burden.

When a clinical supervisor meets with more than one supervisee, the supervisor carefully discriminates interesting discussions from necessary ones. The importance of this is that supervisees who see themselves as performing well and who are likely performing well will want to talk about their clinical work. They are interested and value feedback from others. In contrast, the supervisees who see themselves as performing poorly and who are likely performing poorly may not want to discuss their clinical work. No matter what level of comfort or discomfort a clinical supervisor may feel in response to either of these supervisees, good clinical supervision compels that attention be given to the supervisee who is performing poorly. As an adjunct to this matter, clinical supervisors should place a higher priority on the needs of clients and supervisees than on the economics of meeting with supervisees in triadic supervision or group supervision.

In other words, group supervision may be more economical for an agency or for supervisees, but poorly performing supervisees may be able to conceal their poor performance in group supervision. A clinical supervisor may determine, therefore, that the poorly performing supervisee will meet only in sessions that include the clinical supervisor and the supervisee.

Clinical supervisors maintain a focus on the professional goals of supervisees. This is to say that, during supervision meetings, supervisors initiate conversations about progress toward supervisees' professional goals. In such conversations, "goals" should be defined somewhat broadly so that they include large and agreed-upon goals but also the goals that arise from the existential and evocative encounters with clients. For example, a somewhat broadly framed goal may be something like this: "The supervisee will demonstrate expanding understanding of, identifying, and responding to trauma-related issues." In contrast, maybe conceived of as a "micro-goal," a goal that arises from the existential and evocative encounter with a client may be something like this: [The supervisee speaks.] "I know we've talked about this. But, there's something about this guy that just pisses me off. I feel like I need to achieve some insight into how I get triggered by this guy. You've been helping with this, but I feel like I'm still missing something here. I need some help figuring this out." Both macro-goals and the micro-goals are important.

Clinical supervisors select interventions in a deliberative manner. In contrast with reactive interventions, clinical supervisors place their interventions in the context of the supervisee's level of development, the needs of clients, and the specific needs of a supervisee at the moment. Clearly, during many supervisory sessions, clinical supervisors will exhibit spontaneous, serendipitous feedback. This is likely to be a valuable asset and example. After all, evidence indicates that effective clinicians must adapt to the experience of conducting counseling in the moment. In addition, effective clinicians and effective clinical supervisors provide their spontaneous, serendipitous feedback out of a history of professional development and an ever-enlarging capacity for deliberative decision making and actions.

Clinical supervisors endorse clinical work through their demonstrated commitment to it and to clinical excellence. The value of such an endorsement in delivering clinical supervision is that, among other things, it endorses the positive value of supervisees. Stated in another way, when supervisors endorse clinical work, they contribute to enabling their supervisees to value their work toward developing their professional practice of clinical work. This may help supervisees to work in increasingly effective ways, insofar as they may more strongly believe in the work they do, but it helps supervisees, too, to believe that they can provide services that truly help others. In this kind of clinical supervision, the demands of clinical work no doubt continue, but they continue with a lower level of stress. It helps supervisees to gain needed positive valuing of their work, insights into their work, increased likelihood of effective practice, and, therefore, an elevated sense of well-being. It is validation of the supervisee and of shared, clinical service.

Clinical supervisors invite feedback from their supervisees. Evaluating their supervisions is a feature of providing effective clinical supervision. This is discussed elsewhere in this book. This discussion places emphasis on the practice of soliciting feedback from supervisees during supervision sessions so that both or all participants in supervision sessions will more likely meet their needs. In providing clinical services to clients, feedback informed therapy (FIT) has received strong validation through research. (Recent examples include van Hennik & Hillewaere, 2017; Winkeljohn Black et al., 2017; Tilsen & McNamee, 2015.) The strong validation of feedback informed therapy implies that clinical supervisors who practice feedback informed clinical supervision will likely see superior results. In short, if the evidence from feedback informed therapy may be translated into clinical supervision, clinical supervisors who pursue feedback informed supervision will add a significant tool in their work toward improving their services to supervisees and to clients who are treated by these supervisees.

Conclusion

Clinical supervisors encourage leadership and autonomy for supervisees. In contrast with subordinating supervisees to their will or to the clinical perspectives and practices of a supervisor, adaptable and developmentally oriented clinical supervisors will look for development in their supervisees and confirm it when they see it. With the aim of facilitating the growth of supervisees toward effective functioning as autonomous clinicians, clinical supervisors will nurture and support clinical leadership and autonomy. Based on their own leadership and autonomy, the effectiveness of clinical supervisors may be appropriately assessed through an examination of how well they manage the administrative tasks that inhere in clinical supervision.

SECTION IV

Creating a Philosophy of Clinical Supervision

16

HELPFUL PRACTICES TOWARD DEVELOPING A PHILOSOPHY OF CLINICAL SUPERVISION

Just as good therapy comes from a heightened understanding of the several processes of therapy, good supervision comes from a heightened understanding or the several processes of supervision. A useful, productive, and developmental future of clinical services depends on the acquisition and utilization of this understanding and of a supervisor's ability to articulate a well-developed philosophy of supervision that incorporates this understanding. Because of the importance of a philosophy of clinical supervision, this discussion offers assistance to those who may pursue the development of one.

Therefore, to assist you in developing your philosophy of clinical supervision, we would like to offer some suggestions. Recognizing that that there could be more than these, here are ten of them.

Share your supervision cases with other supervisors.
Write your philosophy of supervision.
Start a workbook.
Create a reflection tool.
Consult with other supervisors.
Review your experience as a supervisee.
Ask your supervisees and former supervisees.
Explore questions about yourself as a good supervisor.
Subscribe to and study supervision journals.
Study codes of ethics.

A longer list of suggestions could be offered. To no one's surprise, these suggestions express the view that growth as a supervisor involves self-examination, along with the belief that shared self-examination enhances the process of growth. Our hope is that they are useful for you.

Share Your Supervision Cases with Other Supervisors

The most important practice for developing a philosophy of clinical supervision and improving the practice of clinical supervision is active and regular consultation with other clinical supervisors. After all, clinical supervisors practice supervision on the basis of the belief that their supervision – consultation of one professional with another – offers valuable benefits for supervisees. Consultation among clinical supervisors, therefore, becomes a matter of "practicing what one preaches." Its value, though, transcends the need to comply with a belief. Instead of this, its value is that it provides specific and lasting benefits for clinical supervisors, their supervisees, and, moreover, the clients who receive treatment from supervisees. Specifically, when clinical supervision cases are shared among clinical supervisors for extended periods of time in ongoing and mutual examination of one another's supervision cases, the professional accountability among them helps to

- Improve clinical supervision skills;
- Enable supervisors to correct their mistakes;
- Utilize guidance for management of sensitive legal and ethical issues;
- Secure personal and professional support within an understanding and responsive community;
- Provide opportunities to help other clinical supervisors;
- Elevate clinical supervisors' confidence in providing services as a clinical supervisor;
- Offer a model of professional development for supervisees;
- Improve clinical services for clients; and
- Identify useful resources, such as referral agencies and counselors, books and articles, training events, and others.

The need for and the practice of supervisor-with-supervisors consultation has been discussed and advocated for almost three decades. Interested supervisors can readily locate useful resources, including Granello et al. (2008), Powell (1996), Benshoff and Paisley (1996), Borders (2012), Crutchfield and Borders (1997), Newman (2013), and Watkins (2012). In addition to these resources, groups of clinical supervisors will likely be able to invent their own development-enhancing approaches to their work.

Write Your Philosophy of Supervision

Because it is useful toward clarifying many activities and goals of supervision, having a clearly articulated philosophy of supervision is important. One way to achieve a clearly articulated philosophy is to write one. While this suggestion may appear to be a daunting thought, it may be better regarded as an ongoing process of development than a completed task. Just as supervisors expect their supervisees to demonstrate a commitment to growth, supervisors need to demonstrate this commitment, too. Writing a philosophy of supervision is one way to demonstrate this commitment.

To begin the process of clarifying your philosophy of supervision, you may want to write your responses to the questions raised earlier and repeated here.

How do I describe counseling/psychotherapy?
What do I believe about conducting mental health care?
What do I believe about clinical supervision?
What is the role of the supervisor?
What is the role of the supervisee?
How do I define the good clinical supervisor?
How do I conceptualize the good or excellent counselor/therapist?

To take increased advantage of what you write, you may want to encourage a colleague or two to write their responses to these questions. Then, you may want to compare your responses to theirs so that all of you may gain insight from one another and develop your skills with them.

Start a Workbook

Create your own workbook through which you develop your philosophy of clinical supervision. While many more questions could be raised, here are some of the questions that you may want to answer, as ways to focus your thinking about clinical supervision:

How do I define good clinical supervision?
What is my preferred role as a supervisor?
What resources – books, mentors, records of supervision, articles – do I or may I utilize to help me clarify my approach to clinical supervision?
What should I tell my supervisees about my approach to supervision?
How do I measure the effectiveness of my clinical supervision?
To which, if any, professional ethical issues am I vulnerable in my approach to supervision?
To which client problems am I drawn? To what degree does this lead to good clinical supervision or inhibit good clinical supervision?
To which client populations am I drawn? To what degree does this lead to good clinical supervision or inhibit good clinical supervision?
How do I handle clinical weakness in my supervisees?
How do I handle clinical strength in my supervisees?
How do I track progress in my supervisees?
How do I affirm progress in my supervisees?
How do I express clear and comprehensive evaluations of my supervisees?
In what ways may I try to ensure that my supervision provides a reasonably good match with my supervisee's needs?

Create – or Borrow – a Reflection Tool

A reflection tool is simply a way to engage a clinical supervisor(s) in a process of reviewing and assessing their work as supervisors. It is somewhat more influential toward positive change when it is processed with other clinical supervisors. Here is one that you may adopt and alter in any way that you wish:

Chart 16–1 A Reflection Tool

Question	Disagree Agree
I enjoy delivering clinical supervision.	1 2 3 4 5
I have a clearly articulated approach to counseling/therapy.	1 2 3 4 5
I utilize an informed consent form with supervisees.	1 2 3 4 5
I consult with others about my supervisions.	1 2 3 4 5
I have grown as a clinical supervisor.	1 2 3 4 5
I have a clearly articulated philosophy of supervision.	1 2 3 4 5
I have recently reviewed the ethics of supervision.	1 2 3 4 5
I have written my philosophy of supervision.	1 2 3 4 5
I have plans for my professional development.	1 2 3 4 5
I have clearly defined good clinical supervision.	1 2 3 4 5
I help supervisees to understand the goals of supervision.	1 2 3 4 5
I bring sufficient clinical experience to supervising.	1 2 3 4 5
I utilize research in my supervision.	1 2 3 4 5
I maintain appropriate boundaries in supervision.	1 2 3 4 5
I advance the counseling profession through supervision.	1 2 3 4 5
I respect the power differential in supervision.	1 2 3 4 5
I demonstrate clinical skill in supervision.	1 2 3 4 5
I engage my supervisees in positive struggles.	1 2 3 4 5
I raise questions about ethics and law with supervisees.	1 2 3 4 5
I have a well-developed plan for supervision emergencies.	1 2 3 4 5

The value of a reflection tool is that it assists supervisors in their ongoing reflection on their work as supervisors. After you complete the ratings, you may want to consider adding features of your supervision that are not represented in the list. Also, if you complete the reflection tool, you may want to invite a colleague to complete it, too, and discuss your results with your colleague.

Consult with Other Supervisors

Experienced counselors and supervisors understand that much of what they do is necessarily done in a cone of privacy. Because of this, supervisors often find themselves in the position of "having to view the picture from the frame." They are close enough to the experience of supervision that they know the limits of their objectivity and self-evaluation. Usually, they conduct supervision alone, as the only supervisor in the room. Understandably, they may need others to help them to view their work as supervisors.

In contrast with the recommendation with which this chapter began, "Share your supervision cases with other supervisors," the emphasis on consultation here is that practicing clinical supervisors make themselves available for one another, assuming that each one of them will inevitably encounter sensitive and difficult supervision-related issues. Each one needs other supervisors as sources of support and assistance in the process of effectively managing her or his work as a clinical supervisor and refining skills and insights. As supervisors and prospective supervisors contemplate this need, they may want to think in terms of becoming a mentor and/or a mentee with at least one other clinical supervisor.

Each consultative relationship should set its own way of working and its own goals. We recommend, though, that the consultation give attention to self-identified needs for support, assistance, and professional development. The expression of these needs may be seen in questions such as "I need to figure out what is happening with a particular supervisee, because there is a disconnect in our relationship. May we talk about this?" or "When I offer feedback, I can sometimes see fear in the eyes of those who hear it. I'm very good at creating safety for my supervisees, but something is happening here. What is it?" or "I find myself being overly reactive to a supervisee. Would you help me with this?"

Review Your Experience as a Supervisee

Take time to review your experience as a supervisee. This may take a while – especially, if you need to locate attendance records and evaluations that you received – but it may be a valuable process through which you clarify your philosophy of clinical supervision, insofar as first experiences with clinical supervision are almost always powerful ones.

Here are some suggestions about how to proceed. Beginning with your first clinical supervisor, write comments in response to the following items:

The name of the supervisor
The manner in which the supervisor provided clinical supervision
What made clinical supervision with this person memorable?
How did your work with this person change or challenge your self-perception as a counselor?
What are the positive and negative things you remember from this supervision experience?

Carefully study these questions before you record your responses to them. Then, take time to consider each one and begin a process of synthesis. How does your past experience inform the present manner in which you offer clinical supervision? Have you created your own "style" of supervision, or are you "mirroring" a past experience that you found "comfortable"? How much is your current supervision challenged by your experience as a supervisee? How much of your current supervision is a fulfilment of the supervision that you received? What are the really good and useful things that you learned from those who supervised you? What aspects of your work as a supervisee did you find unhelpful and of little use to you as a counselor and now as a supervisor? Are you "re-treading" these same issues with your supervisees?

After taking the time to review former clinical supervision and comparing the past with your present supervision style, ask the question, "Am I doing the same things in supervision now that I received back then?" and "Am I mostly repeating my supervisee experience?" Clinical supervisors, like everyone else, get "stuck" in the familiar and that which is "easy." Have you taken the style of supervision that your clinical supervisor(s) used with you because it is comfortable for you? Do you seriously reflect on the manner in which you deliver clinical supervision? Are your actions with supervisees continually "acting" in thoughtful ways based in the present, or are you "reacting" to your past supervision with your current supervisees?

Following your review of your understanding of how the past has influenced your present manner of supervision, give attention to those areas of growth that may need to be addressed. It is my hope you will have discovered places for possible growth as a clinical supervisor. What is your plan of action for addressing your identified areas of growth as a supervisor? If you discovered parts of your present supervision style that are "baggage" from past supervision, what may you do to relieve your burden? How do you plan to refresh your skills, attitudes, and supervisory relationships? As you see positive change in your supervisees, can you describe the "gifts" from the supervisors who supervised you that may be an affirmation of them and you? Are these "gifts" that you may pass to others? Are these "gifts" that you may continue to improve?

Another way to reflect on your experience as a supervisee and the influence of the experience on your current supervision is to list the resources that you consult or to which you usually refer. For many who do this, the list may be as good as it is bad, because observations about the list are likely to be both affirming and challenging. For example, consider asking, "When did I last read or locate research about a clinical supervision challenge?" or "What are the dates of the books to which I usually refer when I need information about clinical supervision?" In other words, reflecting on your experience as a supervisee and the resources to which you refer may indicate that you need to develop plans for updating and refreshing your views about clinical supervision. If you find that your resources are dated, you will likely find that your philosophy of clinical supervision is dated, too. If you suspect that your views of clinical supervision are dated, you may want to pursue the challenge of re-conceptualizing and refreshing your views. Just as clients and supervisees gain from new information, supervisors usually gain from new information and insights about supervision. New information and insights have ways of challenging an old philosophy and prompting new ways to conceptualize a fresh philosophy.

Ask Your Supervisees and Former Supervisees

Clinical supervisors should always be open to and seeking to solicit feedback from supervisees. Do those whom we supervise find meaning, worth, and clinical assistance from what we offer? Could it be that supervisees are merely "sitting" through the process with us because they must? If someone that we supervise is not finding growth from our work with them, is it a reflection of faulty conclusions from our philosophy of clinical supervision?

There are ways to guard against the possibility of ineffectual or stale supervision. One of these is that, at various points in time during the supervision process, you can make yourself vulnerable to your supervisees and ask for their feedback. Here are some questions for your consideration: Is the process of supervision useful to you? In what ways am I being helpful to you as a clinical supervisor? What, if anything, have I missed that you find important but are uncomfortable addressing with me? Are your clients being helped because of the work that we are doing together? What would you like for us to do differently? Do you have goals for supervision that we need to discuss, especially ones that emerged recently?

The value of a philosophy of clinical supervision is seen in its translation into the practice of clinical supervision. Surely, those whom we supervise may be in the best position to help us understand how our philosophy translates into positive help and practice.

Explore Questions About Yourself as a Good Supervisor

If prospective clinical supervisors take each of the statements in Chapter 9 about good supervisors and convert them into questions for self-examination, they may establish major parts of their foundational views of themselves as clinical supervisors as they answer each question. If you are a prospective clinical supervisor, please consider the following questions, adapted from the list of statements in Chapter 9.

- Do I genuinely like providing clinical services to clients?
- What is my level of confidence in believing that I understand good therapy, because I have practiced good therapy?
- How well do I understand and affirm the power differential between my supervisees and me?
- Do I unambiguously support my supervisees in forming clear goals for their supervision so that they gain self-awareness and skill in progress toward being effective practitioners?
- Am I quite willing to demonstrate my clinical skills for my supervisees?
- How well do I understand the real world where human lives are seriously impacted by their supervision, instead of contemplating my supervisory role from a primarily administrative and/or academic point of view?
- Do I ask good questions for those whom I supervise and help them to experience the worth of the struggle to serve clients in a positive fashion?
- Do I help my supervisees to discover that therapy is more a way of being than a way of doing?
- Do I empower my supervisees to confidently conduct clinical work by confronting their inadequacies but, moreover, by affirming their struggle to succeed and their consequent successes?

Do I stay alert to opportunities for helping my supervisees to improve their clinical judgment?

How do I demonstrate respect for the necessary boundaries between clinical supervision and my supervisee's possible need for personal therapy?

How clear am I in my understanding of my responses to clinical situations as responses that are likely some among many clinically appropriate ways of responding?

Do I seek to nurture professional identity in my supervisees?

How clearly do I practice supervision with the knowledge that clients' needs take precedence over my needs and my supervisees' needs?

Do I remain cognizant of my obligation to advancing the profession of which my supervisees and I are members?

How well do I understand that supervision is a process, not an event or a technique?

Do I help my supervisees to pursue their quest for meaning, satisfaction, and personal fulfillment as mental health care providers?

Do I find meaning, satisfaction, and personal fulfillment in providing clinical supervision for my supervisees?

How well can I define the clinical skills that my supervisees need to develop?

How clearly and strongly am I committed to spontaneity, experimentation, inventiveness, and other existential necessities, knowing that my supervision and my supervisees' clinical work should be disciplined and well informed?

How do I hold my supervisees accountable for their professional growth toward becoming effective mental health care providers?

How do I hold myself accountable for my professional growth toward becoming an effective clinical supervisor?

Do I know that my conjoint and occasional incapacity to help clients provides opportunities for growth for me and my supervisees?

Do I place sufficient emphasis on showing that a professional working alliance with supervisees is necessary and mutual?

How well do I increase my supervisees' awareness of transference and counter-transference issues in therapy, but also in supervision?

What are my plans for my own professional development?

Do I demonstrate appropriate cognizance of the potential threats that sometimes attend growth toward healthy and effective therapeutic functioning by my supervisees? (These threats may be within the individual supervisees, imposed by the agency or institution in which they work, constraints from insurance companies or other corporations, legislative initiatives or laws that alter professional functioning, and more.)

How comfortable am I with confronting my supervisees – along with the consequent stress – recognizing that confrontation is necessary in the conduct of clinical supervision?

How comfortable am I with showing tenderness and support with my supervisees, knowing that they may be distressed by their work?

In what specific ways do I demonstrate appreciation for empirical research in counseling and psychotherapy and self-consciously integrate research findings into the process of supervision?

Subscribe to and Study Supervision Journals

Journals that seek to advance the cause of effective clinical supervision may be placed into two categories. One category includes journals that give almost exclusive attention to research about, training in, and the practice of clinical supervision. These journals include the following.

Counselor Education and Supervision

According to the website of the Association for Counselor Education and Supervision (2017),

> *Counselor Education and Supervision* (CES) is the official publication of the Association for Counselor Education and Supervision (ACES), a division of the American Counseling Association. CES is dedicated to publishing manuscripts with original research, theory development, or program applications related to counselor education and supervision. The focus is on the preparation and supervision of counselors in agency or school settings, in colleges and universities or at local, state, or federal levels.
> (CE&S Journal section, para. 1)

The Clinical Supervisor

According to the journal's website (*The Clinical Supervisor*, 2017),

> *The Clinical Supervisor* is the premier journal in the United States devoted exclusively to the art and science of clinical supervision. An interdisciplinary, refereed publication of the highest standards, the journal communicates the ideas, experiences, skills, techniques, concerns, and needs of supervisors in psychotherapy and mental health. You will find what you need to know about supervision to effectively supervise students and trainees.
> (Journal description section, para. 1)

The Journal of Counselor Preparation and Supervision

According to the website of the North Atlantic Region Association of Counselor Education and Supervision (NARACES),

> *The Journal of Counselor Preparation and Supervision* is a service of the North Atlantic Regional Association for Counselors and Supervisors. The mission of the *Journal of Counselor Preparation and Supervision* is

> to provide a high quality platform for research, theory and practices of counselor educators, counselor supervisors and professional counselors. We believe the journal chronicles current issues, concerns and potential solutions that enable counselors to continue to grow and develop as practitioners, educators and human beings. The journal publishes high-quality articles that have undergone a thorough and extensive blind peer-review.
>
> (2019, Journal website, para. 1)

The other category includes journals that collectively offer numerous articles that address multiple aspects of clinical supervision. Their offerings of articles on clinical supervision come irregularly, mainly because these journals attempt to respond to a broad range of professional needs. The following list could easily expand to a much longer list. This one, though, may be a good list with which to begin.

- *American Journal of Psychotherapy*
- *Professional Psychology: Research and Practice*
- *Psychotherapy: Theory, Research, Practice, and Training*
- *The Counseling Psychologist*
- *Journal of Clinical Psychology*
- *Journal of Counseling and Development*
- *Journal of Counseling Psychology*
- *Journal of Mental Health Counseling*
- *The Professional Counselor*

Study Codes of Ethics

Given the very familiar emphasis on professional ethics, the idea of studying codes of ethics may appear to be an invitation to the tedium of redundancy. However, this invitation is something else. Insofar as this may appear to be an invitation to study codes of ethics with which readers are already familiar, the predictable response is likely low or no interest. Instead of studying, again, the most commonly known codes of ethics, such as those from the American Counseling Association (ACA), the American Psychological Association (APA), and the National Association of Social Workers (NASW), clinical supervisors may want to examine some others. The rationale for this is clear. Because most counselors and psychotherapists are expected to comply with more than one code of ethics and because they often work with others whose codes of ethics are different, studying several codes of ethics will likely improve the provision of clinical supervision. To augment this point, because virtually all professional certifications come with their respective code of ethics, the clinical supervisor may need to become familiar with several such codes.

If clinical supervisors or their supervisees hold one of these certifications or aspire to hold one of these certifications, they must know and comply with the standards in the code. A list of professional certifications appears in Chapter 1. The location of each code is provided in Chapter 1, although it may be easily located through an Internet search.

For another thing, some clinical supervisors and their supervisees hold membership in other associations or have certifications by agencies that have their own code of ethics. Among the many associations in which they may have membership, in addition to ACA, APA, and NASW, supervisors and their supervisees may hold membership in one or more of the following associations, each one of which comes with its code of ethics.

American Art Therapy Association (AATA, 2013)
American Association of Christian Counselors (AACC, 2014)
American Association of Marriage and Family Therapists (AAMFT, 2015)
American Association of Pastoral Counselors (AAPC, 2012)
American Association of Sex Educators, Counselors, and Therapists (AASECT, 2014)
American Counseling Association (ACA, 2014)
American Group Psychotherapy Association (AGPA, 2002)
American Mental Health Counselors Association (AMHCA, 2015)
American Psychological Association (APA, 2014)
American School Counselor Association (ASCA, 2016)
Association for Addiction Professionals (AAP, 2016)
International Expressive Arts Therapy Association (IEATA, n.d.)
National Association of Social Workers (NASW, 2017)
National Career Development Association (NCDA, 2015)
United States Association for Body Psychotherapy (USABP, 2007)

All of these professional associations, along with others, expect their members to comply with their respective codes of ethics. Note should be taken of the fact that neither of these lists is intended to be an exhaustive or thorough one. Instead, they are illustrative of the complicated and complex world of clinical supervision and the unusual and extraordinary demands that inhere in this world.

Conclusion

None of these activities will ensure that an individual will become an effective clinical supervisor. Surely, any or all of these activities can help, though. No matter what the professional development activity is, the supervisor's readiness to grow determines whether she or he will become an effective clinical supervisor. Just as clinicians understand that growth in their clients involves risks, growth as a clinical supervisor involves risks, too. The supervisor's readiness to grow includes an openness to receiving feedback, the pursuit of understanding of what clinical supervision is and what it may best become, a willingness to share mutual improvement with other supervisors, a capacity to adapt to new awareness and new understanding, and an enjoyment of providing clinical services. The life of an effective clinical supervisor is one that should be truly and authentically lived, not merely studied, and not be merely one that manages the oversight of other clinicians. Pursued well, the activities described in this chapter require growth. Growth involves risk. And, pursued well, risk has its rewards.

17

PUTTING IT ALL TOGETHER

By now, you have likely identified several components of your philosophy of clinical supervision. The following material serves only to create a list of possible content areas that you may wish to include in your philosophy. You may want to consider the items as a checklist against which you can compare your own. At the end of your attempt(s) to "put it all together," you will likely conclude that having it all together means that you have established a baseline of ideas and practices that aim you toward more questions to answer. This is the nature of growth; it almost never stops, despite our sometimes considerable, large steps toward getting it all together. It is the "getting it all together" that characterizes growth, not the "having it all together."

In the form of questions that you may answer, a philosophy of clinical supervision includes the following parts:

What is clinical supervision?
What is a philosophy of clinical supervision?
What is counseling/psychotherapy?
What do I believe about conducting mental health care?
How do I think about mental and emotional disturbance?
What is my definition of clinical supervision?
What do I believe about clinical supervision?
What is the role of the supervisor?
What is the role of the supervisee?
How do I define the good clinical supervisor?
How do I conceptualize the good or excellent counselor/therapist?
Why is my philosophy of clinical supervision a necessary feature of my supervision?
Is a philosophy of clinical supervision necessary? Why or why not?
What are the qualities of an effective mental health care provider?
What do I want to achieve through clinical supervision?
What are my personal assets that contribute to effective clinical supervision?
What are my professional assets that contribute to effective clinical supervision?
With which primary model of clinical supervision do I most closely identify?

What kind of relationship do I want to develop with supervisees?
What are the ethically sensitive issues that I am likely to encounter in conducting clinical supervision?
What is informed consent in supervision and why would I want to include it?
What do my supervisees need to know about me?
What do I need to ensure that my supervisees know about the process and procedures of clinical supervision?
What records and reports do I need from my supervisees?
What should I include in a supervision contract?
What records about my supervisees should I keep?
What records should I expect my supervisees to keep?
How will crises be handled?
What specific goals should I expect my supervisees to pursue?
How do I describe what happens when I meet with my supervisees?
How will I evaluate my supervisees?
How will I handle diversity issues?
How will I ensure that I continue to develop my supervision competencies?

If you answer all of these questions in a conscientious, professional manner, you will have worked hard to produce a large set of documents. Obviously, the creation of a large volume of material is not the goal. When you have produced a large set of documents, you will have made a substantial claim for your professionalism as a clinical supervisor. Moreover, you will have established a useful wall of protection against anyone who may have doubts about your competence and your commitment to the best welfare of the clients whom your supervisees seek to help and to the development of your supervisees toward increased competence. These are outcomes that are worthy of your efforts. In addition, you will have made a positive statement about clinical supervision and the profession that clinical supervision represents.

As we bring this book to a close, we hope that its potential contributions for you will remain open. The guiding principle for us has been framed by the question, "How may we make clinical supervision better than it is?" Whether we have done this for you is your call, not ours. Nevertheless, with this book, we invite you to consider this question as a guiding principle for your clinical supervision. How may you be a better clinical supervisor than you are? And, together, how may we make our profession better than it is?

The best to you as you pursue the development of your approach to clinical supervision.

REFERENCES

Aasheim, L. (2012). *Practical clinical supervision for counselors: An experiential guide*. New York, NY: Springer Publishing.

Ablon, J. S., & Jones, E. E. (1998). How expert clinicians' prototypes of an ideal treatment correlate with outcomes in psychodynamic and cognitive-behavioral therapy. *Psychotherapy Research, 8*, 71–83. http://dx.doi.org/10.1093/ptr/8.1.71

Alabama Board of Examiners in Counseling. (n.d.). *Educational requirement for licensure*. Retrieved from www.abec.state.al.us/PDFs/Education/EducationalRequirement.pdf

Albert Ellis Institute. (2018). Retrieved from https://albertellis.org/professional-rebt-cbt/trainings/

Alonso, A. (1985). *The quiet profession: Supervisors of psychotherapy*. New York, NY: Macmillan.

American Art Therapy Association (AATA). (2013, December). *Ethical principles for art therapists*. Retrieved from https://arttherapy.org/wp-content/uploads/2017/06/Ethical-Principles-for-Art-Therapists.pdf

American Association for Marriage and Family Therapists (AAMFT). (2015). *AAMFT code of ethics*. Retrieved from www.aamft.org/Legal_Ethics/Code_of_Ethics.aspx

American Association for Marriage and Family Therapists (AAMFT). (2019). *Responsibilities and guidelines for AAMFT approved supervisors and supervisor candidates*. Retrieved from www.aamft.org/AAMFT/supervision/Responsibilities.aspx

American Association for Marriage and Family Therapists (AAMFT). (2019a). *Approved supervisor designation*. Retrieved from www.aamft.org/supervision /supervision.aspx

American Association of Christian Counselors (AACC). (2014). *AACC code of ethics*. Retrieved from http://aacc.net/files/AACC%20Code%20of%20Ethics%20%20Master%20Document.pdf

American Association of Pastoral Counselors (AAPC). (2012, April). *AAPC code of ethics*. Retrieved from www.aapc.org/Default.aspx?ssid=74&NavPTypeId=116American

American Association of Sexuality Educators, Counselors, and Therapists (AASECT). (2014). *Code of ethics & conduct for AASECT certified members*. Retrieved from www.aasect.org/sites/default/files/documents/Code%20of%20Ethics%20and%20Conduct_0.pdf

American Counseling Association. (2014). *ACA code of ethics*. Retrieved from www.counseling.org/resources/aca-code-of-ethics.pdf

American Counseling Association. (2018, December). ACA FY 2018 membership statistics. *Counseling Today, 61*(6), 74. Retrieved from www.counseling.org/docs/default source/counselingtodayarchives/ct_december.pdf?sfvrsn=8790542c_0

American Group Psychotherapy Association. (2002, February). *AGPA and IBCGP guidelines for ethics*. Retrieved from www.agpa.org/home/practice-resources/ethics-in-group-therapy

American Mental Health Counselors Association. (2015). *AMHCA code of ethics*. Retrieved from www.amhca.org/?page=codeofethics

American Psychiatric Association. (2013). *Diagnostic and statistical manual of mental disorders* (5th ed.). Washington, DC: Author.

American Psychological Association. (2014). *APA guidelines for clinical supervision in health service psychology*. Retrieved from http://apa.org/about/policy/guidelines-supervision.pdf

American Psychological Association. (2017). *Ethical principles of psychologists and code of conduct*. Retrieved from www.apa.org/ethics/code/ethics-code-2017.pdf

American Psychological Association. (2018). *Office of program consultation and accreditation*. Retrieved from http://apps.apa.org/accredsearch/?_ga=1.141650421.632455831.1413840772

American School Counselor Association (ASCA). (2016). *ASCA ethical standards for school counselors*. Retrieved from www.schoolcounselor.org/asca/media/asca/Ethics/EthicalStandards2016.pdf

Association for Counselor Education and Supervision. (2011). *Best practices in clinical supervision – 2011*. Retrieved from https://acesonline.net/wp-content/uploads/2018/11/ACES-Best-Practices-in-Clinical-Supervision-2011.pdf

Association for Counselor Education and Supervision. (2017). *Counselor Education and Supervision Journal*. Retrieved from: https://onlinelibrary.wiley.com/page/journal/15566978/homepage/productinformation/html

Association for Play Therapy. (n.d.a). *Registered Play Therapist*. Retrieved from www.a4pt.org/page/CredentialsInfo

Association for Play Therapy. (2015). *School Based Registered Play Therapist*. Retrieved from www.a4pt.org/ page/CredentialsInfo

Association for Play Therapy (APT). (2016). *Play therapy best practices: Clinical, professional & ethical issues*. Retrieved from https://c.ymcdn.com/sites/www.a4pt.org/resource/resmgr/publications/Best_Practices_Sept_2016.pdf?hhSearchTerms=%22code+and+ethics%22

Association of Certified Biblical Counselors. (2017). *Statement of Policy Regarding Gender, Sexuality, and Counseling from the ACBC Board*. Retrieved from https://biblicalcounseling.com/statement-of-policy-regarding-gender-sexuality-and-counseling-from-the-acbc-board/

Auger, R. W. (2004). What we don't know CAN hurt us: Mental health counselors' implicit assumptions about human nature. *Journal of Mental Health Counseling*, *26*(1), 13–24. https://doi.org/10.17744/mehc.26.1.q2r31fh0na9efbv0

Australian Institute of Professional Counsellors. (2011, April 11). *Theories and models of supervision*. Retrieved from www.aipc.net.au/articles/theories-and-models-of-supervision/

Barker, K. K., & Hunsley, J. (2013). The use of theoretical models in psychology supervisor development research from 1994 to 2010: A systematic review. *Canadian Psychology*, *54*(3), 176–185.

Benshoff, J. M., & Paisley, P. O. (1996, January–February). The structured peer consultation model for school counselors. *Journal of Counseling and Development*, *74*(3), 314–318. https://doi.org/10.1002/j.15566676.1996.tb01872.x

Bernard, J. M., & Goodyear, R. K. (2004). *Fundamentals of clinical supervision* (3rd ed.). Boston, MA: Allyn and Bacon.

Bernard, J. M., & Goodyear, R. K. (2009). *Fundamentals of clinical supervision* (4th ed.). Upper Saddle River, NJ: Pearson Education.

Blatt, S. J., Sanislow, C. A., Zuroff, D. C., & Pilkonis, P. A. (1996). Characteristics of effective therapists: Further analyses of data from the national institute of mental health treatment of depression collaborative research program. *Journal of Consulting and Clinical Psychology, 64*(6), 1276–1284.

Blount, A. J., Taylor, D. D., Lambie, G. W., & Anwell, A. N. (2016). Clinical supervisors' perceptions of wellness: A phenomenological view on supervisee wellness. *The Professional Counselor, 6*(4), 360–374.

Bolton, G. (2010). *Reflective practice: Writing and professional development* (3rd ed.). Los Angeles, CA: Sage Publications.

Borders, L. D. (1994). *The good supervisor*. Retrieved from www.counseling.org/resources/library/eric%20digests/94-18.pdf

Borders, L. D. (2012, July). Dyadic, triadic, and group models of peer supervision/consultation: What are their components, and is there evidence of their effectiveness? *Clinical Psychologist, 16*(2), 59–71. https://doi.org/10.1111/j.1742-9552.2012.00046.x

Borkin, S. (2014). *The healing power of writing: A therapist's guide to using journaling with clients*. New York, NY: W. W. Norton & Company.

Boswell, J. F., & Constantino, M. J. (2015). Clinicians self-judgement of effectiveness. *Psychotherapy Bulletin, 50*(4), 15–19.

Bratton, S. C., Landreth, G. L., Kellam, T., & Blackard, S. R. (2006). *Child parent relationship therapy (CPRT) treatment manual: A 10-session filial therapy model for training parents*. New York, NY: Routledge and Taylor & Francis Group.

Brown, H. (2013, March 25). *Looking for evidence that therapy works*. Retrieved from http://well.blogs.nytimes.com/2013/03/25/looking-for-evidence-that-therapy-works/?r=

Bureau of Labor Statistics. (2019). Retrieved from www.bls.gov/careeroutlook/2018/article/social-workers.htm

Calvert, F. L., Crowe, T. P., & Grenyer, B. F. S. (2016). Dialogical reflexivity in supervision: An experiential learning process for enhancing reflective and relational competencies. *The Clinical Supervisor, 35*(1), 1–21.

Campbell, J. M. (2000). *Becoming an effective supervisor: A workbook for counselors and psychotherapists*. Philadelphia, PA: Accelerated Development.

Campbell, J. M. (2006). *Essentials of clinical supervision*. Hoboken, NJ: John Wiley and Sons.

Center for Credentialing and Education. (2016). *Approved clinical supervisor code of ethics*. Retrieved from www.cce-global.org/Assets/Ethics/ACScodeofethics.pdf

Center for Credentialing and Education. (2019). *ACS Approved Clinical Supervisor*. Retrieved from www.cce-global.org/Credentialing/ACS

Center for Substance Abuse Treatment. (2007). *Competencies for substance abuse treatment clinical supervisors*. Technical Assistance Publication (TAP) Series 21 A (Rep. No. HHS Publication No. (SMA) 074243). Rockville, MD: Substance Abuse and Mental Health Services Administration.

Center for Substance Abuse Treatment. (2009). *Clinical supervision and professional development of the substance abuse counselor*. Treatment Improvement Protocol (TIP) Series 52. HHS Publication No. (SMA) 14-4435. Rockville, MD: Substance Abuse and Mental Health Services Administration.

Certification Board for Music Therapists (CBMT). (2011, October 4). *CBMT code of professional practice*. Retrieved from www.cbmt.org/about-certification/code-of-professional-practice/

Church of the Nazarene manual: Manual 2017–2021. (2017). Kansas City, MO: Nazarene Publishing House.

Cimino, A. N., Rorke, J., & Adams, H. L. (2013). Supervisors behaving badly: Witnessing ethical dilemmas and what to do about it. *Journal of Social Work Values and Ethics, 10*(2), 48–57.

Cliffe, T., Beinart, H., & Cooper, M. (2016, January–February). Development and validation of a short version of the supervisory relationship questionnaire. *Journal of Clinical Psychology and Psychotherapy, 23*(1), 77–86.

Clinical Supervision Resources. (2017). *Reflective supervision: Some guiding questions*. Retrieved from www.clinicalsupervisionservices.com.au/client_images/1779598.pdf

The Clinical Supervisor. (2017). *Aims and Scope*. Retrieved from www.tandfonline.com/action/journalInformation?show=aimsScope&journalCode=wcsu20

Cloninger, C. R. (2013). What makes people healthy, happy, and fulfilled in the face of current world challenges? *Mens Sana Monographs, 11*(1), 16–24.

Commission on Rehabilitation Counselor Certification (CRCC). (2009, April). *Code of professional ethics for vocational evaluation specialist, work adjustment specialist, and career assessment associates*. Retrieved from www.crccertification.com/filebin/pdf/VE/VECodeofEthics.pdf

Commission on Rehabilitation Counselor Certification (CRCC). (2017, January 1). *Code of professional ethics for rehabilitation counselors*. Retrieved from www.crccertification.com/code-of-ethics-4

Conway, K. (2018). *Kim Conway—Psychology Today*. Retrieved from www.psychologytoday.com/us/therapists/kim-conway-andover-ma/303227

Cooper, L. D., & Wieckowski, A. T. (2017). A structured approach to reflective practice training in a clinical practicum. *Training and Education in Professional Psychology, 11*(4), 252–259.

Cottone, R. R. (2001). A social constructivism model of ethical decision making in counseling. *Journal of Counseling & Development, 79*, 39–45. doi: 10.1002/j.15566676.2001.tb01941.x

Council for the Accreditation of Counseling Related Educational Programs. (2019). Retrieved from www.cacrep.org/directory/page/6/?state=TN&pt_id&pc_logic=any&accr_status%5B0%5D=A&accr_status%5B1%5D=PA&accr_status%5B2%5D=IP&keywords&submitthis

Crall, J. (2011). *Ethical behavior of supervisors: Effects on supervisee experiences and behavior*. Theses and Dissertations. Lehigh University. Retrieved from https://preserve.lehigh.edu/cgi/viewcontent.cgi?article=2182&context=etd

Crutchfield, L. B., & Borders, L. D. (1997). Impact of two clinical peer supervision models on practicing school counselors. *Journal of Counseling & Development, 75*(3), 219–230.

Curtis, D. F., Duran, P., Elkins, S. R., & Venta, A. C. (2016). Promoting a climate of reflective practice and clinician self-efficacy in vertical supervision. *Training and Education in Professional Psychology, 10*(3), 133–140.

Dass, R. (2011), as quoted by Edelstein, L. N., & Woehler, C. A. (2011). *What do I say: A therapist's guide to answering client questions*. Hoboken, NY: John Wiley & Sons.

Dawes, R. M. (1989). Experience and validity of clinical judgment: The illusory correlation. *Behavioral Sciences & the Law, 7*, 457–467.

Dawes, R. M. (1994). *House of cards*. New York, NY: The Free Press.

Diamond, S. A. (1996). *Anger, madness, and the daimonic: The psychological genesis of violence, evil, and creativity*. Albany, NY: SUNY Press.

Eells, T. D. (1999). What do we know about master therapists? *Journal of Psychotherapy Practice Research*, *8*, 414–317.

Epstein, R. M., & Hundert, E. M. (2002, January). Defining and assessing professional competence. *Journal of the American Medical Association*, *287*(2), 226–235.

Falender, C. A., Shafranske, E. P., & Ofek, A. (2014). Competent clinical supervision: Emerging effective practices. *Counselling Psychology Quarterly*, *27*(4), 393–408.

Faust, D., & Ziskin, J. (1988). Psychologists and psychiatrists as expert witnesses. *Science*, *241*(4870), 1143–1144.

Frick, M. H., & Glosoff, H. L. (2018). Becoming a supervisor: Qualitative findings on self-efficacy beliefs of doctoral student supervisors-in-training. *The Professional Counselor*. Retrieved from http://tpcjournal.nbcc.org/becoming-a-supervisor-qualitative-findings-on-self-efficacy-beliefs-of-doctoral-student-supervisors-in-training/

Gallon, S., Hausotter, W., & Bryan, M. (2005). What happens in good supervision. *Addiction Messenger*, *8*(9). Portland, OR: Northwest Frontier ATTC.

Garb, H. N. (1998). *Studying the clinician: Judgment research and psychological assessment*. Washington, DC: American Psychological Association.

Garb, H. N., & Boyle, P. A. (2003). Understanding why some clinicians use pseudoscientific methods: Findings from research on clinical judgment. In S. O. Lilienfeld, S. J. Lynn, & J. M. Lohr (Eds.), *Science and pseudoscience in clinical psychology* (pp. 17–38). New York, NY, US: Guilford Press.

Garcia, J. G., Cartwright, B., Winston, S. M., & Borzuchowska, B. (2003). A transcultural integrative model for ethical decision making in counseling. *Journal of Counseling & Development*, *81*, 208–277.

Genuchi, M. C., Rings, J. A., Germek, M. D., & Cornish, J. A. E. (2015, February). Clinical supervisors' perceptions of the clarify and comprehensiveness of the supervision competencies framework. *Training and Education in Professional Psychology*, *9*(1), 68–76.

Goldberg, S. B., Miller, S. D., Nielsen, S. L., Rousmaniere, T., Whipple, J., Hoyt, W. T., & Wampold, B. E. (2016). Do psychotherapists improve with time and experience? A longitudinal analysis of outcomes in a clinical setting. *Journal of Counseling Psychology*, *63*(1), 1–11.

Goldfried, M. R., Raue, P. J., & Castonguay, L. G. (1998). The therapeutic focus in significant sessions of master therapists: A comparison of cognitive-behavioral and psychodynamic-interpersonal interventions. *Journal of Consulting and Clinical Psychology*, 66, 803–810.

Goodyear, R., Lichenberg, J. W., Bang, K., & Gragg, J. B. (2015). Ten changes psychotherapists typically make as they mature into the role of supervisor. *Journal of Clinical Psychology*, *70*(11), 1042–1050.

Gosselin, J., Barker, K. K., Kogan, C. S., & Pomerleau, M. (2015). Setting the stage for an evidence-based model of psychotherapy supervisor development in clinical psychology. *Canadian Psychology*, *56*(4), 379–393.

Granello, D. H., Kindsvatter, A., Granello, P. F., Underfer-Babalis, J., & Moorhead, H. J. H. (2008). Multiple perspectives in supervision: Using a peer consultation model to enhance supervisor development. *Counselor Education and Supervision*, *48*(1), 32–47.

Haderlie, M. M. (2011). *Enhancing therapists' clinical judgments of client progress subsequent to objective feedback*. Unpublished dissertation. University of Nevada, Las Vegas. Retrieved from http://digitalscholarship.unlv.edu/cgi/viewcontent.cgi?article=2225&context=thesesdissertations

Harding, T. P. (2007). Clinical decision-making: How prepared are we? *Training and Education in Professional Psychology, 1*, 95–104.

Harner, M. (2018). *The Foundation for Shamanic Studies*. Retrieved from https://shamanism.org/workshops/index.php?gclid=EAIaIQobChMIt6iPzt7S2AIV3rXACh03TAa1EAAYASAAEgLTdfD_BwE

Harrist, S., & Richardson, F. C. (2012, April). Disguised ideologies in counseling and social justice work. *Counseling and Values, 57*, 38–44.

Heisler, E. J. (2017). *The mental health workforce: A primer*. Congressional Record Service. p. 1. Retrieved from https://fas.org/sgp/crs/misc/R43255.pdf

Hightower, E. (1988). Four illustrations of healthy personality: A prescription for living the good life. *Journal of Clinical Psychology, 44*(4), 527–535.

Hill, C. E., Baumann, E., Sjafran, N., Gupta, S., Morrison, A., Rojas, A. E., . . . Gelso, C. J. (2015). Is training effective? A study of counseling psychology doctoral trainees in a psychodynamic/interpersonal training clinic. *Journal of Counseling Psychology, 62*(2), 184–201.

Hill, H. R. M., Crowe, T. P., & Gonsalvez, C. J. (2016). Reflective dialogue in clinical supervision: A pilot study involving collaborative review of supervision videos. *Psychotherapy Research, 26*, 263–278.

Hillman, J. (2017). *James Hillman Quotes-BrainyQuotes*. Retrieved from www.brainyquote.com/quotes/james_hillman_280924

Hindes, Y. L., & Andrews, J. J. W. (2011). Influence of gender on the supervisory relationship: A review of the empirical research from 1996 to 2010. *Canadian Journal of Counselling and Psychotherapy, 45*(3), 240–261.

Holden, G., & Barker, K. (2018). Should social workers be engaged in these practices? *Journal of Evidence-Informed Social Work, 15*(1), 1–13.

How to Become a Licensed Psychologist in Alabama. (n.d.). *Careers in psychology.org*. Retrieved from https://careersinpsychology.org/psychologist-licensing-procedures-in-alabama

Huhra, R. L., Yamokoski-Maynhart, C. A., & Prieto, L. R. (2008). Reviewing videotapes in supervision: A developmental approach. *Journal of Counseling and Development, 86*(4), 412–418.

Huxley, A. (2017). *BookBrowse.com, BookBrowse's favorite quotes*. Retrieved from www.bookbrowse.com/quotes/detail/index.cfm/quote_number/430/experience-is-not-what-happens-to-you-its-what-you-do-with-what-happens-to-you

International Association of Eating Disorders Professionals (IAEDP). (n.d.). *Welcome to IAEDP membership, IAEDP ethics statement*. Retrieved June 19, 2019, from https://iaedp.site-ym.com/

International Coach Federation (ICF). (2015, June). *ICF code of ethics*. Retrieved from https://coachfederation.org/code-of-ethics

International Coach Federation. (2015a). *Professional Certified Coach*. Retrieved from https://coachfederation.org/icf-credential

International Expressive Arts Therapy Association (IEATA). (n.d.). *Code of ethics for registered expressive arts therapists (REAT)*. Retrieved from https://docs.wixstatic.com/ugd/4b548d_e144c2740f534db99a5cffe7a8c61141.pdf

International Expressive Arts Therapy Association. (n.d.) *Registered Expressive Arts Therapists*. Retrieved from www.ieata.org/what-is-reat

Ivey, A., Ivey, M. B., & Zalaquett, C. P. (2014). *Intentional interviewing and counseling: Facilitating client development in multicultural society* (8th ed.). Belmont, CA: Brooks/Cole.

Jennings, L., & Skovholt, T. M. (1999). The cognitive, emotional, and relational characteristics of master therapists. *Journal of Counseling Psychology, 46*, 3–11.

Jensen, J. P., & Bergin, A. E. (1988). Mental health values of professional therapists: A national interdisciplinary survey. *Professional Psychology: Research and Practice, 19*(3), 290–297.

Jung, C. G. (1985). *The practice of psychotherapy: Essays on the psychology of the transference and other subjects.* Princeton, NJ: Princeton University Press.

Justia US Law. (2019). *Jerrie M. Simmons, Plaintiff-appellee, v. United States of America,* Defendant-appellant, 805 F.2d 1363 (9th Cir. 1986). Retrieved from https://law.justia.com/cases/federal/appellate-courts/F2805/1363/107932/

The Kabbalah Center. (2018). *Introduction to Kabbalah.* Retrieved from https://kabbalah.com/en/online-courses/3190-introduction-to-kabbalah

Keyes, C. L. M. (2002, June). The mental health continuum: From languishing to flourishing in life. *Journal of Health and Social Research, 43*(2), 207–222.

Kitzrow, M. A. (2001). A model of supervisory style based on psychological type. *The Clinical Supervisor, 20*(2), 133–146.

Kocet, M. M., & Herlihy, B. J. (2014). Addressing value-based conflicts within the counseling relationship: A decision-making model. *Journal of Counseling & Development, 92*(2), 180–186.

Koocher, G. P., & Keith-Spiegel, P. (2008). *Psychology and the mental health professions: Standards and cases* (3rd ed.). New York, NY: Oxford University Press.

Koocher, G. P., & Keith-Spiegel, P. (2016). *Psychology and the mental health professions: Standards and cases* (4th ed.). New York, NY: Oxford University Press.

Kozlowski, J. M., Pruitt, N. T., DeWalt, T. A., & Knox, S. (2014). Can boundary crossings in clinical supervision be beneficial? *Counselling Psychology Quarterly, 27*(2), 109–126.

Kraus, D. R., Anderson, P., Bentley, J. H., Boswell, J. F., Constantino, M. J., Baxter, E. E., & Castonguay, L. G. (2016). Predicting therapist effectiveness from their own practice-based evidence. *Journal of Consulting and Clinical Psychology, 84*(6), 473–483.

Lafferty, P., Beutler, L. E., & Crago, M. (1989). Differences between more and less effective psychotherapists: A study of select therapist variables. *Journal of Consulting and Clinical Psychology, 57*(1), 76–80.

Lambie, G. (2017). *The counselor competencies scale.* Retrieved from http://webmedia.jcu.edu/counselingdepartment/files/2016/03/CCS-R-Evaluation.pdf

LCSW-1. (2018). Retrieved from www.psychologytoday.com/us/therapists/ellen-stein-weaver-philadelphia-pa/271627?sid=1515549568.8627_29070&city=Philadelphia&state=PA&spec=407&ref=3&tr=ResultsPhoto

LCSW-2. (2018). Retrieved from www.psychologytoday.com/us/therapists/camillecampbellmurrayut/303683?sid=1515702632.5343_9343&state=UT&spec=408&ref=1&tr=ResultsPhoto

LCSW-3. (2018). Retrieved from www.psychologytoday.com/us/groups/shamanic-teaching-and-healing-workshops-and-offers-missoula-mt/117764

LCSW-3a. (2018). Retrieved from www.psychologytoday.com/us/therapists/buffalo-heart-healing-missoula-mt/340512

LEAGLE.com. (2018). *Andrews v. U. S. 1984.* Retrieved from www.leagle.com/decision/19841098732f2d36611030

Lichtenberg, J. W. (2009). Comment: Effects of experience on judgment accuracy. *The Counseling Psychologist, 37*, 410–415.

Ling, T. J., & Hauck, J. M. (2016). *The ETHICS model: Comprehensive, ethical decision making*. Retrieved from https://pdfs.semanticscholar.org/13d3/29ac728e3732849fa6251470457fa5f00dac.pdf

Littrell, J. M., Lee-Borden, N., & Lorenz, J. (1976). A developmental framework for counseling supervision. *Counselor Education and Supervision, 19*, 129–136.

LMFT-1. (2018). Retrieved from www.psychologytoday.com/us/therapists/james-bowen-counseling-duck-creek-village-ut/167435

LMFT-2. (2018). Retrieved from www.psychologytoday.com/us/therapists/victorious-beginningsllc-las-vegas-nv/130731 Lines were here?

LMFT-3. (2018). Retrieved January 8, 2018, from www.psychologytoday.com/us/therapists/joan-cook-glendale-az/155620

Lochner, B. T. (1996). *The relationship between cognitive style, theoretical orientation, and preferences for supervisory style among professional psychology interns*. Dissertation. Texas Tech University, Lubbock, TX.

Loyola University Chicago. (2019a). *MSW Advanced Standing Option*. Retrieved March 2, 2019, from www.luc.edu/socialwork/academics/graduate/msw-advanced-standing/

Loyola University Chicago. (2019b). *Explore the Program PhD in Counseling Psychology*. Retrieved March 2, 2019, fromwww.luc.edu/education/graduate/doctoraldegrees/counselingpsychology/curriculum/

LPC-1. (2018). Retrieved January 9, 2018, from www.psychologytoday.com/us/therapists/noble-counseling-services-pllc-raleigh-nc/132144

LPC-2. (2018). Retrieved January 9, 2018, from www.psychologytoday.com/us/therapists/sherri-lambiase-san-antonio-tx/142699?sid=1515622593.0027_21141&city=Castroville&state=TX&spec=3&ref=1&tr=ResultsPhoto

LPC-3. (2018). Retrieved January 4, 2018, from www.psychologytoday.com/us/therapists/kathy-leigh-glover-hopkinsville-ky/370177?sid=1515697818.8798_22323&city=Clarksville&state=TN&spec=405&ref=9&tr=ResultsRow

Luke, M., Goodrich, K. M., & Gilbride, D. D. (2013). Intercultural model of ethical decision making: Address worldview dilemmas in school counseling. *Counseling and Values, 58*, 177–194. doi: 10.1002/j.2161-007X.2013.00032.x

Mahrer, A. (1999). Embarrassing problems in the field of psychotherapy. *Journal of Clinical Psychology, 55*(9), 1147–1156.

Mann, K., Gordon, J., & MacLeod, A. (2009). Reflection and reflective practice in health professions education: A systematic review. *Advances in Health Sciences Education: Theory and Practice, 14*(4), 595–621.

Martin, F. A. (1975). *Prayers from where you are*. Waco, TX: Word Books.

Martin, F. A. (1990). *Prayers for recovery: Talks with God for your 12 Step program*. Brentwood, TN: New Directions Press.

Martin, F. A. (2004). Confessional writing in the process of therapy: Our shared journey. In J. G. Byers & M. Forinash (Eds.), *Educators, therapists, and artists on reflective practice* (pp. 89–109). New York, NY: Peter Lang Publishers.

Martin, F. A. (2010). *Full life: A workbook for spiritual recovery from addictions*. Nashville, TN: Green Hills Press.

Martin, F. A. (In Press). *Therapy thieves: How to save mental health care from its providers*. Oxford University Press.

Martin, F. A., & Cannon, W. C. (2010). *The necessity of a philosophy of clinical supervision*. Retrieved from http://counselingoutfitters.com/vistas/vistas10/Article_45.pdf

McMahan, E. H. (2014). Supervision, a non-elusive component of deliberate practice toward expertise. *The American Psychologist, 69*(7), 712–713. http://dx.doi.org/10.1037/a0037832

Mead, D. E. (1990). *Effective supervision: A task-oriented model for the mental health professions*. Philadelphia, PA: Brunner/Mazel.

Menninger, K. (2017). *Child and Youth Care (CYC) Net*. Retrieved from www.cyc-net.org/cyc-online/cycol-0711-menninger.html

MFT license requirements in Alabama. (n.d.). *MFT License Requirements in Alabama*. Retrieved from www.mft-license.com/states/alabama-mftlicense.html#context/api/listings/prefilter

Miller, D. J., Spengler, E. S., & Spengler, P. M. (2015). A meta-analysis of confidence and judgment accuracy in clinical decision making. *Journal of Counseling Psychology*, *62*(4), 553–567.

Moore, T. (2016). *Copied from: Inner work: Counseling and psychotherapy*. Retrieved from www.innerwork.info/quotes.htm

Mullen, E. J., & Streiner, D. L. (2004). The evidence for and against evidence-based practice. *Brief Treatment and Crisis Intervention*, *4*(2), 111–121. http://dx.doi.org/10.1093/brief-treatment/mhh009

Multiplying Connections. (2017). *What is reflective supervision?* Retrieved from http://multiplyingconnections.org/become-trauma-informed/what-reflective-supervision

NAADAC, Association for Addiction Professionals. (2016). *NAADAC/NCC AP code of ethics*. Retrieved from www.naadac.org/assets/2416/naadac-nccap-code-of-ethics11–04–16.pdf

NAADAC, Association for Addiction Professionals. (n.d.). *National Peer Recovery Support Specialist Code of Ethics*. Retrieved from https://www.naadac.org/ncprss-code-of-ethics

National Association of Social Workers (NASW). (2017). *Code of ethics of the national association of social workers*. Retrieved from www.socialworkers.org/About /Ethics/Code-of-Ethics/Code-of-Ethics-English

National Association of Social Workers. (2019). *About NASW*. Retrieved from www.socialworkers.org/About

National Board for Certified Counselors (NBCC). (2016). *NBCC code of ethics*. Retrieved from www.nbcc.org/Assets/Ethics/NBCCCodeofEthics.pdf

National Career Development Association. (2015). *NCDA code of ethics*. Retrieved from www.ncda.org/aws/NCDA/asset_manager/get_file/3395

Newman, C. F. (2013). Training cognitive behavioral therapy supervisors: Didactics, simulated practice, and "meta-supervision". *Journal of Cognitive Psychotherapy*, *27*(1), 5–18. http://dx.doi.org/10.1891/0889-8391.27.1.5

North Atlantic Region Association of Counselor Education and Supervision. (2017). *The Journal of Counselor Preparation and Supervision*. Retrieved from http://repository.wcsu.edu/jcps/about.html

North Carolina. (2018). *North Carolina social work licensing requirements*. Retrieved from www.socialworkguide.org /licensure/north-carolina/

O'Donohue, W., & Lilienfeld, S. O. (Eds.). (2013). *Case studies in clinical psychological science: Bridging the gap rom science to practice*. New York, NY: Oxford University Press.

Olds, K., & Hawkins, R. (2013). *Conceptualizing the generic competencies required to provide clinical supervision to Australian psychologists: A thematic analysis*. Retrieved from www.nswiop.nsw.edu.au/images/publications/clin-sup-monograph.pdf

Oregon. (2018a). *Psychology Schools*. Retrieved from www.psychologydegree411.com/schools/oregon/

Oregon. (2018b). *LPC: Degree & Coursework*. Retrieved from www.oregon.gov/oblpct/Pages/degrees.aspx

Oregon Board of Licensed Professional Counselors and Therapists. (2018). *Requirements for licensed professional counselor*. Retrieved from https://secure.sos.state.or.us/oard/displayDivisionRules.action?selectedDivision=3732

Pakdaman, S., Shafranske, E., & Falender, C. (2015). Ethics in supervision: Consideration of the supervisory alliance and countertransference management of psychology doctoral students. *Ethics and Behavior, 25*(5), 427–441.

Pearson, Q. (2004). Getting the most out of clinical supervision: Strategies for mental health. *Journal of Mental Health Counseling, 26*(4), 361–373.

Peck, M. S. (2003). *The road less traveled, timeless edition: A new psychology of love, traditional values and spiritual growth.* New York, NY: Simon and Schuster.

Pelling, N. (2008). The relationship of supervisory experience, counseling experience, and training in supervision to supervisory identity development. *Journal for the Advancement of Counseling, 30*, 235–248.

Pennebaker, J. W. (2016). *Writing and Health: Some Practical Advice.* Retrieved from https://liberalarts.utexas.edu/psychology/faculty/pennebak#writing-health

Pentecostal Theological Seminary. (2017). *Story of PTSeminary.* Retrieved from www.ptseminary.edu/story-of-ptseminary.php

Pentecostal Theological Seminary. (2018). *Academic catalog (2017–2018).* Retrieved from www.ptseminary.edu/uploads/pdf/2017-2018AcadCatalog.pdf

Polk, T. A. (2015). *The addictive brain.* Chantilly, VA: The Teaching Company.

Powell, D. J. (1996). A peer consultation model for clinical supervision. *The Clinical Supervisor, 14*(2), 163–169.

Powell, D. J., & Brodsky, A. (2004). *Clinical supervision in alcohol and drug abuse counseling: Principles, models, methods* (Rev. ed.). San Francisco, CA: Jossey-Bass.

Prest, L., Schindler-Zimmerman, T., & Sporakowski, M. (1992). The initial supervision checklist (ISSC): A guide for the MFT supervision process. *The Clinical Supervisor, 10*, 117–133.

Presti, D. (2016). *The foundational concepts of neuroscience.* New York, NY: W.W. Norton and Company.

Psychologist-1. (2018). Retrieved January 8, 2018, from www.psychologytoday.com/us/therapists/patricehellerphiladelphiapa/158733?sid=1515549568.8627_29070&city=Philadelphia&state=PA&spec=407&ref=9&tr=ResultsPhoto

Psychologist-2. (2018). Retrieved January 8, 2018, from www.psychologytoday.com/us/therapists/jennifer-n-white-duluth-mn/152231

Psychologist-3. (2018). Retrieved January 8, 2018, from www.atlanta-counseling.com/atlanta-christian-counseling

Rainer, S. (2018). The integration of Christianity and psychology. *Christianity Today.* Retrieved from www.christianitytoday.com/edstetzer/2014/september/concerning-psychology-and-christianity-guest-post-by-sarah-.html

Rich, P. (1993). The form, function, and content of clinical supervision: An integrated model. *The Clinical Supervisor, 11*(1), 137–178.

Riggs, S. A., & Bretz, K. M. (2006). Attachment processes in the supervisory relationship: An exploratory investigation. *Professional Psychology: Research and Practice, 37*(5), 558–566.

Rock, D. L., Bransford, J. D., Maisto, S. A., & Morey, L. C. (1987). The study of clinical judgment: An ecological approach. *Clinical Psychology Review, 7*, 645–661.

Rodenhauser, P. (1994). Toward a multidimensional model for psychotherapy supervision based on developmental stages. *Journal of Psychotherapy Practice and Research, 3*, 1–15.

Rogers, C. R. (1961). *On becoming a person: A therapist's view of psychotherapy.* Boston, MA: Houghton Mifflin Company.

Rogers, C. R. (1969). *Freedom to learn.* Columbus, OH: Charles E. Merrill Company.

Russell, R. K., & Petrie, T. (1994). Issues in training effective supervisors. *Applied and Preventive Psychology, 3*, 27–32.

Schanz, A. (2016). *A comparison of the cognitive style similarity and communication style adjustment index methods to study counseling supervision performance.* Denton, TX: University of North Texas Libraries, Digital Library. Retrieved from http://digital.library.unt.edu/ark:/67531/metadc3211/

Schnarch, D. (2017). *Therathrive counseling and consultation, Dr. Grace Malonai's approach.* Retrieved from www.therathrive.com/about/about-dr-grace-malonai/dr-graces-approach/

Shelder, J. (2018). Where is the evidence for "evidence-based therapy?" *Psychiatric Clinics of North America, 41*(2), 319–329.

Simpson-Southward, C., Waller, G., & Hardy, G. (2017). How do we know what makes for "best practice" in clinical supervision for psychological therapists? A content analysis of supervisory models and approaches. *Clinical Psychology and Psychotherapy, 24*, 1228–1245.

Singer, M., & Lalich, J. (1996). *Crazy therapies: What are they? Do they work?* San Francisco, CA: Josey-Bass.

Six, T. (2014). *Characteristics of highly effective therapists.* Master's Thesis. Gent University. Retrieved from http://lib.ugent.be/fulltxt/RUG01/002/166/096/RUG01-0021660962014_0001_AC.pdf

Skovholt, T. M. (2001). *The resilient practitioner: Burnout prevention and self-care strategies for counselors, therapists, teachers, and health professionals.* Boston, MA: Allyn & Bacon.

Skovholt, T. M., & Jennings, L. (2004). *Master therapists: Exploring expertise in therapy and counseling.* New York, NY: Merrill Publishing.

Smith, H. D. (2006). *A stage development theory of counselor competence.* Adapted from e-mail correspondence, June 2016.

Soul Entrainment. (2019). *Soul Entrainment Training and Certification.* Retrieved from: https://createheaven.com/soul-entrainment-training/

South Dakota. (2018). *Licensing Professional Counselor (LPC).* Retrieved January 3, 2018, from www.counselor-license.com/states/south-dakota-counselor-license.html#section1

South Dakota. (2018a). *Psychology Schools in South Dakota.* Retrieved January 4, 2018, from www.psychologydegree411.com/schools/south-dakota/

South Dakota. (2018b). Untitled. Retrieved from https://sdlegislature.gov/Statutes/Codified_Laws/DisplayStatute.aspx?Type=Statute&Statute=36-33-9

Spengler, P. M., & Pilipis, L. A. (2015). A comprehensive meta-reanalysis of the robustness of the experience-accuracy effect in clinical judgment. *Journal of Counseling Psychology, 62*(3), 360–378.

Spengler, P. M., White, M. J., Ægisdóttir, S., Maugherman, A. S., Anderson, L. A., Cook, R. S., . . . Rush, J. D. (2009). The meta-analysis of clinical judgment project: Effects of experience on judgment accuracy. *The Counseling Psychologist, 37*(3), 350–399.

Stoltenberg, C. D. (1981). Approaching supervision from a developmental perspective: The counselor-complexity model. *Journal of Counseling Psychology, 28*, 59–65.

Stoltenberg, C. D., & Delworth, U. (1987). *Supervising counselors and therapists: A developmental approach.* San Francisco, CA: Josey-Bass Publishers.

Stoltenberg, C. D., & McNeill, B. W. (1997). Clinical supervision from a developmental perspective: Research and practice. In C. E. Watkins, Jr. (Ed.), *Handbook of psychotherapy supervision* (pp. 184–202). New York, NY: John Wiley and Sons.

Stoltenberg, C. D., McNeill, B. W., & Delworth, U. (1998). *IDM supervision: An integrated developmental model of supervising counselors and therapists*. San Francisco, CA: Josey-Bass.

Storm, C. I., & Todd, T. C. (2002). *The reasonably complete systematic supervisor resource guide*. New York, NY: Authors Choice Press.

Sturmey, P. (2009). *Clinical case formulation: Varieties of approaches*. Chichester, West Sussex: Wiley-Blackwell.

Styczynski, L. E. (1980). The transition from supervisee to supervisor. In A. K. Hess (Ed.), *Psychotherapy supervision: Theory, research, and practice* (pp. 29–40). New York, NY: John Wiley and Sons.

Tanenbaum, S. (2005, January). Evidence-based practice as mental health policy: Three controversies and a caveat. *Health Affairs, 24*(1), 163–173.

Thomas, J. T. (2007). Informed consent through contracting for supervision: Minimizing risks, enhancing benefits. *Professional Psychology: Research and Practice, 38*(3), 221–231. http://dx.doi.org/10.1037/0735-7028.38.3.221

Thomas, J. T. (2010). The ethical practice of supervision and consultation. In J. T. Thomas, *The ethics of supervision and consultation: Practical guidance for mental health professionals* (pp. 3–14). Washington, DC, US: American Psychological Association. http://dx.doi.org/10.1037/12078-001

Thompson, T. C. (2010). Psychological treatments to avoid. *The Alabama Counseling Association Journal, 36*(1), 39–48.

Thyer, B. A., & Pignotti, M. G. (2015). *Science and pseudoscience in social work practice*. New York, NY: Springer Publishing Company.

Tibetan Medicine Education Center. (2019). *The Tibetan Medicine Course*. Retrieved from www.tibetanmedicine-edu.org/index.php/tibetan-medicine-course

Tilsen, J., & McNamee, S. (2015). Feedback informed treatment: Evidence-based practice meets social construction. *Family Process, 54*, 124–137.

Tracey, T. J. G., Wampold, B. E., Goodyear, R. K., & Lichtenberg, J. W. (2018). Improving expertise in psychotherapy. *Society for the Advancement of Psychotherapy*. Retrieved from https://societyforpsychotherapy.org/improving-expertise-in-psychotherapy

Tracey, T. J. G., Wampold, B. E., Lichtenberg, J. W., & Goodyear, R. K. (2014). Expertise in psychotherapy: An elusive goal? *American Psychologist, 69*(3), 218–229.

Umstead, L. K. (2019). *Exploring counselors' use of research in practice: A CQR Study*. (Unpublished dissertation). Greensboro, NC: University of North Carolina at Greensboro. Retrieved from NC Digital Online Collection of Knowledge and Scholarship (NC DOCKS), https://libres.uncg.edu/ir/uncg/f/Umstead_uncg_0154D_12857.pdf

United States Association for Body Psychotherapy (USABP). (2007). *Ethical guidelines*. Retrieved from http://usabp.org/wp-content/uploads/2013/12/USABPethics2.pdf

University of South Dakota. (2019). Retrieved from http://catalog.usd.edu/preview_program.php?catoid=26&poid=4504#doctorofphilosophyinpsychology

University of Tennessee School of Social Work. (2018). *Master of science in social work (MSSW) program*. Retrieved from www.csw.utk.edu/mssw/index.htm

van Hennik, R., & Hillewaere, B. (2017). Practice based evidence based practice: Navigating based on coordinated improvisation, collaborative learning and multi-methods research in feedback informed systemic therapy. *Journal of Family Therapy, 39*(3), 288–309.

Walfish, S., McAlister, B., O'Donnell, P., & Lambert, M. J. (2012). An investigation of self-assessment bias in mental health providers. *Psychological Reports, 110*(2), 639–644.

Waller, G., Stringer, H., & Meyer, C. (2012). What cognitive behavioral techniques do therapists report using when delivering cognitive behavioral therapy for the eating disorders? *Journal of Consulting and Clinical Psychology, 80*, 171–175.

Watkins, Jr., C. E. (2012). Educating psychotherapy supervisors. *American Journal of Psychotherapy, 66*(3), 279–307.

Watkins, Jr., C. E. (2012a). Development of the psychotherapy supervisor: Review of and reflections on 30 years of theory and research. *American Journal of Psychotherapy, 66*(1), 45–83.

Watkins, Jr., C. E. (2018). Educationally corrective experiences as a common factor in psychotherapy supervision. *Journal of Psychotherapy Integration, 28*(2), 22–252.

Wedding, D., & Faust, D. (1989). Clinical judgment and decision making in neuropsychology. *Archives of Clinical Neuropsychology, 4*(3), 233–265.

Winkeljohn, B. S., Owen, J., Chapman, N., Lavin, K., Drinane, J. M., & Kuo, P. (2017, November). Feedback informed treatment: An empirically supported case study of psychodynamic treatment. *Journal of Clinical Psychology, 73*(11), 1499–1509.

Wolfsfelda, L., & Haj-Yahiaa, M. M. (2010). Learning and supervisory styles in the training of social workers. *The Clinical Supervisor, 29*, 68–94.

Woodman, M. (2016). *Marion Woodman*. Retrieved from www.greatthoughtstreasury.com/author/marion-woodman

Woolfolk, R. L. (2015). *The value of psychotherapy: The talking cure in an age of clinical science*. New York, NY: Guilford Press.

Wright, J., & Bolton, G. (2012). *Reflective writing in counseling and psychotherapy*. Thousand Oaks, CA: Sage Publications.

APPENDIX

Assessment of Supervisee Form

Assessment of Supervisee Form

SUPERVISEE ____________________ EVALUATION DATE ________________

INCOMPETENCE > > > > > > COMPETENCE

LOW COMPETENCE< > HIGH COMPETENCE

Knowledge		
1	Development of recognition and validation	1 2 3 4 5 6 7 8 9 10
2	Development of growth and enrichment	1 2 3 4 5 6 7 8 9 10
3	Development of expanded knowledge	1 2 3 4 5 6 7 8 9 10
4	Growth of meta-knowledge	1 2 3 4 5 6 7 8 9 10
	(e.g., complex thinking, clinical reasoning, curiosity)	
Clinical Skills and Transcendent Skills		
Clinical Skills		
5	Relational skills	1 2 3 4 5 6 7 8 9 10
6	Self-management skills	1 2 3 4 5 6 7 8 9 10
7	Clinical leadership skills	1 2 3 4 5 6 7 8 9 10
8	Engagement skills	1 2 3 4 5 6 7 8 9 10
9	Activity-oriented skills	1 2 3 4 5 6 7 8 9 10
10	Assessment skills	1 2 3 4 5 6 7 8 9 10
Transcendent Skills		
11	Emotional attunement/self and/or client	1 2 3 4 5 6 7 8 9 10
12	Adaptability	1 2 3 4 5 6 7 8 9 10
13	Clinical judgment	1 2 3 4 5 6 7 8 9 10
14	Critical thinking	1 2 3 4 5 6 7 8 9 10
15	Conceptualization skills	1 2 3 4 5 6 7 8 9 10
Outlook/Attitude		
16	Proclivity for relationships	1 2 3 4 5 6 7 8 9 10
17	Appropriately valuing self	1 2 3 4 5 6 7 8 9 10
18	Attitudes toward self and others	1 2 3 4 5 6 7 8 9 10

19 Facility with feelings	1 2 3 4 5 6 7 8 9 10
20 Adaptability/reactivity	1 2 3 4 5 6 7 8 9 10
21 Meta-emotions	1 2 3 4 5 6 7 8 9 10
22 Relevant personal values	1 2 3 4 5 6 7 8 9 10
23 Tolerance of ambiguity	1 2 3 4 5 6 7 8 9 10
24 Motivation	1 2 3 4 5 6 7 8 9 10

Task Completion Competencies

[This may be most anything that needs to be done in relation to clinical work. To utilize this form for evaluating supervisees, tasks should be clearly identified and defined by supervisors and supervisees.]

25 Keeping accurate and current documentation	1 2 3 4 5 6 7 8 9 10
26 Timely attendance of meetings	1 2 3 4 5 6 7 8 9 10
Preparing for sessions with clients	1 2 3 4 5 6 7 8 9 10
Nurturing referral network / managing referrals / contacts	1 2 3 4 5 6 7 8 9 10
Following normative organizational policies and procedures	1 2 3 4 5 6 7 8 9 10
Consulting with numerous others (e.g., probation officers, physicians, attorneys)	1 2 3 4 5 6 7 8 9 10
Testifying in court/depositions	1 2 3 4 5 6 7 8 9 10
Preparing letters for schools, employers, and others	1 2 3 4 5 6 7 8 9 10
Handling billing and related matters	1 2 3 4 5 6 7 8 9 10
Attending to licensing and certification requirements	1 2 3 4 5 6 7 8 9 10

INDEX

Note: Page numbers in **bold** indicate a chart on the corresponding page.

Taylor & Francis Group
an informa business

Taylor & Francis eBooks

www.taylorfrancis.com

A single destination for eBooks from Taylor & Francis with increased functionality and an improved user experience to meet the needs of our customers.

90,000+ eBooks of award-winning academic content in Humanities, Social Science, Science, Technology, Engineering, and Medical written by a global network of editors and authors.

TAYLOR & FRANCIS EBOOKS OFFERS:

- A streamlined experience for our library customers
- A single point of discovery for all of our eBook content
- Improved search and discovery of content at both book and chapter level

REQUEST A FREE TRIAL

support@taylorfrancis.com

Routledge
Taylor & Francis Group

CRC Press
Taylor & Francis Group

Made in the USA
Monee, IL
12 November 2026

664d00cf-b3bf-4130-a74f-fa4ff679b2e0R01